The Power of Chinatown

The publisher and the University of California Press Foundation gratefully acknowledge the generous support of the Lisa See Endowment Fund in Southern California History and Culture.

The Power of Chinatown

SEARCHING FOR SPATIAL JUSTICE IN LOS ANGELES

Laureen D. Hom

UNIVERSITY OF CALIFORNIA PRESS

University of California Press
Oakland, California

© 2024 by Laureen D. Hom

Library of Congress Cataloging-in-Publication Data

Names: Hom, Laureen D., 1982– author.
Title: The power of Chinatown : searching for spatial justice in Los Angeles / Laureen D. Hom.
Other titles: Searching for spatial justice in Los Angeles
Description: Oakland, California : University of California Press, [2024] | Includes bibliographical references and index.
Identifiers: LCCN 2023056340 (print) | LCCN 2023056341 (ebook) | ISBN 9780520391215 (cloth) | ISBN 9780520391222 (pbk.) | ISBN 9780520391239 (ebook)
Subjects: LCSH: Gentrification—California—Los Angeles. | Chinatown (Los Angeles, Calif.)—Social aspects.
Classification: LCC E184.C5 H65 2024 (print) | LCC E184.C5 (ebook) | DDC 979.4/9400451—dc23/eng/20231214
LC record available at https://lccn.loc.gov/2023056340
LC ebook record available at https://lccn.loc.gov/2023056341

33 32 31 30 29 28 27 26 25 24
10 9 8 7 6 5 4 3 2 1

*For Los Angeles Chinatown. Thank you for being a space
for so many to find community.
To Gilbert Hom (not related), a community leader
who helped countless people.
And to my family and friends for everything.*

CONTENTS

ILLUSTRATIONS

MAPS

FIGURES

TABLES

I moved to Southern California in 2012 to start my PhD program in urban planning and public policy with the intent to study gentrification and community development issues in Asian American communities. I chose to attend UC Irvine in Orange County, the southern neighbor of Los Angeles County that consisted of smaller satellite cities to Los Angeles and home to a growing Asian American population. I consider myself a Chinese American urbanite, as I had only lived in older urban areas that were home to the major historic Asian American ethnic enclaves in the United States, including Los Angeles, San Francisco, and New York, so this was a major lifestyle shift for me. It also did not escape me that my move was part of a broader trend and recognition of these newer urban and suburban spaces eclipsing the older urban ethnic spaces as the cultural, residential, and economic centers for Asian American communities, especially Chinese Americans like me. I also assumed that my move meant that Orange County would be the focus of my intellectual and personal development, as well as civic engagement. However, this did not quite go according to plan. What I did not anticipate was that this same year I moved back to Southern California, there was a major development conflict about a Walmart Neighborhood Market being proposed in one of the most recognized and oldest Asian American spaces in the region and a neighborhood that my family would often visit when I was a child, Los Angeles Chinatown. My curiosity about the conflict would take me back to the city that was my first home.

Still, the path that led me to Los Angeles Chinatown was not simply due to an intellectual curiosity about urban development and Asian American communities. Like so many other Chinese Americans, what brought me to the neighborhood was also spurred by personal reasons. During the winters of 2013 and 2014, when I was trying to solidify my dissertation plans, both my grandmothers, Zem Ping Dong and Lin Choi Hom, passed away. As my grandfathers, Don Moon Dong and Henry Hom, had already passed in my youth, the passing of my grandmothers now meant that both sides of my family had lost the generation that went through immense struggles to make the United States our permanent home, and they did so in the Chinatown I grew up with, San Francisco. While I had past experiences volunteering and working in San Francisco and New York City's Chinatowns prior to my academic career, I did not anticipate dedicating my research to urban Chinatowns. I dismissed Chinatown as too personal and wanted to move on, like so many other Chinese Americans of my generation and age. But with the loss of my grandmothers and the questions I had about what Chinatown now meant to my family and myself, I inevitably began to think about how the changes I was seeing in my own family were intimately related to the changes happening in urban Chinatowns today. I wanted and needed to explore that more fully.

Thus, I have learned to embrace that my best research is as much personal as intellectual, and because of that, I would first like to thank my family and friends for their unwavering support. I would not be here without my family. Endless gratitude to my mom and dad, Lorraine Dong and Marlon Hom. It was extremely daunting to venture down this path in their shadows, both in the university and the community. But I also know that my writing and analytical skills, as well as constant reminders to think beyond myself, come from them and have helped me to develop an identity and voice independent from them. I also am grateful for my siblings: my brother, Elan Hom, and my cousins, Brian Yee and Allen Yee. Along with my parents, they raised me, and they continue to shape me as a person. Arthur Dong, Reed Dong-Gee, Young Gee, Pauline Hom, Cindy Lai Yee, Derek Yee, and Tyson Yee also provided a sense of family and home for me in Los Angeles and San Francisco that anchored me throughout the research.

I also am incredibly grateful for my friends who were there for me in countless ways throughout this book journey. For my friends who knew me before my academic career: Jaime Anno, Allen Beck, Lisa Blonder Ohlenkamp, Shekinah Elmore, Krittika Ghosh, Christine Kao, Jeehye Kim, Jeeyoung Kim, Diana Kung, Adrian Meza, Tammy Michel, Jen Lemberger, CJ Lee, Kim Ma, Walter Quiroga, and Jennifer Schwarz. I am appreciative of your friendship through the years (decades!) and that despite different life trajectories, we always were there for each other. For the friends I met during my time at the PhD program: Elaine Andres, Erica Maria Cheung,

Rafael Contreras, Santina Contreras, Edward Curammeng, Allison Laskey, Jonathan Magat, Phil Posen, and Ray San Diego. Thank you for defying the expectations I had that academia was going to be a solitary experience. I am in awe of you as fellow scholars and am grateful that we also had fun times amid the pressures of academia. Thank you to all my family and friends for the encouragement, sympathetic ear, and laughs in between the research and writing. You are all brilliant, and I am constantly inspired by you.

I also want to express my gratitude to those in my academic community for helping me in every step of this research, from the dissertation proposal to the final publication of the book. Maria G. Rendón and Linda Trinh Võ were incredible mentors to me at UC Irvine. Their encouragement helped me believe that I could—and should—do an ethnography about Los Angeles Chinatown. Through them, I learned so much about being a woman of color faculty and how to accept my positionality as not just a part of my academic identity, but a strength. In addition, I would like to thank Victoria Basolo, Scott Bollens, Jim Lee, Judy Tzu-Chun Wu, and Rodolfo Torres for their enthusiasm for my research while I was a graduate student. My peers were also critical to my research and writing. Hiroshi Ishikawa and Brian Hui connected me to several people in Chinatown during the beginning of my fieldwork. Ashley Camille Hernandez, Ray San Diego, and Michelle Zuñiga, generously reviewed manuscript drafts, while Elaine Andres, Erica Maria Cheung, and Santina Contreras were always a text away to provide affirmations and brainstorm ideas on the fly, from wording sentences to design ideas.

I was also fortunate to find encouragement beyond the intellectual community I found at UC Irvine. My interest in urban life and gentrification was first nurtured by my advisors in my MPH program at Columbia University, Mindy Thompson Fullilove and Lourdes Hernandez-Cordero. My conversations with William Gow and Oliver Wang, along with feedback from Lon Kurashige and Nayan Shah when I presented my work, were also critical to the evolution of my ideas when I was a doctoral student. Peter Burns and Dani Denardo also supported me when I was a postdoctoral scholar at Soka University of America and in the initial stages of putting together the manuscript. At Cal Poly Pomona, the College of Letters, Arts, and Social Sciences, and specifically the Department of Political Science, was my home base as I wrote this book. I thank my colleagues, Neil Chaturvedi, Brady Collins, Mario Guerrero, Shayda Kafai, Anthony Ocampo, and Renford Reese, for their advice and resources that assisted me with the book. The RSCA and Teacher-Scholar awards were invaluable for helping me to complete the manuscript while I navigated junior faculty life. I also am appreciative of the Department of Political Science administrative coordinators, Kim Alm, Jessica Castillo, and Beatriz Garcia, for the behind-the-scenes administrative work that I could not do alone. I also presented this research at several conference venues, including the Association for Asian American Studies, Association for Collegiate Schools of Planning, American Sociological Association, Pacific Coast Branch-American Historical Association, and Urban Affairs Association. The questions and feedback that I received from scholars at these conferences helped to strengthen my interdisciplinary thinking for this book.

A special thank you to the students in my undergraduate and graduate classes at Soka University of America and Cal Poly Pomona with whom I shared bits and pieces of my research over the years, which led to generative discussions and became a source of motivation. I am especially grateful for Breanna Li, Natalie Kassar, and Jenny Tseng who helped me at various points of the research and writing during their undergraduate studies.

I am thrilled that I was able to publish with UC Press, a press that I have admired since I was an undergraduate student. I would like to extend my deep appreciation to my editor, Kim Robinson, and editorial assistant, Aline Dolinh, for their guidance and patience in every step of the publication process. Thank you for making what is undoubtedly an overwhelming experience as smooth and straightforward a process as possible. I also thank Gary Hamal for meticulously reviewing and copyediting the manuscript. Additionally, James Zarsadiaz generously shared tips and resources. I am especially humbled and grateful that Wendy Cheng and Jan Lin also reviewed the initial manuscript drafts. Their incredibly constructive feedback motivated and challenged me throughout the writing process.

No words can capture how thankful and indebted I am to the people that I met in Los Angeles Chinatown. Every conversation (from a quick hello to the four-hour conversation), piece of paper (sometimes boxes full of them!), willingness to connect me with more people, pat on the back, and insistence that I take leftover food at the end of meetings was so critical to helping me become a better scholar and person. These relationships allowed me to dig deeper into the history and social connections that defined Chinatown. I was able to critically think about my understandings of community, identity, and space that would not have been possible if I had stayed within the traditional confines of academia.

I am especially grateful to Suellen Cheng, Gilbert Hom, Munson Kwok, Eugene Moy, and Steve Wong for having the first conversations that kick-started both my project and civic engagement in Chinatown, as well as inviting me to spaces and connecting me to others in the community. Munson Kwok shared the archive of materials he had preserved throughout his time as a community leader in Los Angeles Chinatown. His archive was critical in providing an understanding of the Los Angeles Community Redevelopment Agency and Chinatown Community Advisory Committee, as much of these documents had yet to be organized and archived for the public. Gilbert Hom also thoroughly read my dissertation (twice!), and we had multiple conversations where he encouraged me to further develop the research as a book. He passed before I could hand this book to him in person, a moment that I was looking forward to sharing with him, but I am happy that he was, at the very least, able to see iterations of the research and to know the book was happening. David Louie also helped to connect me with several individuals whom I was told would be impossible to reach, and I am especially grateful for his support. I also want to acknowledge Phil Choy for passing along what he had collected about the neighborhood early on in my research and for joining me on an unexpected Northern California interview. He was a generous community leader and scholar who was based in San Francisco but was influential for Chinese American communities beyond the Bay Area. Additionally, I thank the Chinese Historical Society of Southern California and the Chinese American Citizens Alliance–Los Angeles Lodge for providing parking and the occasional working space, two things that are not so easy to find in Chinatown. I was extremely privileged to have access to both.

Lastly, every person I met throughout my fieldwork shaped my understanding of Chinatown as a neighborhood and community, which will continue to evolve. This book would not have been possible without the following people: Dennis Arguelles, Linda Bentz, Lillian Burkenheim-Silver, Jean Chan, Scott Chan, Patrick Chen, Sophia Cheng, Suellen Cheng, King Cheung, Deborah Ching, Phyllis Chiu, Chester Chong, Ruth Chu, Wendy Chung, Susan Dickson, Fenton Fong Eng, Rick Eng, Mike Fong, Stephen Fong, Gerald Gubatan, Maryanne Hayashi, Gilbert Hom, Gordon Hom, William Chun-Hoon, Susan Hum, Daniel Huynh, Frances Huynh, Vincent Huynh, Larry Jung, Alan Kumamoto, Munson Kwok, Collin Lai, Lawrence Lan, Wendy Lau, Judy Lee, Martin Lee, Patrick Lee, Peter Lin, Richard Liu, Don Loo, David Louie, Emma Louie, Ron Louie, Sharon Lowe, Lawrence Lue, Daisy Ma, Robert Ma, Tom Majich, Eugene Moy, Angelica Lopez Moyes, Peter Ng, Sophat Phea, Alexis Readinger, Gerry Shu, Kerry Situ, Al Soo-hoo, Edmund Soohoo, Cooke Sunoo, Don Spivack, Diane Tan, Paul

Tea, Ted Tongsak, Don Toy, Jim Tsai, Connie Vuong, Bill Watanabe, Craig Wong, Dorothy Fue Wong, Martin Wong, Steve Wong, Mike Woo, Peter Woo, Wanda Wu, Annie Yee, Anson Yew, Cynthia Yparraguiree, George Yu, Gay Yuen, Bibiana Yung, Xiayi Zhang, and the countless Chinatown residents, workers, and activists with whom I shared both passing moments and routine interactions each time I was in the neighborhood. Thank you for making Los Angeles Chinatown a special place for so many.

ABBREVIATIONS

AAFE	Asian Americans for Equality
BID	Los Angeles Chinatown Business Improvement District
CACA	Chinese American Citizens Alliance–Los Angeles Lodge
CAM	Chinese American Museum
CCAC	Chinatown Community Advisory Committee
CCED	Chinatown Community for Equitable Development
CHSSC	Chinese Historical Society of Southern California
CPA	Chinese Progressive Association
CRA	Community Redevelopment Agency
CSC	Chinatown Service Center
FACES	Friends and Alumni of Castelar Elementary School
HCNC	Historic Cultural Neighborhood Council
HCNNC	Historic Cultural North Neighborhood Council
LACPA	Los Angeles Chinatown Project Association (now the Los Angeles Chinatown Corporation)
PAC	Chinatown Project Area Committee
SEACA	Southeast Asian Community Alliance
UDLUC	Historic Cultural Neighborhood Council's Urban Design and Land Use Committee

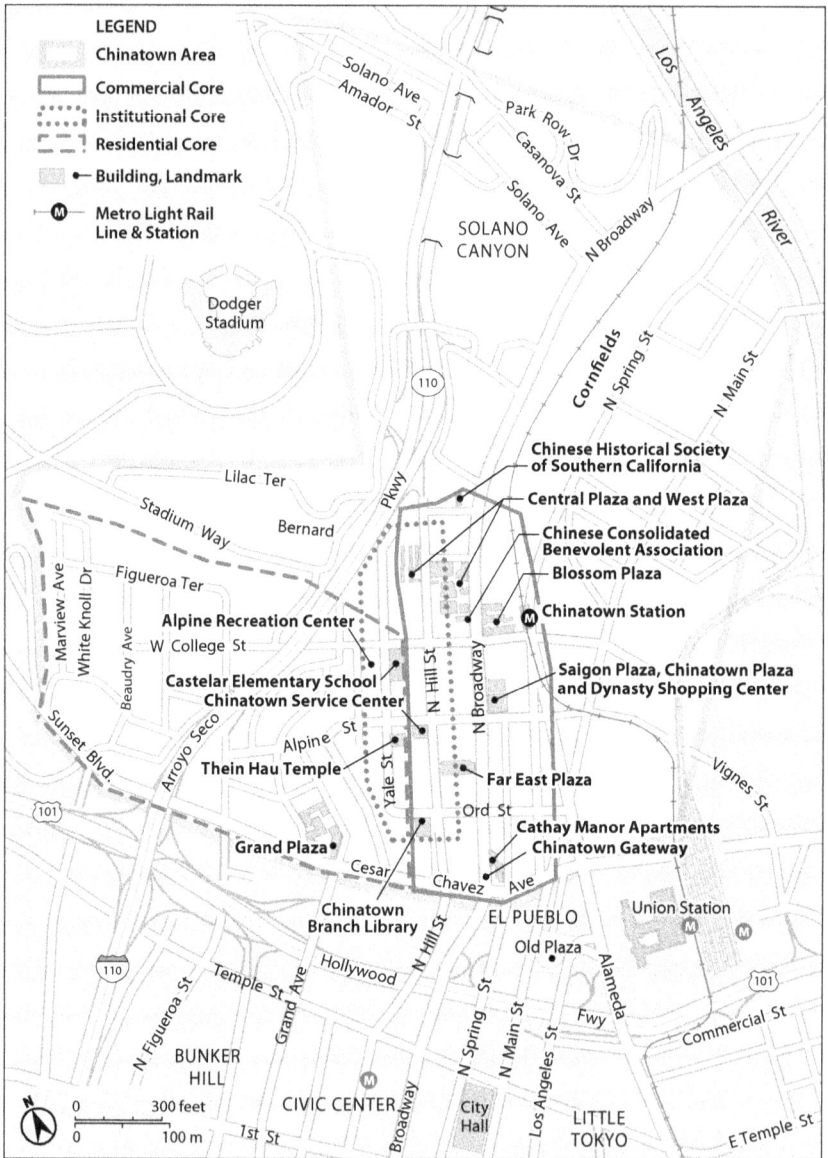

MAP 1. Current Chinatown neighborhood with select landmarks. Map created by Ben Pease.

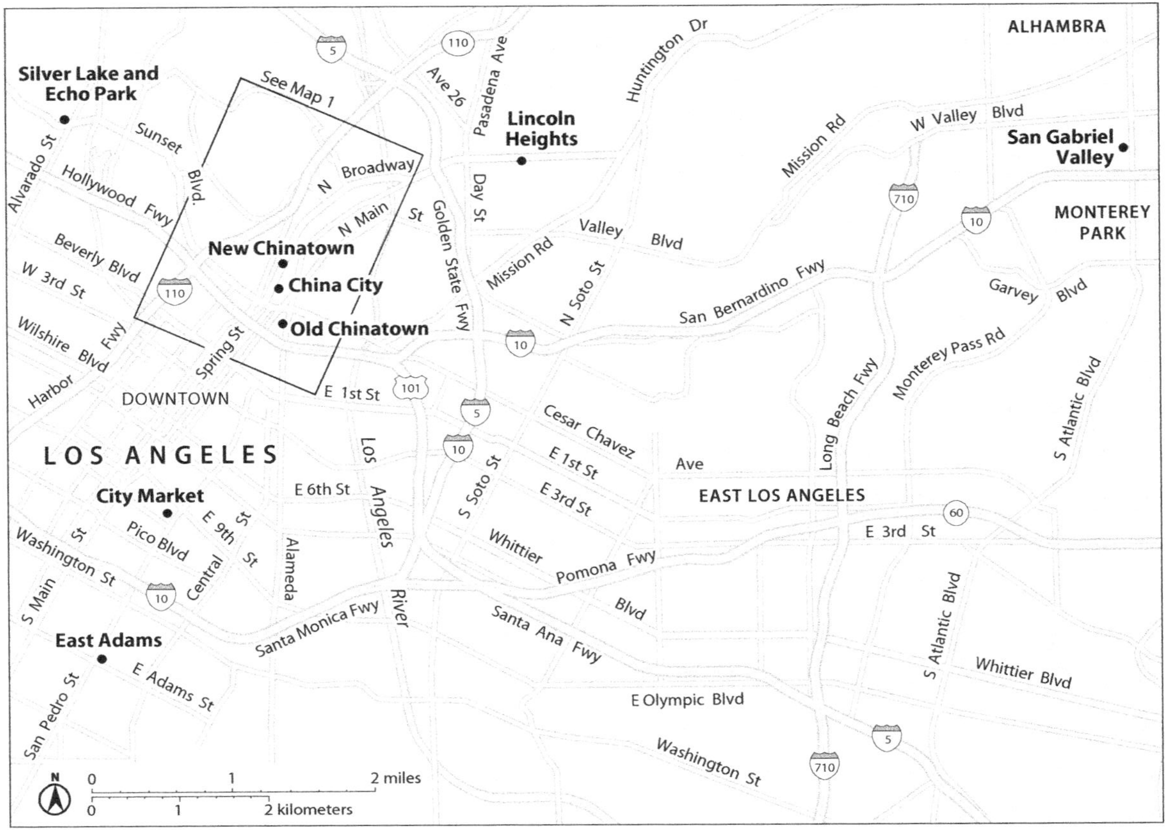

MAP 2. Areas with Chinese American settlements in the Los Angeles region (1870s to present day). The areas highlighted are select places that were mentioned during interviews and archival research. Map created by Ben Pease.

Introduction

WHY CHINATOWN STILL MATTERS

Chinatown has two or three percent of the Chinese population
in the county. So, does L.A. Chinatown matter as a community?
Is it relevant? How important is it? . . . Are we [Chinese Ameri-
cans] going to knit ourselves into the fabric of Chinatown so
that there's room for others?

—EUGENE MOY, community leader since the 1970s

IN 2013, a Walmart Neighborhood Market opened in Los Angeles Chinatown. Its presence and the conflict leading up to its eventual opening raised
important questions about the future of Chinatown for the Chinese American community across the region. The market was located in Grand Plaza,
a mixed-use development that was home to affordable senior citizen housing units on the southwestern border of Chinatown and downtown. When
Grand Plaza was originally proposed in the 1980s and opened in 1992, an
on-site grocery store was an especially critical amenity for the senior citizens
who would move directly into the building. A grocery store in this location was also more physically accessible to the Chinatown residents than
the smaller grocery stores located in the neighborhood's commercial area,
which residents would have to walk through hilly terrain to access. At the
time, the grocery stores in Chinatown primarily consisted of small butcher
shops and produce stores, as well as one major ethnic supermarket, Ai Hoa
Market. While at one point there was another major ethnic supermarket,
99 Ranch, a Chinese supermarket chain started by a Taiwanese American
in Southern California in the 1980s, it was only in operation for a few years
before shutting down. Some saw the inability of a 99 Ranch to thrive in
the neighborhood as a sign that Chinatown was no longer a center for the
Chinese American community. In the 1980s, at the same time Grand Plaza
was being developed, the smaller cities and suburbs in the San Gabriel Valley

emerged as competition for Chinatown, as it not only had several 99 Ranch markets, but other ethnic grocery and retail stores. Amid these changes across the region, this space in Grand Plaza remained vacant for over two decades and was a major unfulfilled promise for the Chinatown community. There were rumors in the community about different markets moving into the space, but none came into fruition until the proposal for the Walmart neighborhood market in 2012.

As the Chinatown community learned about the possibility of a Walmart Neighborhood Market opening in the vicinity, different community voices began to publicly express either their resistance or support—while some maintained a purposeful silence about it. Some community leaders, including those involved with the Chinatown Business Improvement District (BID) and some of the long-standing organizations such as the Chinese Consolidated Benevolent Association (CCBA) and the Chinese American Citizens Alliance (CACA), not only were relieved that the space would no longer be vacant, but argued that Walmart would bring resources to a predominantly low-income community and address a retail gap in the neighborhood. Walmart also promised community benefits, which included financial support to some of the community organizations. Progressive activists representing the Chinatown Community for Equitable Development (CCED) and the Southeast Asian Community Alliance (SEACA) countered by pointing to the long history of Walmart's labor violations and the potential to drive out the immigrant-owned small businesses. They also saw its presence as fundamentally at odds with the cultural and historical character that made the neighborhood a distinct place of community for generations of Asian American immigrants. Walmart's presence was a part of the homogenization of urban spaces, as corporations would start to displace small business owners, which would ultimately have ripple effects on low-income residents. Labor activists across the city were also a part of the conflict in Chinatown, having historically campaigned against Walmart establishing a presence in the city. They aligned with the new progressive groups in Chinatown and organized a protest in the neighborhood to try to prevent its opening. Recognizing the resistance to Walmart, the City Council proposed an interim ordinance to prevent the Walmart from opening. But this ordinance was not specific to Chinatown; it generally blocked major box stores from opening throughout the city, which generated even more political conflict. This ordinance ultimately was a moot point, as Walmart obtained the building permit a day before the ordinance unanimously passed.

While this conflict played out publicly in the media and in local politics, it also played out privately in community spaces in Chinatown. Intense debates would happen among community organization leaders and members about the value of the Walmart Neighborhood Market for the community, even after it opened. In these debates, people were often silenced by the questioning of their personal stake in the neighborhood. *How could they speak with authority about the community if they did not live, work, or own property here?* For some, it also led to a confusion about what gentrification meant for Chinatown. *If Chinatown has been grappling with empty storefronts and vacant lots for decades, isn't the Walmart Neighborhood Market a benefit? Would it not help bring vibrancy and resources to the community, especially low-income households?* They also had to contend with the contradictions of trying to define what a contemporary Chinatown should look like. *Were they concerned that it was not an ethnic-specific supermarket? Would a 99 Ranch be more of a Chinatown business?* The debates about Walmart were magnifying and creating conflict within the community.

The Walmart Neighborhood Market was ultimately only in operation for two and a half years. A corporate decision shut down all the neighborhood markets across the United States in January 2016. A press release was announced on a Friday and shared through email among different community leaders that weekend. Two days later, the sign was removed, and the space was empty. While Walmart's physical presence in Chinatown was now gone, the conflict surrounding this space lingered, revealing the complexities of how the community grapples with gentrification and forced displacement. It showed the different hopes and fears of change in a neighborhood that is intrinsically a part of the history and identity of Chinese and Asian Americans.[1] But it also reflected the tenuous relationship that Chinese Americans now have with Chinatowns. Los Angeles Chinatown is no longer the only residential or commercial center for the Chinese American community in the city or region. A small proportion of the Chinese American population in the county live in Chinatown—and it is specifically a concentration of low-income, working-class Chinese Americans. As one of those Chinese Americans who did not live in Chinatown, but was concerned about the consequences of the Walmart, I had to also step back and pose questions for myself and my community: Why does the Walmart Neighborhood Market in Chinatown even matter for the Chinese and Asian American community today, especially for Chinese Americans like me, who no longer live and work there? Even as a symbolic site of heritage, what role do Chinese Americans play in shaping

Chinatowns today? And how can we critically examine our political engagement in controlling preservation and change in urban Chinatowns?

The Power of Chinatown examines why historic urban Chinatowns continue to matter and how place-based ethnic community politics are reshaping these spaces as a physical neighborhood, as well as a political and cultural community, amid the threats of gentrification and forced displacement. Chinatowns are historic urban neighborhoods that continue to persist; however, these spaces are not ahistorical and static. They persist and change simultaneously, shaped by the continuous and evolving political engagement that happens in Chinatown, especially among Chinese Americans. Yet Chinese Americans are not a political monolith, and their political engagement is informed by class and socioeconomic status, generation, immigration history, and ideologies. Chinatown also remains a home for many community organizations that promote civic engagement for Chinese Americans, providing a sense of community, belonging, and shared heritage across different generations. But the neighborhood is first and foremost a residential home for low-income, working-class immigrant communities who have been an integral part of shaping the neighborhood's physical, social, and cultural landscape since its establishment. While Chinatown has been a space for the broader Chinese American community to come together and assert political representation, as the Walmart conflict showed, their engagement also cannot be divorced from addressing local community needs and material conditions of the neighborhood.

Urban Chinatowns across North America are experiencing the pressures of gentrification, contributing to concerns that they will soon disappear from the urban landscape.[2] Los Angeles Chinatown is no exception, especially in the past two decades. In the late 1990s, art galleries began to open in old trinket shops in West Plaza, one of the oldest commercial spaces in the neighborhood. In the early 2000s, along the border of Chinatown and downtown, Geoffrey Palmer, a controversial real estate developer in Los Angeles, constructed the Orsini Apartments, an all-market-rate housing development a couple of blocks away from the former Walmart market that many in the community continue to see as an incongruent space that is not truly part of Chinatown. In the 2010s, the Jia Apartments, a mixed-use market-rate apartment development also opened and is now home to the neighborhood's first Starbucks. Along with the Walmart market, new retail and restaurants were also opening in older storefronts. These changes and pressures facing Los Angeles Chinatown—and other urban Chinatowns—raise important questions about how this may be threatening to displace the cultural heritage of these spaces and the low-income, working-poor residents and workers, exacerbating social and economic inequities across the city. They also raise important questions about how the civic engagement of Chinese and Asian Americans in the neighborhood addresses these changes.

Thus, the political responses to gentrification in urban Chinatowns are not simply about identity and representational politics; it is an issue of how Chinese and Asian American communities engage in spatial justice. Spatial justice centers the importance of geographies and place in understandings of urban inequities. Spaces provide the material resources and social conditions that shape our social and everyday lives, but they are also socially constructed and in constant flux by the communities and individuals that interact with this space. Edward Soja argues that an analysis of urban development must consider not just the outcome, that there is a fair and equitable distribution of resources and opportunities across spaces, but also the process of development, as whoever has access to urban public spaces and the political power to determine how these spaces develop can also contribute to producing "unjust geographies."[3] In his theorizing about the right to the city, Henri Lefebvre critiques urban policies for supporting capitalist production over human rights that have led to these spatial injustices.[4] The right to the city demands transformative political changes so that historically marginalized groups have the power to control the trajectory of change in their neighborhood and community's future.[5]

Embedded within these arguments is the conflict between collective rights and individual rights in the creation of a just city.[6] Collective rights prioritize the creation of public spaces that address the needs of those who have been historically disadvantaged and oppressed, while individual rights often ultimately prioritize the economic and political elite in maintaining their control over property and development and, ultimately, in shaping the urban landscape.[7] Spatial justice is also intrinsically linked to mobility justice, as the ability to freely traverse spaces is differentiated by political and economic power, which is intrinsically linked to race.[8] In places like Chinatown, spatial justice has unique complexities; residentially it is home to low-income, working-class Chinese and Asian American immigrants, but it also continues to hold symbolic and historic meaning, as well as economic value, for a geographically dispersed Chinese American community. Their various attachments to Chinatown shape if and how they are politically engaged in the neighborhood and whether their advocacy is in the collective interest of both the local and ethnic communities.

This book highlights the perspectives and experiences of Chinatown's community leaders, who are engaging in community development efforts that may resist or encourage gentrification and the implications of this political engagement on our understandings of spatial justice among racialized groups. Community leaders have been active place makers, contributing to the political decision-making and practices that determine the housing, economic, and cultural character of the neighborhood throughout its history. However, they are also working within the institutions and policies that structure Chinatown's development and navigating the racialization of Asian Americans that marginalizes the residents and workers of Chinatown. Their political engagement raises important questions about how Chinatown continues to be represented as an ethnic space and how much control both the Chinese American and local Chinatown community have in steering neighborhood change amid these contemporary threats of gentrification. Who is representing Chinatown and what representations of neighborhood and community are they producing? What are the implications of their political engagement for creating a just, equitable present and future for Chinatown and Los Angeles?

RECOGNIZING GENTRIFICATION IN URBAN CHINATOWNS

The term *gentrification* was first formally introduced by British sociologist Ruth Glass to describe the "back-to-the-city" movement of the middle-class to working-class spaces in London in the 1960s.[9] Since then, *gentrification* has become a somewhat ubiquitous term in the debates and discussions about contemporary urban change. With that ubiquity, there are now many ways to define and identify gentrification, which has contributed to general confusion over the term, as it can be conflated with a depoliticized perspective of neighborhood change.

This book is guided by a specific definition of *gentrification* as a type of neighborhood change that is politically contested and contributes to an urban restructuring that continues to segregate and limit opportunities for low-income communities, especially non-White racialized groups. Gentrification occurs when public and private investment into low-income neighborhoods results in changes that indicate socioeconomic improvements, such as increases in household income and property values. Yet these changes are not necessarily an indicator of new opportunity structures that were created for the current residential and business tenants. Instead, these changes are attracting relatively wealthier newcomers to the neighborhood, contributing to the forced displacement of long-time community members who experience socioeconomic and cultural barriers to their ability to freely move to and live in other spaces. This book emphasizes that gentrification is a process, and different policies set the conditions for the practices, interactions, and activities of different community and political actors to respond to the threats of forced displacement. Furthermore, the historical and social context of the community matters in understanding how gentrification unfolds and whether a community has a choice to be in these neighborhoods and, relatedly, to leave these spaces.

While gentrification is often described as a movement and displacement of people across space, structural and political forces create the economic and sociocultural conditions for these movements.[10] Since the early 1900s, urban policies that sought to upscale and modernize urban areas have often led to the forced displacement of the working poor and non-White racialized communities.[11] Neighborhoods that were close to urban downtown cores were often home to Black and immigrant communities. They were targets for urban redevelopment and revitalization because of their perceived "slum" conditions. However, these determinations were often made by the city and those outside the community. Furthermore, rather than creating opportunities for social mobility for the community living and working in these spaces, these strategies often sought to attract a relatively wealthier and upwardly mobile population from outside the area to spend and invest in these spaces, whether through commercial or housing developments. These urban revitalization and redevelopment policies and practices tend to favor economic growth and profit for the city, property owners, and developers. This criticism has characterized revitalization strategies throughout time, from the City Beautiful Movement and post–World War II federal urban renewal programs to contemporary policies and programs, including business improvement districts and economic empowerment zones.

A distinct outcome associated with gentrification is forced displacement. The forced displacement that happens due to gentrification is also multifaceted, as it includes material and symbolic forms of displacement. Often gentrification is measured through demographic changes, including racial turnover and population shifts toward a higher socioeconomic status, and changes to the built environment, from the increased presence of boutique small businesses, such as coffee shops and restaurants, to large-scale commercial developments, such as stadiums, shopping malls, and chain businesses.[12] Yet documenting the neighborhood's demographic and physical changes has not always provided a holistic understanding of the process of gentrification in neighborhoods. Most notably, research examining demographic changes among residents in Harlem, a historic Black neighborhood in New York City that was popularly recognized as gentrifying in the late 1990s, led to debates as to whether rapid forced displacement was occurring.[13]

Scholars have thus also argued that gentrification can lead to other forms of displacement that are not always evident in short-term economic or demographic indicators. In addition to direct displacement through new developments, there can be a relatively slower secondary displacement process, or what Peter Marcuse has described as displacement pressures.[14] New developments that may be built in neighboring areas or in vacant spaces and promote upscaling can lead to potential rent increases for neighboring areas, eventually leading to economic displacement.[15] Gentrification can contribute to cognitive and social disruptions that challenge a sense of place and community for longtime stakeholders, which can be a form of cultural displacement.[16] These community stakeholders also may experience political displacement as more affluent and educated newcomers begin to outnumber them in gentrifying neighborhoods.[17] The threat of gentrification can vary and include concerns of not just physical displacement of buildings and people, but also the symbolic displacement of the current community who may feel psychologically, culturally, and politically disconnected from their neighborhood because of the physical changes.

Forced displacement distinguishes gentrification from other types of neighborhood change, and it is one reason why Chinatowns may often be misinterpreted theoretically in both gentrification studies and public discourses. Often recognized as ethnic enclaves, Chinatowns are a distinct immigrant and racialized space. In contrast to *ethnic ghettos*, which have limited opportunity structures for residents, *ethnic enclaves* have a neighborhood social structure that can lead to social and residential mobility.[18] Spatial assimilation theories have traditionally framed the logic of neighborhood change in ethnic enclaves, which argue that changes occur due to voluntary migration in and out of the neighborhood.[19] Ethnic enclaves are steppingstone neighborhoods for first-generation immigrant communities who will use the social networks and resources in these spaces for their socioeconomic mobility and political incorporation. Due to voluntary out-migration, the neighborhood transitions to support a new immigrant community. Chinatowns are often framed as ethnic enclaves because of their robust social and economic infrastructures that have provided social capital, support, and resources for the ethnic community throughout history.[20] Furthermore, with the striking down of residential segregation, post–World War II residential patterns suggested that Chinatowns fit this spatial assimilation model, as Chinese Americans were more likely to live in suburban areas and were more residentially dispersed than other non-White groups.[21] Thus, the theories of ethnic enclaves assume that neighborhoods such as Chinatowns were never meant to be a permanent part of the urban landscape and instead would change with the ebbs and flows of different immigrant groups as they "assimilated" into mainstream society.

Yet Chinatowns have persisted and are still present today. The liberalization of immigration policies after World War II struck down exclusionary immigration policies targeting Asian nation-states, which led to an increase of immigration from these areas. However, the residential populations of Chinatowns are a specific segment of new immigrants and refugees. Many low-income Chinese American immigrants continued to move into and remain in the neighborhood because of ongoing social, cultural, and economic exclusion.[22] Furthermore, upwardly mobile Chinese Americans did not necessarily have to reside in urban Chinatowns, but these spaces continued to hold important economic purposes for the Chinese American community. Since the 1980s, immigration scholars have argued that the enclave economy has been a driving force in sustaining historic urban ethnic enclaves for subsequent generations.[23] The upwardly mobile segment of the ethnic community maintained social ties and economic investments in ethnic enclaves, regardless of whether they lived there or not. For working-class community members, especially first-generation immigrants living in the neighborhood, the economy provides socioeconomic opportunities through ethnic networks. Min Zhou argues that the Chinatown economy is a protected sector of the labor market for immigrants to obtain jobs through co-ethnic ties in the neighborhood that they would not have in the mainstream labor market.[24] While the theorizing of ethnic enclaves has evolved to account for why urban Chinatowns have sustained themselves, it alone does not suffice in explaining the politics of urban redevelopment that have also contributed to both the persistence of these spaces and the ongoing threats of displacement.

Today, most urban Chinatowns remain predominantly Asian American residential spaces, even if they are not home to a majority of the Chinese or Asian American population within that region. But they are also predominantly low-income neighborhoods that are close to downtown cores, which historically have been targeted for redevelopment initiatives that have ripple effects to surrounding neighborhoods. Chinatowns may go unnoticed, as they are relatively small downtown-adjacent neighborhoods and the socioeconomic, cultural, and regional differences of Chinese and Asian Americans are not always accounted for in statistical and quantitative studies that traditionally inform public policy.[25] Yet Chinatown is a place where forced displacement can occur and is occurring. Chinatowns, and specifically Los Angeles Chinatown, are critical and contested sites that can expand upon our understanding of gentrification and urban inequities. By presenting the story of the community politics that have come to define Los Angeles Chinatown and its struggles with gentrification, we can start to unpack how gentrification may similarly and differentially impact different racialized communities in the urban landscape. We can further understand how community actors are impacted by the larger structural forces of gentrification, while also recognizing that they are agents of change who can both resist and contribute to this process as they assert a community voice in urban politics.

POLITICAL AND ECONOMIC POWER IN CHINATOWN: CONTROLLING COMMUNITY AND SPACE

As much as it is important to understand how the outcomes of gentrification contribute to urban inequities, it is also just as critical to understand the procedural and deliberative processes that create the conditions for gentrification and the forced displacement of the most economically and socially vulnerable in the neighborhood. Gentrification is a politically and economically contested process in which those who have the power to steer neighborhood change may not always represent the most marginalized in the neighborhood. According to political economy perspectives, neighborhood change occurs through political conflicts over the production of space.[26] These conflicts determine the economic and social value of neighborhoods. Whoever has the right to define those values ultimately contributes to the rearticulation of the neighborhood identity and who it serves.

When framed as a commodity, places are defined by their use-value, which represents the function and role of the space in providing services and goods, and an exchange-value, which is the monetary value of the land as determined through the market and expressed through rent and property values. According to Neil Smith's rent gap theory, gentrification occurs in areas where there is a disparity between the current rent and the potential rent that can be obtained.[27] Public and private actors, including the city, private developers, and property owners will thus speculate and support developments and businesses that are "the highest and best use of land" to maximize the profits of the exchange-value of land. They are also assumed to not have the same emotional attachments as residents and other community actors who may emphasize the use-value of space more than the exchange-value.[28] These place-based elites form growth coalitions and engage in competition with other elites to control changes and secure their economic interests. Thus, gentrification is a power conflict over how land has become commodified and valued based on the economic potential of that land rather than by the collective needs of a community.

The evolving role of community actors is critical to understanding how these power conflicts unfold in gentrifying spaces. Derek Hyra argues that contemporary urban redevelopment differs from early post–World War II urban renewal in that the emergence of community actors can now gain financially from the revitalization of low-income neighborhoods because of the striking down of past exclusionary policies.[29] They include upwardly mobile members of the community, ethnic political leaders, and professionals within the ethnic community, such as developers, property owners, real estate agents, and other for-profit business interests, some of whom may even transcend national boundaries as transnational corporations invest into these same neighborhoods. The investment from co-ethnics may not always be recognized as gentrification because of assumptions that they intuitively understand the needs of the community and that their individual benefits translate to broader community benefits. Yet, in their analysis of co-ethnic gentrification, or *gentefication*, in a Latine[30] barrio, Emanuel Delgado and Kate Swanson argued that low-income Latine residents were still facing displacement pressures and forced displacement despite co-ethnic investment.[31] Similarly, studies on redevelopment in historic urban Black neighborhoods have documented how middle-class Black professionals are investing in these neighborhoods; however, these investments may still encourage development that does not directly benefit the urban poor and working-class living in these neighborhoods.[32]

These tensions also exist in urban Chinatowns, reflecting the political and economic differences within both the local Chinese American community and transnational Chinese networks. In Asian American communities, business leaders often have had the most political influence, as they often mediate between the community and mainstream institutions.[33] However, these economic elites also have a financial interest in shaping spaces that may maximize the exchange-value of land. Furthermore, Asian American business leaders have formed immigrant and ethnic growth coalitions to position ethnic spaces as unique sites of urban and global capital accumulation.[34] The global economy has been especially critical to gentrification as the flow of global capital has been facilitated through the transnational networks and institutions located in ethnic neighborhoods.[35] Global Asian investment, in particular, has shaped economic development for both older historic ethnic enclaves and contemporary multiethnic suburbs in the United States.[36] While these global investors may be considered co-ethnics, this does not necessarily translate to a shared lived experience with the local communities that they are investing in. Thus, the ongoing presence of ethnic social and economic ties, whether local or global, may not be protective factors that can combat displacement in gentrifying neighborhoods. This has implications for how we define and enact community, especially in the political representation and organizing of non-White racialized groups as they respond to gentrification.

Neighborhood governance and community power in Chinatown is also distinguished by an ethnic power structure, which includes generations of community organizations. Historic ethnic neighborhoods like Chinatowns have a robust social and political infrastructure because they originated as a racialized space in a city. Despite their contemporary framing as an ethnic enclave, Chinatowns were originally racially segregated urban ghettos that formed in the late 1800s when early Chinese immigrant laborers were socially and legally excluded from mainstream society. In the face of this exclusion, an internal social structure, which included a network of organizations and a local economy, provided resources and a sense of community.[37] The ethnic organizations were especially critical in many historic Asian American spaces as a de facto structure of local governance and social control.[38] Robert Park originally argued that these organizations in ethnic enclaves were meant to replicate the intimate village structure of immigrant homelands.[39] They were theorized to be insular institutions that only provided resources for immigrants who had yet to assimilate into the mainstream. However, these ethnic organizations have persisted and continue to hold meaning for multiple generations and cohorts of new immigrants. They are the basis for the community power structure in Chinatowns, and generations of organizations in the neighborhood are present today.

While providing spaces of political inclusion for some, these ethnic organizations can also be exclusionary, serving the needs of ethnic community elites. The Chinatown elite has historically consisted of members of older organizations that have been critical in the development of the political, organizational, and commercial infrastructure of these spaces. These organizations have also historically represented business interests in the community. In his work on New York City Chinatown, Peter Kwong argues that Chinatown is a polarized community of *uptown Chinese* and *downtown Chinese*.[40] The uptown Chinese are the Chinese Americans who left Chinatown after experiencing upward mobility but still have economic investments in Chinatown and are part of the older institutions that continue to hold political power in Chinatown. The downtown Chinese include poor and working-class Chinese Americans who are unable to leave Chinatown and rely on housing and employment from the uptown Chinese. Kwong further argues that the downtown Chinese face dual oppression in which they may be oppressed by both mainstream society as well as within their community. Community elites have hidden the neighborhood's social problems, including poverty, labor exploitation, and juvenile delinquency, conveying Chinatown as a presentable neighborhood to encourage economic development and assert a sense of national belonging.[41] The ethnic elite, and the organizations that they are a part of, hold much political and economic power in Chinatown and have been important in representing the ethnic community, but they are also often only representing specific interests and segments of the community.

In response to these inequities, new community organizations and types of organizing in urban Chinatowns have contributed to a complex neighborhood political structure representing different generations and political interests. As Asian Americans engaged in the New Left movements that emphasized self-determination, anti-racism, and anti-imperialism in the 1960s, they became involved in labor and housing activism on behalf of working-class immigrants and seniors living in older ethnic enclaves like Chinatown that disrupted the power of the older elite community leaders and organizations.[42] This engagement led to new political leadership that addressed issues of urban poverty and continues to be a political voice representing immigrant working-class interests today.[43] This grassroots organizing has not only highlighted class struggles within the community, but has been critical of both outside investment and the older power structure in contributing to gentrification.[44] Some of them have also since transformed into formal community institutions and nonprofits that are now part of the community power structure.

These ethnic politics and organizational dynamics are especially critical to understanding gentrification and spatial justice in places such as urban Chinatowns. The organizations and groups that form in ethnic spaces serve as critical sites for community leadership to develop and ultimately to enact power over community development and land use conflicts. Yet the representation of community is contested and political, especially in community development practices among non-White immigrant communities.[45] The neighborhood has a long-standing ethnic community elite whose political and economic power has been challenged and reshaped throughout history, especially with the arrival of new immigrant cohorts and political activism from the younger generation. Furthermore, through their political engagement, the different segments of the ethnic community who do not live there also continue to make political claims that have implications for local development. They are engaging in placemaking efforts that reconstruct the meaning of the neighborhood for the ethnic community and the meaning of the ethnic community itself.

SPATIAL-RACIALIZED REPRESENTATIONS OF CHINESE AMERICA

The politics that define Chinatowns and the process of gentrification in these spaces also necessitates an analysis of how racialization is spatially informed. Gentrification studies have traditionally approached race as an outcome measure, that racial turnover in historical non-White ethnic spaces is an indicator of forced displacement. However, this understanding of race within gentrification is simplistic. It provides a static representation of race and race relations and how that is expressed through space.[46] While Chinatowns may be framed as ethnic enclaves, they are ultimately racialized spaces. They began as neglected slums, originally formed in response to the racialized othering and segregation of early Chinese immigrant laborers, who were treated as socially and culturally inferior. Today, as multiculturalism and diversity have become of increasing value in urban areas, Chinatowns are now recognized as cultural and historical assets.[47] The transformation of Chinatowns and their shifting values and meanings is intrinsically linked to racialized understandings of Chinese Americans and their positioning within race relations.

The process of gentrification should thus be understood in relation not simply to race, but to the process of racialization. Michael Omi and Howard Winant define the racialization of groups as an othering process that "signifies and symbolizes [historically situated] sociopolitical conflicts and interests in reference to different types of human bodies."[48] The cultural and political representations of different racialized groups contribute to ongoing social stratification and power inequities across groups based on these perceived physical markers and ethnic culture.[49] While race is a persistent, structural force that stratifies groups, racial categories are unstable and politically contested. In their theory of racial formation, Omi and Winant further argue that individuals, groups, and institutions participate in historically situated racial projects in which groups negotiate current racial ideologies, meanings, and representations to organize and distribute cultural, economic, and political resources. These racial projects can be anti-racist, challenging White supremacy and racial hegemony, but they can also reinforce racial inequities.

Gentrification conflicts can be seen as what Clement Lai defines as spatialized racial projects in which this rearticulation and negotiation of a group's racialized social and political standing are anchored in place and neighborhoods.[50] Wendy Cheng further explains that as individuals and organizations negotiate the material and social conditions of spaces, they are in accommodation and resistance to racial ideologies that shape identities and relations.[51] Land use and development conflicts, the segregation and migration of groups across space, and the social interactions and activities within a geographically defined space all not only shape the identity and material conditions of places, but also contribute to the production of race and community.[52] Thus, the political processes that contribute and respond to gentrification can also be seen as a critical racial project.

The racialization of groups has played a significant role in urban development throughout history, resulting in an uneven distribution of resources and precarity among communities of color.[53] George Lipsitz argues that a racialized moral and political economy of place contributes to a *White spatial imaginary*.[54] The ongoing private and public investment that contributes to the segregation of White and non-White communities has shaped the exchange-value of places, homeownership opportunities, and neighborhood amenities, with specific privileges and political power held in White spaces. Traditional top-down approaches to planning, such as urban renewal policies and practices, have been critiqued as pathologizing low-income Black, Latine, Asian American, and non-White immigrant neighborhoods as socially disorganized to justify the characterization of these communities as blighted.[55] Contemporary debates on land use changes, from housing to commercial developments, continue to draw from negative framings of the poor, immigrants, and racialized groups to resist development and promote slow growth.[56] These racialized framings also differ across groups as non-White communities have been differentially framed in revitalization efforts reflecting their racialization, histories of migration, and residential segregation.[57]

For Asian Americans, historic urban ethnic enclaves have been critical sites where ascribed racialized community identities are reproduced, challenged, and rearticulated. In the late 1800s, Asian Americans were socially and legally excluded as non-Whites and seen as unassimilable others. In the post–World War II context, the racialized identity of Asian American communities has been the image of the assimilated, upwardly mobile "model minority" that valorizes them relative to other racial groups.[58] This ascribed identity persists to contemporary times. While seemingly presenting a positive image of the community as model citizens, this identity homogenizes the experiences of Asian American communities and obscures the ongoing economic, cultural, and political oppression facing many Asian Americans, especially those still living in ethnic enclaves like Chinatown. When the model minority identity was extended to Asian Americans, community elites steered community development in Chinatown to support this image of Chinese Americans as model citizens, emphasizing their possibility for socioeconomic mobility and assimilation.[59] This reframing of Chinatown was part of the neighborhood's transition from an urban ethnic ghetto that formed through racial exclusion to an ethnic enclave facilitating ideologies of assimilation. By extension it further facilitated the racial positioning of Chinese Americans as model minorities who, although still culturally foreign, could socioeconomically incorporate and contribute to society. These images of the community were juxtaposed against the portrayal of Black communities, who continued to be pathologized and criminalized as "bad" citizens.

Yet the development of progressive Asian American politics that countered these model minority perceptions was also rooted in the place-based political engagement in older urban ethnic enclaves.[60] This activism, which emerged during the 1960s, resisted assimilationist perspectives and articulated an Asian American identity that was situated in anti-racist, anti-capitalist, and anti-imperialist philosophies as they fought for working-class immigrant residents and laborers in these older ethnic spaces. Politically progressive Asian Americans specifically protested urban redevelopment in ethnic enclaves as a part of the politicization. This resistance was not simply to preserve the historical importance of these spaces, but also to highlight the urban poor and working-class Asian immigrants who still lived in these places, thus purposely resisting assimilation narratives. Today, anti-gentrification organizers continue to use the ideological frameworks of anti-imperialism and anti-racism that were rallying cries for the Asian American movement to connect the current forced displacement of working-class immigrants and refugees to the longer history of forced displacement that they faced in their home countries due to US militarism and imperialism. This is especially true for many Chinese and Asian Americans who migrated from Southeast Asian countries and now have settled in neighborhoods like Chinatown. As Diane Fujino argues, the social conditions and relationships in older urban spaces have nurtured an oppositional political culture that openly questions democracy and equality.[61] Historic urban ethnic enclaves have thus been critical sites for Asian Americans to develop politicized ethnic community identities that have broader implications for their racialization, while also having broader material impacts on these neighborhoods. Despite the uneven racialized development of space, communities of color have created solidarities that hold the possibilities of countering the *White spatial imaginary* and to create spaces of their own.

Spaces are an expression of prevailing ideologies about race, class, and culture. We can see this in both the built environment as well as how these spaces are governed, whether from within or external to the community. Thus, the disputes over neighborhood change in Chinatown are at an intersection of conflicts about how we define community, the commodification of land, and the impacts of the racialization of our communities. This negotiation is also happening in response to urban policies that are not just restructuring the physical conditions of neighborhoods, but are also contributing to racial and socioeconomic inequities. By asserting specific histories, stories, and images of Chinese and Asian Americans, different political actors are constructing specific representations of Chinatown as both a community and physical space, which shapes how spatial justice is defined in Chinatown and whether it can be realized.

ETHNOGRAPHIC RESEARCH
IN LOS ANGELES CHINATOWN

The narratives, stories, and data presented in *The Power of Chinatown* are from my ethnography about the political culture of Los Angeles Chinatown that I conducted from 2014 to 2018.[62] This was a very specific, but critical moment in the neighborhood's history. I arrived in Chinatown after the statewide dissolution of redevelopment agencies in 2011, which had guided much of the neighborhood's development for three decades, but before the COVID-19 pandemic in 2020, which undeniably exacerbated the concerns about how Chinatown residents and small businesses were vulnerable for displacement due to not just gentrification, but also the rise of anti-Asian sentiment. While this book is centered on a specific moment in Chinatown's contemporary history, the 2010s, I also consider how these dynamics are reflective of how Chinatowns, as well as Asian America more broadly, have changed since the 1965 Immigration and Nationality Act. This ethnography is also specifically about the neighborhood that developed from the New Chinatown development, which was established in 1938 and has evolved into a roughly 1.5 square miles area located in the northeastern area of Los Angeles.[63] I situate this neighborhood as a distinct physical geography that is not inclusive of the entirety of the former Old Chinatown area (currently Union Station and the El Pueblo Historical Monument), nor the cities in the San Gabriel Valley that have been labeled the "new suburban Chinatowns."[64] However, as explained in subsequent chapters, these areas are external influences that shape the neighborhood and concerns about gentrification.

During my fieldwork, I gathered data through observations of the neighborhood and community events, interviews, and local archives. I observed over ninety public meetings and events in Chinatown hosted by community organizations and local government. I chose these sites with the expectation that community leaders would learn about, share, and deliberate neighborhood development issues, which was not always the case. However, the absence of these discussions was also critical in understanding the community power structure and how there was a distinction between ethnic politics and place-based politics in Chinatown, a major theme that will be the focus of chapter 2. As I routinely attended these meetings, I became a more active participant-observer by the end of my first year of fieldwork, which often included volunteering to help with meeting logistics and note taking for meeting minutes. Additionally, I conducted observations of the neighborhood, which included attending major cultural events and routine neighborhood visits. Neighborhood visits provided additional contextual understandings of Chinatown, as I saw patterns of foot traffic during different times of the day, the physical and spatial arrangement of the neighborhood, and the progress of new developments that were being proposed and constructed. Through the process of participant-observation and my regular presence in the neighborhood, many in the community became familiar with me, which allowed me access to a range of individuals for interviews.

I conducted both informal and formal interviews with various types of Chinatown stakeholders. During my observations, I had many open-ended and unstructured interviews that provided a contextual understanding of development issues in Chinatown. A majority of these stakeholders were community leaders; however, I also interacted and had informal interviews with residents, business owners, and various individuals who worked in local government. The informal, unstructured interviews were especially helpful in constructing a general history of Chinatown, the organizational landscape, and the Chinese American community in Southern California that was not available through archival research. This book primarily includes excerpts from fifty-two formal semi-structured interviews with community leaders. I broadly defined and identified community leaders as individuals who publicly represented and spoke on behalf of the Chinatown community, whether as community-based organization leaders, staff, or members; grassroots organizers; or individual stakeholders not tied to any one organization but actively engaged in the community. These community leaders are reflective of the complexities of Chinatown and its intersecting identities and meanings for the Chinese American community. They represent the different interests that stakeholders have in Chinatown, specifically business, cultural, and residential interests, and they vary in age, gender, generation, years of involvement, and political perspectives. Community leaders provided perspectives based on their community work that recognized the interests of other members of the neighborhood and community, as well as their own. While I critically analyzed these perspectives, as they were not always opinions or perceptions that came directly from residents or workers of Chinatown, their narratives and actions provided important insight about the social and political relationships in Chinatown.[65]

Archival research was also critical to understanding the broader context and history of the neighborhood. I collected various documents that consisted of media, community publications, social media accounts of community organizations, government documents and reports, and census data, which I was able to access via my observations and visits to community organizations, as well as personal and online public archives. Through my archival research, I was able to construct a social history of Chinatown to understand the trajectory and pattern of development, which is further detailed in chapter 1. Limited academic work was available in this area, thus archival research, especially the community-based publications, served as important sources to understand the historical context. Furthermore, these documents allowed for an analysis of how urban revitalization and neighborhood change in Chinatown was framed to the public. Similar to the interviews, I approached my archival research from an interpretivist and critical perspective as I analyzed the various archives as reflective of specific institutional perspective and/or the person's role in the community.[66]

Following the reflexive science approach to ethnography, I situated myself as an active participant in meaning making and the construction of knowledge during my fieldwork.[67] As a 2.5 generation Chinese American woman (one parent born in China who immigrated as a teenager and the other born in the United States) who has family members involved in Chinese American heritage and cultural activities in San Francisco and Los Angeles, I was aware that my identity and background would provide specific privileges, and at times barriers, to developing community relationships. Some community gatekeepers had prior knowledge about my family without ever meeting me, which created a sense of familiarity and trust from the very start of my fieldwork. Others viewed me as a stranger and were hesitant to engage with me until some time had passed.

While I was able to develop relationships and trust with many in the community, I never situated myself as a complete insider or outsider to the community.[68] I was a co-ethnic, so many naturally assumed I would have some predetermined insight into the community, which I did to some extent. I was also praised for visiting the neighborhood so often and commuting between Irvine and Los Angeles, as it was a sign of my commitment to the Chinatown community. Yet my gender, age, generational status, occupation, language skills, and background as nonnative to Los Angeles also influenced my access and ability to develop rapport with different stakeholders.[69] These various aspects of my identity both enhanced and limited my understandings in the field. My identity as an academic researcher also situated me as a perceived neutral entity in the community. This perception of my neutrality was further magnified as I visited different community leaders and stakeholders simultaneously, often without a consistent gate-keeper introducing me. I also volunteered for several organizations, and I eventually became an official member of two organizations, the Chinese Historical Society of Southern California and the Chinese American Citizens Alliance–Los Angeles Lodge. Despite my membership, I still was never associated with any one group throughout my fieldwork. This position allowed me to navigate the different organizations with the same amount of depth, but concurrently limiting my ability to be a true insider with any one organization. Even as a member of some organizations, I was not always privy to insider information because I was not in a leadership position and many in the community prioritized my identity as an academic researcher, which made me distinct from a typical community stakeholder. I was also considered to be a young person—and specifically a young woman participating in spaces that continue to be male-dominated—still learning the ins and outs of both the Chinatown community and Southern California Chinese American community, with the expectation that my involvement would be limited.

My relationships were not static and, at times, were tenuous. I was in contact with individuals and groups that were in conflict but often not in direct contact with one another. As someone who was in a privileged position to learn and gather information about the community that was often not shared or easily accessible across spaces, I quickly realized that I was also situated within the community social structure and had a source of potential power: information and technical knowledge about urban planning.[70] I was asked by several people about my opinions about other groups in Chinatown, advice on interpreting land use policies, and my initial policy recommendations based on what I learned so far. I was enthusiastic to help when I could, but had to be mindful about how to share and present information when I was asked by others. I not only did not want to jeopardize my relationship and trust with different individuals, but I also did not want to contribute to the reproduction of community conflict and power struggles. Thus, while this book presents the experiences and narratives of community leaders, my analysis and interpretations also account for my positionality and relationships to ensure that I provide as faithful an account of both the community and my experiences.

The following chapters are a synthesis of the fieldwork I conducted in Los Angeles Chinatown. The analysis presented in this book reflects both my academic training as an ethnographic researcher and my personal experience as a Chinese American woman learning about the community and becoming involved in the community political structure. These chapters show how community leaders represented the Chinatown community and asserted control and power in Chinatown through several mechanisms: the creation and participation in both grassroots community organizations and the local formal governance structures; the construction of symbolic boundaries to define community belonging; and the framings of neighborhood change and identity that regulated the neighborhood's physical character. I specifically focus on housing, economic development, and cultural heritage, as these were the most salient issues underlying the broader debates about gentrification and forced displacement in Chinatown. Additionally, I underscore that forced displacement can manifest in different forms, whether a direct, physical displacement, indirect displacement pressures, or symbolic ruptures to a sense of community and place. The chapters show how and why community leaders varied in their interpretations of neighborhood change and representation for the neighborhood, both of which have implications for envisioning a just and equitable Chinatown.

I begin with a brief history of Los Angeles Chinatown from an urban planning and racialization perspective to set the context for the contemporary development issues in the neighborhood. Unlike past histories that center the Chinese American community in Los Angeles, in chapter 1, I center the physical neighborhood of Chinatown and its changes throughout time. Forced displacement is not only a contemporary issue but has been a defining part of Chinatown's history that community leaders have constantly responded to. They also did so in ways that navigated their racialization during specific time periods. In addition, this chapter sets the context for gentrification in Los Angeles Chinatown as a neighborhood located in a Pacific Rim global city that promoted low density and suburban development, which continue to shape race relations and residential patterns in the region. This unique aspect of Los Angeles also structured the role of the Chinatown neighborhood as an important economic, political, and cultural hub for the Chinese American community. While Chinese Americans have faced racial segregation, historically they also have been geographically dispersed to certain areas, which has implications for the role and meaning of Chinatown for the local Chinese American community today.

The meaning and articulation of community is constantly contested in Chinatown. Through an analysis of the organizational landscape of Chinatown, chapter 2 examines how community stakeholdership is redefined and challenged in Chinatown. Chinese Americans who did not live in the neighborhood continued to be involved in organizations and organizing that represent the neighborhood in gentrification, community development, and other land use conflicts. Their involvement showed how Chinatown is not simply a cultural or economic center for Chinese Americans, but also an ongoing center for political engagement for the ethnic community across Los Angeles and Southern California. Community organizations served as those spaces for politicization and belonging, and it was in these sites that community leaders became neighborhood representatives. However, the legitimacy and role of different community organizations, old and new, were being questioned as a part of the internal power conflicts in the community. Community leaders engaged in symbolic boundary work to assert their legitimacy and to delegitimize others to control community representation. Through this boundary work, they negotiated their community belonging and personal identities as nonresidents, while still trying to assert political power. Ultimately, it was not enough to identify as Chinese American to represent Chinatown, as community leaders and their organizations needed to demonstrate how they are effectively representing the lived experiences of the Chinatown residents and workers.

Chapter 3 further delves into this question of community in Chinatown and the role that the state has in shaping community politics and representation. Through an examination of the spaces of local control that were implemented through state and local public policies, I show how these spaces have contributed to a political displacement and restructuring that reproduced power imbalances in community representation. Local organizations were still integral for community representation, but the city provided formal spaces to promote citizen participation, including the Chinatown Community Advisory Committee and the Historic Cultural Neighborhood Council. These spaces attempted to expand and provide more holistic community representation in local politics. Yet they also had a counter-impact on democratizing representation and instead facilitated in the evolution and legitimization of the community business leaders as the dominant political voice despite the emergence of progressive political representation. Progressive activists, while seen as dominant in spaces of citizen participation, have had difficulty sustaining their presence in Chinatown politics beyond certain individuals, leading to fundamental questions about leadership and representation in Chinatown. Furthermore, the Chinatown Business Improvement District (BID) formed in relation and in response to these spaces, while also stressing that this was a form of local control. However, it is ultimately a neoliberal tool that legitimized a new cohort of business leaders as the community voice to advise the city and developers. This chapter shows the limits and possibilities of these formal spaces of local control in promoting equitable development.

The term *gentrification* is a politicized one, and in my fieldwork, I found that rather than directly engaging with the term *gentrification*, community leaders often spoke of the need for diversity and wanting balance for Chinatown. Chapter 4 examines how community leaders invoked these terms to discuss gentrification. The rhetoric and discourses about balance and diversity were not simply about promoting a social mixing of socioeconomic and racial demographics in the community. They situated their views in response to the development history of Chinatown, as well as its relationship to other areas in the region. Specifically, community leaders drew from Chinatown's recent history of affordable housing development as a Community Redevelopment Agency (CRA) project area and its relation to both downtown and the San Gabriel Valley to understand how the neighborhood can or should remain a unique ethnic space. Community leaders used these reference points to justify and resist specific changes that were displacing the physical and social character of Chinatown that would sustain it as a low-income immigrant neighborhood. However, organizers have also created counterframes of diversity and balance that emphasized an equity framework to ensure that low-income, working-class members of the Chinatown community are recentered in conversations and decision-making for the neighborhood.

In chapter 5, I interrogate how, amid a lack of policy tools to protect and preserve the neighborhood, community leaders attempted to regulate the neighborhood culture through the built environment, businesses, and cultural events. Because Chinatown is associated with a Chinese American identity and culture, Chinatown's culture is shifting in relation to the changes within the Chinese American community in Southern California, as well as in response to the global Chinese diaspora and increasing economic power of China. These dynamics not only define the possibilities of a shared ethnic identity and culture in Chinatown, but it is also shaping how Chinese and

Asian Americans engage in Chinatown. While community leaders sought to maintain Chinatown as a Chinese American community space, these cultural expressions are contested as they reflect differences in socioeconomic status, generation, and migration histories. Furthermore, the economic contributions of Chinese and Asian Americans as producers or consumers of the neighborhood was often privileged in cultural strategies, emphasizing that the role of neighborhood culture is to promote economic growth rather than to help empower and build community capacity to resist displacement. Despite the ongoing efforts to maintain Chinese Americans as the key actors in defining the neighborhood culture, these efforts can still encourage gentrification that lead to cultural and economic displacement.

This book ends with a consideration of how the histories and perspectives captured in my ethnography can provide insight into gentrification and the place-based ethnic politics that drive neighborhood change. The opening and closing of the Walmart Neighborhood Market was just one event in the longer, complex story of development conflicts in Los Angeles Chinatown. The insight and experiences presented throughout this book may be specific to the Los Angeles Chinatown community, but it is ultimately part of a global, ongoing effort to actively include working-class immigrant communities like Chinatown in both academic and policy conversations about gentrification and urban change. By doing so, we not only can learn more about cities and neighborhoods and how they are changing, but we can also plan for its future in a way that centers the people who continue to call these places their home.

ONE

The Making and Remaking of Chinatown

> Central City North is not only the birthplace of Los Angeles,
> but the symbolic cultural centers for three of the region's most
> prominent ethnic groups. The plan area encompasses China-
> town, parts of Little Tokyo, and parts of the original Mexican
> pueblo. Ironically, the majority of each of the major ethnic popu-
> lations that settled [in] Central City North now live outside the
> plan area, yet each regards the original locations as the heart of
> their heritage in Los Angeles.
>
> —Excerpt from the Central City North Community Plan
> for the City of Los Angeles

LOS ANGELES CHINATOWN is a site of heritage for the city and Chinese
American community. It is also one of the oldest urban Chinatowns remaining in the United States. The neighborhood remains an important ethnic
and cultural space, but it has also experienced major upheavals and transfor-
mations throughout its history. The contemporary landscape of Chinatown
that we see today has been shaped by a combination of forces both internal
and external to the community. The physical changes in the neighborhood
are intrinsically linked to the changes in the Chinese American community.
In Los Angeles, the community has been constantly reshaped demographi-
cally and culturally by regional migration and immigration trends that
reflect the global Chinese diaspora. But external forces outside of the Chinese American community have also influenced Chinatown's development,
as neighborhood changes were often in response to the city's development
initiatives, whether in alignment or in resistance to these broader trends.
Los Angeles has gone through various stages of development and redevelopment to maintain its power as a global urban economic and cultural
center. Concurrently, development in Los Angeles supported a fragmented
city of low-density, decentralized development that contributed to a region-
ally specific racial segregation.[1] As a downtown adjacent area, Chinatown
has been subject to the pressures of these urban changes and development

trends that sought to constantly modernize the city. These development pressures have contributed to Chinatown being one of several destinations, albeit a very critical one, for Chinese Americans across Los Angeles today.

In this chapter, I trace the trajectory of Chinatown's development with a specific emphasis on how the neighborhood has been shaped by the intersection of immigration and urban development policies. These are two forces that contribute to the ongoing restructuring of urban spaces and racialization of ethnic communities. These policies have structured Chinatown as an ongoing, contested site for not just urban development, but for the expression of a Chinese American community identity. The different stages of Chinatown's development as an immigrant gateway and ethnic space are a spatial expression of the changing racial ideologies and positioning of Chinese Americans, from the early history of racial exclusion targeting Asian immigrants to the current era that embraces and commodifies global, multicultural identities. The racial formation of Chinese Americans has physical and spatial implications as it has also reshaped the value of Chinatown from a neglected urban neighborhood to a cultural asset. While it is recognized today as an integral historical and "symbolic cultural center" in the city, it has also been a living neighborhood that continues to be a home for working-class immigrants, especially Asian Americans. The development pressures and the threats of gentrification in the neighborhood today are calling into question how Chinatown will support community formations and a sense of belonging for the Chinese American community in the years to come.

FROM OLD CHINATOWN TO NEW CHINATOWN: ASSERTING BELONGING IN THE FACE OF EXCLUSION (1870–1940)

The first major wave of Chinese immigrants to the United States occurred in the mid-1800s. There has been documentation of Chinese Americans in the Los Angeles area since the 1780s, with the 1850 city census listing two house servants of Chinese descent.[2] Due to political and economic instability in China that was exacerbated by European and US imperial interests in the mid- to late 1800s, Chinese laborers migrated to the United States for economic opportunity. US corporations also recruited laborers to work in various industries, such as railroads, mining, and agriculture. Chinese migrant laborers were especially critical to the construction of the Central Pacific and Southern Pacific railroads and experienced dangerous working conditions. A select few also came as merchants and students, representing a more elite class. The early Chinese immigrants were primarily from the Guangdong, or Canton region in China, and primarily migrated from the Siyi, or Szeyup, counties.[3] These migration flows contributed to the Cantonese culture as the dominant cultural identity of early Chinese Americans and many urban Chinatowns.

In response to the mass migration of Chinese laborers, xenophobia and racism emerged, which influenced US policies. Chinese migrant laborers were seen as part of a Yellow Peril in which individuals of Asian descent were positioned as economic, social, and moral threats. During this time, employers paid Chinese and Asian migrant laborers lower wages compared to their White counterparts. Labor unions thus saw them as threats, specifically accusing Chinese Americans of stealing jobs from the White working class. Meanwhile, public officials saw them as health threats responsible for spreading major infectious diseases emerging at the time, including the Bubonic Plague and cholera.[4]

This sentiment led to different policies and practices that limited immigration and legally excluded the rights of Chinese and Asian Americans. The Naturalization Act of 1790 already established that the naturalization of immigrants was limited to those who were "free Whites," and Chinese Americans were classified as non-White. The Page Act of 1875 restricted Asian women from immigrating to the United States, deeming them "undesirables." This policy created a gendered migration stream from China and led to the development of early Chinatowns as bachelor societies. The Chinese Exclusion Act of 1882, which was the first federal policy to explicitly prohibit immigration based on race and national origin, banned Chinese laborers from entering the United States for ten years and prohibited Chinese immigrants currently living in the United States to apply for citizenship. They were legally classified as "aliens ineligible for citizenship." The Geary Act of 1892 required each Chinese resident, regardless of immigration status, to register and obtain a certificate of residence. It also extended the restrictions of the Chinese Exclusion Act for another ten years, and the act would not be officially repealed until 1943. The Immigration Act of 1924 further restricted immigration to the United States by creating national quotas that heavily limited Asian immigration. This policy set preferences for those who have at least one relative who was a naturalized citizen or for those who were merchants or skilled in a certain trade or industry, such as agriculture.

These restrictive immigration policies were the foundation for the structural racism that explicitly denied Chinese Americans, especially first-generation immigrants, to receive rights and privileges as citizens.

As these exclusionary policies against Asian immigrants were passed at the federal level, Los Angeles was developing as a major urban center with one of the most racially diverse populations in the United States.[5] By the early twentieth century, the city had become a major immigrant gateway for Asian and Mexican migrants, while also attracting Black migrants from the South and the White middle class from the Midwest.[6] Yet Los Angeles was also a segregated city, with land use policies that reinforced the xenophobia and racism that othered Chinese Americans and contributed to a White/non-White racial binary. In 1908, the city implemented the Residence District Ordinance, which was a series of zoning ordinances enacted throughout the city to separate residential and industrial use spaces. The zoning patterns not only separated uses but also laid the foundation for a racially segregated city, as the zoning decisions reflected the racial and class divisions within the city.[7] Wealthier neighborhoods in the west enforced more restrictive zoning measures to ensure that they would remain low-density residential areas. The southern and eastern neighborhoods were unrestricted areas and tended to have more industrial uses or were underdeveloped.[8] Asian American, Black, and Latine, primarily Mexican American, communities were clustered in these areas.[9] The Residence District Ordinance also targeted Chinese American businesses by restricting laundry houses and other businesses commonly owned by Chinese merchants to industrial zones. This restriction was a part of the moral and public health panic that was used to further marginalize Chinese Americans at the time.[10]

State-level property ownership laws further shaped local community formation and neighborhood development. The California Alien Land Acts of 1913 and 1920, which initially targeted Japanese Americans, further excluded Chinese Americans by prohibiting any "aliens ineligible for citizenship" from owning and leasing property. While not as racially overt as the Exclusion Act, it still had racial undertones by further restricting the rights of noncitizens, which were primarily immigrants of Asian descent. These policies systematically placed Chinese Americans outside of mainstream society, socially and legally. In 1917, the Supreme Court declared racial zoning ordinances illegal in their ruling of *Buchanan vs. Warley*. This ruling only applied to legal statutes and not private agreements, which included restrictive covenants on private property. These covenants continued racial segregation, barring many non-White groups from renting and owning property in many neighborhoods. This racial segregation made Chinese Americans, as well as other non-White communities, especially vulnerable for early redevelopment projects that aimed to modernize Los Angeles at the turn of the century.

Development and Displacement of Old Chinatown

The restrictive policies against Chinese Americans, from the federal to the local level, shaped the formation of Chinese American settlements in Los Angeles. Old Chinatown formed as Chinese immigrants increasingly began to settle in Pueblo de los Ángeles, near the location of the Old Plaza, which was in the city's eastern industrial area near the railway terminals. The vicinity around the Old Plaza was not only home to Old Chinatown, but also Sonoratown, a primarily Mexican migrant community, and thus Chinese and Mexican Americans were living in proximity to each other.[11] Old Chinatown formed around the street, Calle de los Negros, or Negro Alley, which is present-day Los Angeles Street (Figure 1). The street name reflects the racial caste system of Spanish colonialism in Mexico that marginalized and segregated by skin color and African descent. The settlement of early Chinese immigrants in this street can be seen as a part of a legacy of racism and segregation in the Los Angeles area that predates California statehood. By 1870, a little less than two hundred Chinese Americans lived in the area, which was roughly half of the Chinese American population in Los Angeles. By 1910, the neighborhood included over three thousand Chinese Americans, and by 1920, the community also included second-generation, or native-born, Chinese Americans.[12] The presence of native-born Chinese Americans was critical for the community, as they could claim birthright citizenship and thus had the legal rights of citizens.[13]

Old Chinatown was home to the largest concentration of Chinese Americans in Los Angeles by the early 1900s, yet it was not the only Chinese American settlement during this time. Just south of Old Chinatown, on Ninth and San Pedro near the present-day Fashion District, was the City Market community. This market was established in 1909 in partnership with Chinese and Japanese Americans produce distributors. City Market is considered one of the first satellite Chinatowns in the Los Angeles area. The market not only employed Chinese American workers. The surrounding area also had a noticeable concentration of Chinese American residents, along with ethnic restaurants, grocery stores, and churches.[14] The Chinese

FIGURE 1. Calle de los Negros, the site of Old Chinatown, and now present-day Los Angeles Street, 1882. Photo from the C.C. Pierce Collection of Photographs. Image courtesy of the Huntington Library.

American presence in City Market declined following World War II. However, the existence of multiple early settlements for Chinese Americans highlights that while they were a racially segregated community, they were not hyper-segregated into one area. They lived in specific areas in proximity with other groups who were considered non-White at the time. Different Chinese American settlements would continue to develop, but primarily in the eastern areas of the city and county.

Despite Old Chinatown growing as a residential and business community, the city treated the neighborhood as a slum. Because it was located in one of the oldest areas in the city, the formation predates most of the city's formal planning institutions and tools, including the establishment of the Los Angeles Planning Commission in 1924 and the adoption of the Residence District Ordinance of 1908 and Comprehensive Zoning Ordinance in 1946. This area was a physical legacy of Los Angeles during Mexican and Spanish colonial rule and included adobos and the homes of the older Californio elite families. Isabella Seong Leong Quintana documents how Old Chinatown residents, especially the few women residents, reordered the structure of the housing in Old Plaza that challenged traditional norms of Western European nuclear families. However, to outsiders, these spaces were still seen as disorderly, which reflected the racialized marginalization of Chinese Americans during this time.[15] Yet there were no attempts to improve the neighborhood conditions. While other areas in Los Angeles received structural improvements and municipal services during this time, Chinatown was mostly neglected. It not only had older housing, and what the city deemed as the worst housing in the area, but it was also a place that had gambling houses and opium dens, and it was associated with gang wars, which furthered its image as a slum and an immoral community undeserving of services. Chinese Americans were compared to animals and depicted as preferring to live in crowded conditions because of their cultural traits, which further justified the city to neglect the community.[16] This was not uncommon to Los Angeles as other urban Chinatowns across the United States were neglected and ostracized by elected officials, the media, and the public.[17]

Chinese Americans faced both structural and everyday marginalization outside of their communities. Moreover, they were also vulnerable to racial violence in their places of residence. On October 24, 1871, a public lynching of Chinese Americans occurred on Calle de los Negros. This street was already considered to be one of the most violent streets in Los Angeles even prior to the annexation of California, and its reputation continued as it became a home for Chinese Americans. This public lynching occurred as racism against Chinese Americans was heightening. During an incident of gang conflict, police officers were wounded, and a local saloon owner died. In response, a violent mob of approximately five hundred people converged into Chinatown and murdered at least seventeen Chinese Americans, many of whom were reported to not be associated with the gangs.[18] This event is recognized as the Chinese Massacre of 1871, one of the largest mass lynchings in the United States. This was also a mass killing of approximately 10 percent of the Chinese American population in Los Angeles at the time. As Chinese Americans were excluded from many of the rights of citizenship at the time, including testifying in courts, the community could not legally defend themselves.[19] This event was symbolic of how Chinatowns were not always sanctuary spaces for the early Chinese American community. In many ways, the massacre was also the first major forced displacement of Chinatown. The racial violence caused a major unsettling of the Chinese American community, signaling that they did not belong there or anywhere in the city. Furthermore, the massacre did not necessarily contribute to public sympathy for Chinese Americans and instead contributed to the ongoing public perceptions of Chinatown as an unsafe, blighted area that the city needed to address since it tarnished the reputation of Los Angeles.

Because of its location near the downtown core and railyards, as well as the poor neighborhood conditions and the xenophobia against Chinese Americans, Chinatown was vulnerable for redevelopment projects that aimed to modernize the city. In the 1920s, Los Angeles began to develop its civic center in the downtown area which followed the larger City Beautiful Movement to revitalize cities through grand monuments and open streetscapes. This urban design promoted an image of a moral social order in contrast to the overcrowded slums that had come to characterize most cities. It was also a means for local government to continue the flows of capital and investment into cities.[20] As a part of this movement, Los Angeles built its major civic institutions near the Old Plaza, including City Hall in 1928. The city also had plans to regulate the transit corporations, which were all privately owned monopolies. One of the solutions was to develop a "union" train station near the Old Plaza area that would consolidate all the different independently owned terminals.[21]

Both the city and the media framed the construction of a central railroad station at the site of Old Chinatown as beneficial for the public. They argued that the station would provide connections to the downtown civic center development projects, revitalize and beautify the Old Plaza area, and "the present unsightly Chinatown will be eliminated."[22] By 1920, the *Los Angeles Times* declared that the old Chinatown spirit was "dead," and the neighborhood was now "slumbering in the path of progress."[23] The major property owners of Old Chinatown, the Apablasa family, had also begun to sell to private investors in the 1910s. Private investors and corporations slowly acquired the land, which paved the way for the area to be redeveloped. In May 1931, the California Supreme Court condemned all the property in Chinatown. The city used eminent domain to demolish the buildings in Chinatown and allow for the construction of Union Station. In 1933, the city began the eviction of Chinatown residents and business owners. Union Station eventually opened in 1939 and is still in operation today.

The construction of Union Station led to the removal of the largest Chinese American settlement in the city at the time. This event is also recognized as the first major forced displacement of Chinatown and Chinese Americans in Los Angeles, as Union Station led to the demolishment of most of the physical infrastructure of Old Chinatown. The Old Chinatown community of residents and businesses were forcibly removed and had to relocate. Some who were not citizens migrated back to China. Others moved to areas where Chinese Americans were not excluded, including the City Market area. However, some Chinese American residents and business owners would relocate nearby, as new Chinatowns were developing near Union Station.

Claiming Space and Belonging:
Developing a New Modern Chinatown

Less than a decade after Old Chinatown's demolishment, two new Chinatown developments were established, New Chinatown and China City. These developments were located slightly northwest of Union Station and, at the time, was proximate to European immigrant enclaves and Mexican American settlements. Remnants of the different European immigrant groups are still present today, including St. Anthony's Croatian Church and the French Hospital building. These new Chinatown developments were not just resettlement areas, but also aimed to contribute to the tourism economy of Los Angeles, intending to attract visitors who would arrive through Union Station. Their establishments also reflected the importance of Hollywood and the movie industry as major economic drivers for the city. At the time, Hollywood had an increasing fascination with "Oriental" culture, which facilitated the reestablishment of Chinatown as a potential site of economic growth for the city.[24]

China City opened first in 1938 and was developed by Hollywood socialite Christine Starling. Starling had previously developed Olvera Street, a tourist-friendly destination in the Old Plaza area that commercialized the older Spanish colonial and Mexican history of Los Angeles. China City continued Starling's commercialized plans for cultural tourism in the area with the development and presentation of Hollywood images of China, including props and sets from the movie, *The Good Earth*. Despite the Hollywood and tourist overtones, it also became a thriving Chinese American community space, housing several Chinese American businesses, which also provided jobs for the community.[25] This area was eventually devastated by several fires and disappeared by 1949. Today, there is no remnant of China City other than a sign in the area where it was originally located. Despite its short presence, China City was an example of how a Chinatown could be conceptualized and built by outsiders to the community, which did not go unnoticed by the Chinese American business community leaders at the time.

A group of first- and second-generation Chinese American business leaders also had plans for their own Chinatown development and formed the Los Angeles Chinatown Project Association (LACPA). Peter Soohoo Jr., a second-generation Chinese American, became a prominent community leader who promoted this development. To justify the value of their development, the LACPA openly criticized China City. In an open letter that circulated in the 1930s, they promoted their development as a more authentic Chinatown:

> The Chinese have not been consulted in this promotion [of China City] and no reputable Chinese merchants have approved this plan which was announced in the newspapers, nor are any Chinese merchants likely to participate in such a plan because there is already an official New Chinatown project.... This project is exclusively Chinese in conception and management.[26]

Starling responded to these critiques by stating that Chinese American business leaders did not have the resources to build a successful Chinatown.[27] While Chinese and Asian Americans were facing legal exclusions, Soohoo and other Chinese American business leaders still asserted their belonging and community control over the few spaces that they could have access to. By proposing their own Chinatown development, New Chinatown, they also were controlling the representation of their community.

New Chinatown is the current site that grew into the urban Chinatown in Los Angeles that we know of today. This development was also established in 1938, a few months after China City, with the opening of Central Plaza, a one-square block plaza that consisted of several mixed-use commercial and residential buildings (Figure 2). An additional plaza, West Plaza, was constructed across from Central Plaza in 1948. These developments were purposely designed to be modern, open-space plazas that distanced Chinatown from its prior characterization of an urban slum home to gambling, vice, and disease. The buildings in the plaza were infused with traditional Chinese architectural motifs, such as the pagoda awnings and gateways, and housed restaurants and trinket stores that appealed to tourists. This style of architecture has become a unique and quintessential physical identity of many urban Chinatowns. The roads were paved and originally allowed for automobiles to drive through the plaza, although it eventually was limited to a pedestrian plaza. The buildings are individually owned, some of which are still owned by descendants of the original owners. The LACPA also still manages the shared spaces of the plaza and is currently known as the Los Angeles Chinatown Corporation.

The New Chinatown developments served as a physical symbol of Chinese Americans asserting a claim to space and sense of belonging in an era

FIGURE 2. People walking in Central Plaza, circa 1940. Photo from the Peter Soohoo, Sr. Papers, 1883–2007 (bulk 1923–1945). Image courtesy of the Huntington Library.

of overt and legal racial exclusion. On the opening day of New Chinatown, Peter Soohoo Jr. said that this would become the new center for the Chinese American community that was now scattered throughout Los Angeles.[28] Similarly, a *Los Angeles Times* article from September 21, 1934, noted this new development would reflect the new assimilated second generation:

> Barbara Jean [Wong, descendant of the oldest living resident of Old China-town and child movie star] along with hundreds of other Chinese children whose American educations have made them more conversant with present happenings than are their parents, knows that their homes of her ancestors are passing away. But they will arise, clean, sanitary, carefully planned, when the new Chinese village, which will lie between Ord and College streets, Broadway and Alameda Street, is completed a few months from now.[29]

The New Chinatown development was a response to the exclusion Chinese Americans were experiencing at the time. The development was a way to show that the community could emulate and assimilate into mainstream ideals of urban modernity. It also signaled that with this new generation of Chinese Americans, the community saw themselves as permanently settling and as-serting their presence in the city. The establishment of New Chinatown was a political claim of their identity as Americans that was spatially expressed in a modernized commercial plaza that contrasted with the slum-like conditions of Old Chinatown. Through the clean, orderly design of New Chinatown and the positioning of the development as having economic value for the city, Chinese American leaders were resisting their racialization as an unassimilable other. New Chinatown was a physical expression that showed that they could be model citizens, legally and culturally.

While New Chinatown was community-led and framed as a community space that reflected the new generation of assimilated Chinese Americans, the development was also deliberately proposed as a tourist destination. While Chinese American business leaders were the leaders in its development and New Chinatown has the "typical" Chinatown architecture, movie set designers planned and conceived of the aesthetics of the development, indicating that aspects of New Chinatown were still meant to appeal to outsiders and Orientalist imaginaries of China. In anticipation of its opening, the *Los Angeles Times* advertised New Chinatown as a "delightful bit of the Orient re-created in America."[30] While Chinese American business leaders critiqued the inauthenticity of China City, New Chinatown was also not necessarily a natural development, nor was it primarily an insular, community-serving settlement for Chinese Americans. It was built in response to urban renewal and designed from its inception to also be a place of cultural tourism to serve non-Chinese Americans who were interested in experiencing Chinese culture. By purposely establishing a tourism element to the neighborhood, the neighborhood's economic strategy was not exclusive to, but heavily relied on a specific cultural identity of the neighborhood to encourage cultural consumption and economic development. This reliance on cultural tourism is a legacy of Chinatown that continues today.

WORLD WAR II AND THE EARLY COLD WAR ERA:
THE FLOURISHING OF NEW CHINATOWN AMID
GROWING SUBURBANIZATION (1940–1965)

The racialization of Chinese and Asian Americans began to shift as global relations were changing after World War II and transitioning into the Cold War era. As a part of asserting a global political dominance, the United States emphasized racial liberalism and equality to highlight the superiority of Western democracy over communism. As a part of these geopolitics, Chinese Americans were now shifting from "aliens ineligible for citizenship" to a model minority that while culturally different, could economically incorporate and contribute as Americans.[31] After World War II, the United States began to strike down exclusionary policies alongside these changes in race relations, which impacted the demographics and legal rights of Chinese Americans. The Magnuson Act of 1943 repealed the Chinese Exclusion Act. All Chinese Americans could now become citizens, which provided legal opportunities that were previously unavailable to them. In addition, the 1945 War Brides Act and 1946 Alien Fiancées and Fiancés Act allowed for family reunification as Chinese American bachelors could sponsor their wives to the United States. The 1948 Displaced Persons Act and 1953 Refugee Relief Act allowed for educated and professional Chinese to immigrate to the United States, many of whom were escaping communism from the People's Republic of China. By the 1950s, over 40 percent of the Chinese American population in Los Angeles identified as women and the number of US-born Chinese Americans was increasing.[32]

With these immigration policies, Chinatown was further distancing itself from the image of an urban slum. Ellen Wu argues that urban Chinatowns were "de-ghettoized" and framed as ethnic enclaves as a part of the shift in their racial positioning to model minorities. During this time, sociologists also theorized that Chinatowns would decline and become symbolic spaces as Chinese Americans were positioned as an exceptional group able to assimilate despite the history of racial exclusion.[33] Chinese Americans and other ethnic groups were not accepted because their culture was seen as an integral part of American culture; rather, they would be accepted because of their potential to become similar, but never equal, to White middle-class Americans. As this uplifting narrative emerged, Chinese Americans were still facing systemic and everyday discrimination. Chinatown also endured as an important cultural and residential space for Chinese Americans despite the shifting perceptions and increasing geographic dispersal of the community.

The Growth of New Chinatown in a Multiethnic Immigrant Neighborhood

Following World War II, the New Chinatown grew and thrived as a destination neighborhood for both Chinese Americans and tourists during these years. Al Soo-hoo, a community leader active in various cultural and civic organizations, recalled growing up in Chinatown and helping with the family business, South China Gifts, located in Central and West Plazas. He shared his observations about the active nightlife of Chinatown in the 1950s and 1960s:

> Because it was Chinatown. And it was a destination. And it was a place to go to. . . . Unique, exotic, mysterious. The closest thing to Asia that the Americans could get to. Especially during New Year, when all these people from the Midwest would come out to the Rose Bowl. There was no travel to China, to Asia. And so, this was the closest thing. They couldn't tell if that egg foo yung was real! [laughs] What's real Chinese food? And what's not real Chinese food?

As international travel was still limited, Chinatown was what Soo-hoo described as "the closest thing" to China for many people. Thus families like the Soo-hoos who owned businesses in New Chinatown thrived on tourism. Chinatown was an accessible space of difference for locals and tourists to visit, even if the authenticity was questionable.

However, the economic and physical growth of Chinatown was not simply due to tourism that appealed to imaginaries of China. During my fieldwork, the Chinese Americans who grew up in Los Angeles in the 1950s and 1960s often referred to Chinatown as the hub for the Chinese American community in Los Angeles. Chinatown businesses and institutions continued to develop and expand beyond Central and West Plazas, and many Chinese Americans frequented these businesses. Community leaders who grew up outside of Chinatown during this time also recalled how the neighborhood was still a community space for their families. David Louie, who has a family history of involvement in civic organizations in Chinatown, grew up in the Crenshaw area in South Los Angeles. He recalled how he frequently visited Chinatown with his family, explaining that it was a convening space for Chinese Americans across Los Angeles, "Historically, Chinatown was the center—the cultural center, the religious center. All your professional services were here, lawyers, doctors. You did your grocery shopping here. When you had a celebration, the restaurants were here." Other community leaders of the same generation shared similar memories of Chinatown and spoke about how they would visit on weekends to shop or visit the Chinatown banquet halls for special occasions.

While the growing commercial area around the New Chinatown development was often the focal point for nostalgia for Chinese Americans of this generation, the neighborhood surrounding the plazas was also home to a multiracial, working-class immigrant community. The neighborhood residents near the New Chinatown plazas included Southern and Eastern European and Mexican immigrants along with an emerging Chinese American presence as they were resettling after the demolishment of Old Chinatown. One long-term resident, Mary Anne Hayashi who is of Croatian descent and whose family lived in the neighborhood prior to the establishment of Old Chinatown shared her observations of the residential community at the time. As a youth, she saw few Chinese American residents and primarily lived with Italian, Croatian, and Mexican Americans. Despite being of different ethnic and racial backgrounds, they shared commonalities because they were all working-class immigrant families. She explained the sense of community along her block, "This apartment house next door was that family. It was the only Chinese family on the block. And it's still the same family. . . . But it was interesting because we were all kind of the same socioeconomic [status]. All our fathers were blue collar workers."

The Chinese Americans I met during my fieldwork who grew up in Chinatown during the time also recall growing up in a similar multiracial immigrant neighborhood, from their neighbors to their classmates at the local elementary school, Castelar. Those who had no connection to the families who founded the New Chinatown plazas also shared the challenges of growing up in working-class Chinese immigrant families. Don Toy, who became active in Chinatown progressive groups in the 1970s, described how he often had to translate for his parents, from Castelar teachers to the telephone company, as they struggled navigating mainstream institutions. Despite its public identity as an exotic destination area to experience Chinese culture, Chinatown was also a home to a working-class, multiracial immigrant community.

A Growing Suburban Community?
Residential Mobility and Legacies of Segregation

During this time, suburban housing development was also increasing, which had major impacts on the landscape of the city of Los Angeles. The 1949 Fair Housing Act (FHA) was a major federal legislation that encouraged urban renewal in Los Angeles and other metropolitan areas to address postwar housing and economic concerns. The policy supported new housing development, but it ultimately encouraged suburbanization as most of the loans financed through the FHA supported construction of single-family housing.[34] As suburban development increased, policymakers and the media began to promote these areas as a pathway for immigrant groups to assimilate. Cindy I-Fen Cheng documents how the Commission on Race and Housing, an independent commission led by the University of Chicago, facilitated this image of suburbanization.[35] From 1955 to 1958, they published a series of reports that examined housing problems facing racial and ethnic communities. To combat residential segregation, the Commission recommended that immigrants and racialized minorities move to the suburbs to expose them to White middle-class values and to discourage them in sustaining a distinct ethnic identity.

Chinese Americans were positioned to support these assimilationist arguments about suburbia, and as a result, Chinatown was being framed as a neighborhood in decline. In 1952, the California Supreme Court deemed the Alien Land Acts illegal, which allowed for all Chinese Americans to become property and homeowners, an integral part of achieving the American Dream. The *Los Angeles Times* published an article on October 26, 1959, with the headline "Chinatown Changing as Suburbs Call Residents." The article notes that out of twenty-two thousand Chinese residents in the city, only a few hundred remained in Chinatown. The article declared, "There is nothing startling about this. These are Americans. As which, they wish to live as Americans—to own homes and breathe the fresh air of the suburbs, where there is greenery for their children to play."[36]

Despite this image of assimilated Chinese Americans, housing discrimination persisted. While the Supreme Court decision for *Shelley vs. Kraemer* specifically deemed housing covenants illegal in 1948 at a federal level, other discriminatory practices would not officially be deemed illegal until the Civil Rights Act of 1968. In addition to the federal act, state laws, including the Rumford Fair Housing Act of 1963, outlawed housing discrimination based on race, color, religion, sex, national origin, disability, and family status. However, most non-White groups were still denied loans and other opportunities for home ownership in the suburbs.[37] Of the one million new single-family homes constructed in the suburban areas of Los Angeles between 1940 and 1957, only 1.5 percent were occupied by non-White households.[38] Chinese Americans were not residentially integrated, as they still faced barriers to finding housing in historically White areas.

Chinese Americans continued to settle in residential areas that were primarily in the eastern and southeastern areas of Los Angeles. The East Adams area, which is south of the downtown area, also became another major settlement where they lived in proximity with Black and Japanese American communities. Many of the older generation Chinese Americans interviewed for this research grew up near this area and in other southeastern neighborhoods. Some also grew up in the Silverlake and Echo Park areas neighboring Chinatown, which was home to a small middle-class Chinese American community. In particular, Chinese American business families and celebrities, including actress Beulah Quo, lived in this area. These families moved to this area because it was an area of single-family homes close to Chinatown that did not have restrictive covenants against Chinese Americans. These individuals who grew up in this area reminisced about how they were not simply neighbors; they were a close-knit community that carried over to Chinatown, as their parents were some of the most prominent early Chinatown community leaders who helped to establish major community institutions, including Central Plaza and Cathay Bank, the first Chinese American bank.

Additionally, the San Gabriel Valley, located in the northeastern area of Los Angeles County, was a unique space that was open to Asian Americans and Latines because it included unincorporated cities that historically were not subject to municipal regulations. While it had a history of racial exclusion in the 1920s, the San Gabriel Valley had relatively looser racial restrictions on property ownership, especially in the southern area.[39] In the 1950s, Monterey Park and other suburbs in the area experienced an increase in housing development, and non-White immigrants who had the financial means began to take advantage of these opportunities. These policies structured the San Gabriel Valley to eventually become another node in the broader network of Chinese American settlements along the eastern area of the county. The community's geographic dispersal was not necessarily a sign of assimilation, but one that reflected the pattern and legacy of racial segregation in Los Angeles.

Surrounding Downtown Redevelopment and Shrinking of Old Chinatown

While the neighborhood experienced its growth as a Chinatown—and specifically a working-class immigrant neighborhood with a growing number of Chinese American businesses and institutions—the city's urban renewal projects surrounding the neighborhood continued. Urban renewal policies at the federal, state, and local levels sought to produce more housing, but also were encouraging economic growth in major cities that were beginning to decline due to increased suburbanization. These renewal policies allowed for public agencies to determine neighborhoods as "blighted," a judgement often based on the physical characteristics of the neighborhood, to justify slum clearance and redevelopment. However, this determination of blight often did not consider the social structure and community bonds that also characterized these spaces, which contributed to criticisms that urban re-vitalization practices reproduce racial and socioeconomic inequities, a cri-tique that continues today.[40]

In 1945, the California state legislature passed the Community Redevel-opment Act, which would structure urban renewal within the state. The act gave local authority for a city to establish a community redevelopment agency (CRA) to oversee urban renewal, which included the determination of "blighted" areas to become redevelopment project areas and the creation of redevelopment plans to guide development in these areas. The Commu-nity Redevelopment Law of 1951 further structured the trajectory and pat-terns of redevelopment throughout the state as it established property tax revenues and tax increment financing (TIF) as the mechanism to fund CRA project areas. The TIF structure forecasts anticipated increases in property taxes that would ultimately be used to subsidize future housing and eco-nomic development in the area. Because of the financing structure of rede-velopment, CRA project area plans tended to favor development that would be the "highest and best use of land" to increase property values, which often included assembling land for private developers to build high-density com-mercial and market-rate housing developments.

The Los Angeles CRA formed in 1948, and one of its first activities was to work with the city planning commission to conduct a survey of the inner-city downtown area of Los Angeles. This survey deemed that 20 percent of the area was blighted and a drain on local resources, while also discouraging the development of public housing, arguing that it would further encourage blight.[41] In 1955, Chinatown's neighbor Bunker Hill was declared blighted, and historic Victorian houses were demolished for high-rise, market-rate apartment complexes.[42] The Mexican American residents in Chavez Ravine, which is the northern neighbor of Chinatown, were also forcibly displaced for the construction of Dodgers Stadium despite initial promises of pub-lic housing through redevelopment. Black and Latine communities were so disproportionately targeted for early urban renewal projects that crit-ics of urban renewal efforts nicknamed the process "Negro Removal," and in Los Angeles, the CRA was known as the "Chicano Removal Agency."[43] Chinatown was not directly impacted by the CRA during this time—most likely because it had already faced slum clearance two decades earlier and the business leaders had strategically positioned Chinatown as a modern neighborhood. However, the forced displacement of neighboring communities positioned Chinatown to experience the ripple effects of any changes in these areas that were meant to support the city's plans for revitalization and redevelopment in the downtown area.

The city also began investing in the freeway system in the 1920s, and it had grown fivefold between 1950 and 1954. The eastern area of the city, which not only included Chinatown and industrial areas but was also home to many older barrios that were home to Mexican American communities, were targeted as sites for the network of freeways that sought to increase both regional and statewide travel.[44] In 1941, the county adapted a Master Plan for Highways, and in 1947, the Collin-Burns Act, a state law, would provide over $76 million to improve highway infrastructure. In 1949, plans for the Hollywood (101) Freeway expansion included constructing a major freeway segment through Chinatown, which devastated the remaining buildings of Old Chinatown. Today, the only physical remnant of Old Chinatown is the Garnier Building, and it is preserved as the location for the Chinese American Museum. The 110 freeway was also extended through Chinatown, and both freeways became physical barriers that spatially isolated Chinatown from downtown and other neighborhoods to the north and west. At the same time, this network of freeways also made Chinatown and other downtown neighborhoods accessible to the cities in the San Gabriel Valley, which would eventually be home to many Chinese Americans by the 1980s.

A "NEW" NEW CHINATOWN IN AN ERA OF GLOBAL MULTICULTURALISM (1965–2000)

As Asian Americans continued to be repositioned as model minorities, immigration policies and urban development also shifted to reflect these changes and situated urban Chinatowns as important to the development of a multicultural urban landscape. Most notably, the 1965 Immigration and Nationality Act, or Hart-Cellar Act, contributed to the persistence of major urban Chinatowns through ongoing Chinese migration to the United States. This policy further built on the initial post–World War II immigration policies that opened immigration from China and other Asian countries. This act struck down the national origin quota system that severely restricted Asian immigration and instead placed hemispheric quotas on immigration.

It also prioritized family reunification, as well as immigrants who were of professional work status and had higher education arriving in the United States, a stark contrast to many of the early Chinese immigrants who were low-skilled laborers.[45] The passage of the 1990 Immigration Act further prioritized family reunification, along with encouraging professionals and skilled workers to migrate to the United States by increasing the number of work visas for certain professions.

In addition to the 1965 Immigration Act, refugee policies, including the 1975 Indochina Migration and Refugee Assistance Act and 1980 Refugee Act, contributed to the growth and reshaping of Chinatowns. The refugee policies reflected global tensions during the Cold War era, as they targeted refugees in Asian countries that were subject to US militarism and imperialism to combat communism. Through these policies, there was an increased migration of ethnic Chinese from areas outside of the People's Republic of China.[46] Some Chinese immigrants and refugees arrived from Hong Kong and Taiwan in response to the growing political instability in China. There were also ethnic Chinese migrants who arrived as refugees from Vietnam and Cambodia. While early Chinese immigration history predominantly reflected a Cantonese Chinese heritage, with many immigrating directly from China, the contemporary migration was much more diverse. Some of the ethnic Chinese refugees and immigrants were not only immigrating from Southeast Asian countries, including Vietnam, Cambodia, Laos, and Malaysia, but they also did not always speak or identify as Cantonese. In Los Angeles, new immigrants and refugees also had roots in the Fujian and Chaoshan regions of China. The Chinese American community identity was defined by both the global diaspora dynamics, as well as the local dynamics among the generations of US-born Chinese Americans.

Los Angeles was also establishing itself as a major Pacific Rim global city during this time, which positioned Chinatown and other historic ethnic neighborhoods as important spaces for the city. They were not just homes for new immigrants and refugees, but they could also contribute to economic growth, as they could potentially attract investment via the global economy. Tom Bradley was elected as the city's first Black mayor and was mayor from 1973 to 1993. During his tenure, Bradley often prioritized projects that would support the flow of global capital into the city, from large-scale transportation and downtown redevelopment projects to the 1984 Olympics. As a means to gain support and encourage investment for these efforts, Bradley emphasized multiculturalism as a defining part of Los Angeles. Asian countries were emerging as economic powers, and Asian Americans as model minorities with possible transnational connections played an important role in supporting a multicultural urban identity, and thus contributed to the city's economic growth.[47]

However, the city was also experiencing many social problems that led to racial and class disparities, including ongoing poverty, labor issues due to deindustrialization, and persistently tense relations with law enforcement. The Watts Rebellion in 1965 and the L.A. Uprising in 1992 were two critical moments signifying the ongoing inequities in a diversifying Los Angeles. In Chinatown, new immigrants and refugees sustained the neighborhood as an important Chinese immigrant gateway, but one that was a predominantly poor and working-class community. These population changes placed pressures on Chinatown and the city to support development that served the needs of the new immigrants and refugees despite any potential plans to position Chinatown as a downtown neighborhood to facilitate global capital. With the recognition of this urban poor within the ethnic community, there was now a recognition of the diversity of the Chinese and Asian American community that further challenged their ascribed model minority position.

Defying the Decline Narrative: The Growth and Cultural Diversification of Chinatown

The new immigration policies had a direct impact on Chinatown as both a physical and cultural community. Following the 1965 Immigration Act, Chinatown experienced population increases that continued throughout the decades (Table 1).[48] The overall neighborhood population increased by over 40 percent from 1970 to 1980, whereas the previous decade had a 10 percent decline. Similarly, the foreign-born population declined 26 percent from 1960 to 1970 and then increased 89 percent from 1970 to 1980. In one of the only studies that examined property ownership and demographics of Chinatown during this time, Lucy Hirata observed that Spanish surnames, which at the time was used as an indicator of a Latine presence, was the majority demographic of Chinatown in 1970.[49] But according to the 1980 Decennial Census, Asian Americans, specifically individuals who identified as Chinese, became the majority of residents (68%). While the residents may not have been property owners, the Census data indicate that the neighborhood was transitioning from a multiethnic immigrant space to a majority Chinese immigrant enclave.[50]

Recognizing the growth and changes in Chinatown, the *Los Angeles Times* declared that "Chinatown has gone Chinese" in 1977, citing how the residential changes in the 1970s have made it a predominantly Chinese American residential and commercial neighborhood that was serving the needs of Chinese American residents rather than visitors and tourists.[51] It was also during this time that the Italian and European immigrant businesses were having less of a presence in the commercial core along Broadway Street. Chinese American businesses and new commercial plazas developed by Chinese Americans began to dominate the neighborhood landscape. Chinese immigrants and refugees from Southeast Asia distinctly transformed the commercial character of Chinatown as they opened stores in newer shopping plaza developments, including Saigon Plaza and Chinatown Plaza, the latter of which is home to jewelry stores, many of which are owned by Chinese Americans who have roots in Cambodia.[52] The changes to immigration policy had a ripple effect to the local level, leading to a shift in Chinatown's identity that challenged one of its popular identities as a tourist destination for outsiders. It affirmed and uplifted Chinatown as a neighborhood that existed to primarily serve its residents and a culturally diverse Chinese American community.

However, Chinatown was not just revitalized as a new immigrant enclave, but one that was also becoming a home to a new urban poor community. Despite an opening of immigration following World War II, the policies created a polarized flow of immigration to the United States that impacted the demographic, cultural, and political compositions of Asian American communities.[53] These new policies also created a spatial segmentation of the Chinese American community. The US Immigration Services estimated that limited-English-proficient, low-income Chinese immigrants and refugees moved directly to Chinatown.[54] While there were Asian middle-class professionals immigrating to the United States, they could directly move to the suburbs. Working-poor Asian immigrant laborers, especially those who identified as ethnic Chinese, continued to settle in urban Chinatowns and other older urban neighborhoods, which were still home to low-wage jobs through the ethnic economy, as well as manufacturing jobs, such as garment factory work.[55] By 1980, over two-thirds of individuals living in Chinatown were considered poor, a characteristic that has remained steady over the following decades.[56] Because it had an established infrastructure, Chinatown continued to be the primary space for poor immigrants and refugees with limited English proficiency to rely on social networks and institutions for housing, jobs, and other resources as they adjusted to life in the United States.

TABLE 1. Socioeconomic Characteristics and Trends of Chinatown Residents, 1960–1990

	1960	1970		1980		1990	
	Number of Residents (% of total pop)	Number of Residents (% of total pop)	% Change	Number of Residents (% of total pop)	% Change	Number of Residents (% of total pop)	% Change
Total population	8,875	8,001	–10	11,287	41	12,846	14
			RACE				
Asian	1,963 (22.1)	4,136 (51.7)	111	7,648 (67.8)		9,779 (76.1)	28
Other							
Hispanic or Latine	4,225 (47.6)	3,142 (38.9)		2,488 (22.0)	–21	2,386 (18.6)	–4
Spanish surname							
Non-Hispanic White	6,854 (77.2)	3,854 (48.2)	–44	652 (5.8)	–83	520 (4.1)	–20
Black/African American	58 (0.7)	11 (0.1)	–81	64 (0.6)	482	292 (2.3)	356

ASIAN ETHNIC GROUPS

Chinese	6,101 (69)		6,004 (53.2)		7,903 (61.5)	32
Cambodian					722 (5.6)	
Vietnamese	(13.3)		1,496	(5.5)	712	-52
Foreign-born	4,527 (57.3)	-26	8,543 (76.6)	89	9,497 (74.1)	11

SOURCE: US Census Bureau Decennial Census for 1960–1990 prepared by Social Explorer.

The population pressures and changes in Chinatown also impacted neighboring areas. Chinatown continued to grow, but it only accounted for approximately 10 percent of the Chinese American population in the county.[57] Most Chinese Americans were living in other neighborhoods and cities. Chinatown's northeastern neighborhood, Lincoln Heights, also became a home for the Chinese American community, especially those who arrived from Southeast Asian countries. Prior to the 1970s, Lincoln Heights was a predominantly Latine neighborhood, but by the early 1980s the neighborhood experienced an increasing Chinese and Vietnamese American presence. Community leaders who witnessed this change reasoned that this shift in Lincoln Heights was related to Chinatown's limited housing supply. New immigrants and refugees still wanted to be proximate to the resources in Chinatown and moved to areas that were still accessible to the neighborhood. Along with an increase in Asian American immigrant residents, new businesses and institutions were established to support them, such as the America Vietnam Chinese Friendship Association and Buddhist temples. With these changes came media coverage about the new Asian American presence increasing housing prices and displacing the Mexican residents who were already displaced from other communities, including Chavez Ravine.[58] While the media highlighted potential Asian and Latine conflict, these racial tensions also stem from the legacy of urban renewal and segregation in Los Angeles that has led to cross-racial conflict as residents claim their right to space to prevent future displacement.

Cities in the San Gabriel Valley also continued to grow and flourish, ultimately becoming a new economic and cultural center for Chinese Americans. The city of Monterey Park was marketed as "Beverly Hills" for Mexican and Asian Americans by the 1970s, solidifying it as an aspirational, symbolic suburb for non-White groups.[59] However, unlike predictions that Asian Americans would incorporate and adapt to mainstream institutions, the San Gabriel Valley was home to *ethnoburbs* that had a multiethnic residential and commercial character.[60] This was not a smooth demographic transition, though, as there were slow growth movements that specifically resisted many of the ethnic businesses and development, some of which came from overseas Asian investment.[61] As these political and economic tensions unfolded, Monterey Park and other areas in the San Gabriel Valley were recognized as new spaces of economic and political power for Chinese and Asian Americans. Monterey Park and Chinatown were both changing and growing from new immigration, albeit on different paths and facing different development pressures.

Redevelopment in Chinatown (Again)

The city was reenvisioning its growth in the new global economy, especially in the downtown area. In 1970, the city released *Concept Los Angeles* to guide the new general plan. Recognizing the population growth and scarcity of land to develop, this plan envisioned a polynucleated city where there were different centers of activity, along with suburban, open space, and industrial areas, that were interconnected through a comprehensive transportation system. The downtown area was identified as a regional core of Los Angeles with higher population density and intensity of uses and thus the redevelopment of downtown focused on realizing this vision.

Chinatown continued to be a part of these revitalization efforts for the city. The city adopted the Central City North Community Plan in 1979, which was one of thirty-five community plans that provided planning guidelines for individual areas. While the plan included parts of Little Tokyo and what is now the Arts District, Chinatown was the only neighborhood fully included in the plan. The planning area was primarily zoned for industrial use, but the residential and commercial sections of the area were concentrated in Chinatown. Additionally, the plan described Chinatown's residential and commercial character as primarily low-rise developments.[62] However, in 1996, the city's General Plan Framework Element also designated the Chinatown commercial core as a regional center that contrasted with the preexisting land use and development of the neighborhood. The city described regional centers as places that "cater to many neighborhoods and communities and serve a population of 250,000 to 500,000 residents," by having a variety of uses, including corporate offices and major entertainment and cultural facilities, with buildings that could range from six to twenty stories.[63] This designation promoted higher density and mixed-use projects in anticipation of economic growth for the city. Chinatown's commercial core area thus was part of the city's vision for the broader downtown area to become a major destination for tourism and commercial businesses.

Despite the city's vision, Chinatown's commercial core has remained a relatively low-density neighborhood, especially in relation to downtown development. Many of the Chinatown buildings were considered low-scale developments, not exceeding five-stories, with the majority being two to three stories with retail space at the bottom; however, this trend was starting to shift during my fieldwork, as explained in chapter 5. The city also proposed an International Zone that ultimately did not materialize, but would have formalized Chinatown, along with Olvera Street, and Little Tokyo, as tourist areas to support the growth of the downtown area. Despite the population growth and specific needs to support the working-poor immigrant residents, the city's vision for Chinatown was to serve a much broader economic purpose beyond the neighborhood community.

The CRA also had a major impact on Chinatown's development during this time. In the 1970s, state policies, specifically Senate Bill 90 and Proposition 13, further incentivized local redevelopment agencies to expand the number of planning areas to generate more revenue through the TIF structure as other financing options became limited. In Los Angeles, the CRA began to designate more redevelopment areas and increasingly emphasized downtown as a central area for the headquarters of global corporations, while the surrounding neighborhoods were seen as potential residential spaces for upwardly mobile professionals working downtown. This specific type of reinvestment to the downtown core encouraged a reverse urban movement in which affluent individuals were attracted to the urban core rather than the suburban outskirts. While this back-to-the-city movement of the middle class would potentially contribute to economic growth, it also threatened to forcibly displace poor, working-class communities of color who historically lived in these areas and had limited mobility.

The city designated Chinatown as a CRA project area in 1980. In the 1970s, Asian flight capital also led to land speculation that began to increase real estate values in Chinatown and positioned it for potential new development. The designation of Chinatown was a part of a larger trend of historic urban Asian spaces across the United States being targeted for redevelopment. Philadelphia and Boston Chinatowns, Los Angeles Little Tokyo, San Francisco Manilatown, and Seattle's International District were a few of these historic spaces that were impacted by urban renewal projects, from freeway construction to new commercial development.[64] In Los Angeles, Little Tokyo, which is a mile south of Chinatown, was designated a CRA project area in 1970 amid much controversy. The redevelopment plans for Little Tokyo explicitly supported global business, tourism, and the expansion of civic institutions, as they neighbored City Hall and the downtown civic area. Japanese American senior citizens in Little Tokyo were forcibly displaced to build the New Otani Hotel, which was backed by overseas Japanese investors. Similar hotels were proposed for the downtown area to target Asian businessmen, especially from Japan, which was becoming a major economic power. These hotels were a part of the city's plans to focus on redeveloping the downtown infrastructure to cater to global business exchanges.

The struggles in Little Tokyo did not go unnoticed by Chinatown, as there were concerns about how the CRA designation would impact Chinatown. The Los Angeles formation of Asian Americans for Equality (AAFE), a progressive group that was a part of the New Left political movements of the 1970s, submitted a letter of opposition to the City Council, which critiqued the city's community engagement methods in securing community support for the designation as only being inclusive of community business interests. However, AAFE was one of the few community letters of opposition to the CRA, as most of the older community organizations and business groups wrote letters of support for the designation. They saw it as an opportunity to improve the physical infrastructure of Chinatown, particularly housing and economic development.[65] The differences in community support reflected not simply a tension between business and residential interests in Chinatown and whether to prioritize the local economy or housing. It also reflected the various approaches on how to achieve this for the neighborhood and whether these state interventions from outside the community would effectively address community needs. These tensions are further explained in chapters 3 and 4.

A DIVERSE DOWNTOWN AND CHINATOWN? CONTEMPORARY GENTRIFICATION TRENDS (2000 TO TODAY)

The decades following the 1965 Immigration Act coincided with the growth of the global economy and a recognition of the diversity among Chinese Americans. Yet how this embrace of multiculturalism and diversity has promoted social equity is a prominent debate, especially as Los Angeles has become one of the most expensive urban areas in the country. Issues of housing affordability, homelessness, and living wages are having immediate and material impacts on the livelihood of many communities today. There are continuing concerns about how current urban policies and planning tools may be perpetuating and worsening inequalities through gentrification. By the 1990s, Chinatown was one of several neighborhoods in the city experiencing displacement pressures.[66] In Chinatown, demographic and physical shifts indicate that it is becoming a more "diverse" neighborhood, but these changes have become points of debate about the potential repercussions on the Chinatown community and the relationship Chinese Americans will continue to have with the neighborhood.

Since the establishment of Central Plaza in 1938, Chinatown has grown into what some urban planners would call a complete neighborhood, with a commercial, institutional, and residential core that are interrelated to support the thriving of the neighborhood. The built environment in each of these core areas today reflects the layers of Chinese American and immigration history in Los Angeles. The commercial core runs primarily along Broadway, Hill, Spring, and New High Streets, and is home to different generations of businesses and some of the oldest Chinese American community organizations (Figure 3). This is the area that media, tourists, and community outsiders tend to identify as Chinatown.

However, there are also subtle spatial differences regarding whom the businesses serve. Among Chinese Americans who grew up in Chinatown or routinely visited the neighborhood, they note a north-south divide within the commercial area. In the northern end above College Avenue and between Broadway and Hill Street are the New Chinatown Plazas, Central and West Plaza, which are the historical anchors of the development of this new Chinatown and home to the legacy businesses that established the Chinatown neighborhood. South of this area is home to some of the oldest buildings in the city that predate the New Chinatown and China City developments in the 1930s. Community leaders recognize this area as having a concentration of community-serving retail stores, vendors, and restaurants that primarily serve co-ethnics and residents. Residential developments also exist in the commercial core, which have increased since the 1980s. Most prominently, along Broadway, the major commercial street, is Cathay Manor, a sixteen-story affordable senior housing complex and Chinatown's first subsidized affordable housing development. Other recent mixed-use residential spaces along Broadway, include Jia Apartments, across from Cathay Manor on the southern border of Chinatown, and Blossom Plaza. These newer mixed-use spaces include market-rate apartments and new retail that represent the contemporary changes that community stakeholders often associate with gentrification today.

To the west of the commercial core are the institutional and residential cores. The institutional core of Chinatown is located along Hill and Yale Streets and includes most of the neighborhood's public institutions, including Castelar Elementary School, Chinatown Library, and Alpine Recreation Center (Figure 4). Community organizations, as well as religious

FIGURE 3. Surface parking lot and small businesses along Broadway Street, one of the major streets of the main commercial core of Chinatown, 2023. Photo taken by author.

FIGURE 4. Yale Street with Alpine Recreation Center in the foreground and the Southern California Fukienese Association and multifamily housing in the background, 2016. Photo taken by author.

institutions, both old and new, such as the Thien Hau Temple and Chinese Baptist Church are also along Yale Street, as are the major social service spaces, such as the Chinatown Service Center. Most of the residential area of Chinatown sits on a hillside that begins on Yale Street and continues westward to Marview Avenue. The area is primarily multifamily apartment dwellings with a few single-family homes that are a remnant of the older history of the neighborhood. While many associate Chinatown with the commercial area, it is this part of Chinatown that is home to the people who are especially vulnerable to displacement from any of the changes that occur throughout the neighborhood.

The impact of state and city revitalization policies continues to shape these different areas in Chinatown. The CRA redevelopment plan structured and guided the development of Chinatown for over thirty years, despite its controversies. As explained in chapter 4, the CRA became one of the city's primary financing and policy mechanisms to require affordable housing. However, in 2011, Governor Jerry Brown dissolved community redevelopment agencies across the state, and thus the CRA plan for Chinatown, and the financial resources and political representation that came with it, are now gone. With its dissolution there has yet to be a policy to replace this requirement for former CRA project areas like Chinatown that is not related to opt-in developer incentives, such as density bonuses, which few choose to do. Given the larger affordable housing crisis in Los Angeles, the development of new affordable housing and preservation of the current affordable housing stock have become critical issues in Chinatown.

Chinatown business leaders also established a business improvement district (BID) in 2000 to support economic development. The BID structure is supported by the 1994 California Business and Property District Law which enabled cities to create districts that could levy annual tax assessments to support additional resources for economic development through public-private partnerships. The Chinatown BID is one of forty-two BIDs in the city and is a property-based assessment district, meaning that property owners pay into the assessment and govern the operations of the BID. Through the assessments, funding is redistributed back to the neighborhood to fund activities such as additional street cleaning, private security, and marketing, with the goal of promoting investment and spending in the area. Yet, as described in the following chapters, the BID has a controversial presence in Chinatown. The BID provides a mechanism for neighborhood governance and resources, but one that focuses primarily on economic development strategies that prioritize the economic interests of property owners. While it is technically governed from within the community, other community leaders are concerned that their practices are positioning Chinatown to be a part of downtown redevelopment trends that may contribute to gentrification and forced displacement.

Along with the dissolution of the CRA and the emergence of the BID, the city's official community plan and planning tools for Chinatown are also changing. At the time of the fieldwork, the city was revising its Comprehensive Zoning Ordinance and Central City North Community Plan. The Central City North Community Plan update has been included in the larger DTLA2040 initiative by the Department of City Planning (DCP). The DCP and the Southern California Association of Governments projected that by 2040 the downtown area, which includes Chinatown, will increase by one hundred twenty-five thousand residents, seventy thousand housing units, and fifty-five thousand jobs. The community plan revisions were to accommodate for this growth in the larger downtown vision. As one of the few historically residential and low-density neighborhoods in this planning area, the city's plans for Chinatown included specific zoning tools to preserve its low-density residential and commercial cores, but also to support growth along the neighborhood's eastern and southern borders. Similar to the 1970s, the city is once again planning for growth in Chinatown, but is encouraging incremental growth in the area that borders downtown and around the Metro Station that opened in 2003.[67] Furthermore, while the revisions to the community plan help to preserve the low-density character of the neighborhood—or maintaining it as an "urban village"—there is little in place to help maintain the cultural identity of the built environment, which arguably is what helps to distinguish Chinatown from other neighborhoods.

These development pressures along Chinatown's boundary with the downtown area have been increasing over time. The area to the east of Chinatown is often referred to as Cornfields and Dogtown and is primarily an industrial area that was home to warehouses and distribution centers, some of which are Chinese American owned. The remnants of the Chinese American ownership can be seen in the bilingual signs on the warehouses. Most notably, the Cornfields area has another planning overlay, the Cornfield-Arroyo Specific Plan (CASP), which was adopted in 2012. The CASP was developed through participation of community representatives from the northeastern Los Angeles neighborhoods, including Chinatown, Lincoln Heights, and other surrounding communities along the Los Angeles River. This area has been historically targeted to support economic development in the downtown area, including a proposed industrial warehouse park in the mid-2000s that community leaders resisted. The CASP emphasized open space and pedestrian-oriented development, while also requiring affordable housing depending on the proposed floor-to-area ratio, or FAR, which is one indicator of the development's density.

However, even with the CASP, which some argue has been restrictive for development, there still have been changes that arguably are contributing to gentrification. In 2017, the Los Angeles State Historic Park opened in the CASP area, a result of years of community advocacy. While the park was a much-needed green space, outside developers have proposed mixed-use developments with market-rate housing and retail space for restaurants and bars in anticipation of the park being an economic booster for the neighborhood. One proposed development, the College Station project, was filed before the adoption of the CASP and the developers have challenged its inclusion in the CASP, particularly the affordable housing requirements. To put pressure on the city and developer to honor the CASP, the Chinatown Community for Equitable Development (CCED), one of Chinatown's politically progressive organizations, sued the city in 2019, but was unsuccessful. College Station was just one of the many different developments proposed for the neighborhood that are aligned with downtown trends and have the potential to be major forces of change in Chinatown.

The neighborhood's demographic trends continue to be an important indicator in understanding the trajectory of change in Chinatown. According to the 2014–2019 American Community Survey, the neighborhood was over 90 percent renters, indicating that almost all Chinatown residents are vulnerable for forced displacement and displacement pressures. While the demographics in Chinatown today suggest that it is still an immigrant enclave, there are indications that it may be slowly moving away from that identity. The Asian immigration to Los Angeles continues to grow and has been outpacing Latine immigration.[68] However, only approximately 2 percent of Chinese Americans in the county live in the Chinatown area. While there is a small proportion of Chinese Americans in Chinatown, the neighborhood does continue to experience steady population increases and remains a majority Asian American residential community. Over 60 percent identify as Asian and over two-thirds of Asian Americans identify as Chinese, though the Asian American residential presence may be slowly declining as shown in Table 2. As previously shown in Table 1, from 1980 to 1990 there was a 28 percent increase of Asian Americans, and according to Table 2 the increases have been less than 5 percent since then. The demographic trends suggest that the percentage is now decreasing, both among Asian Americans generally and individual ethnic communities, especially Chinese and Vietnamese Americans. Furthermore, while the Latine population has remained steady throughout the years, representing approximately 25 percent of the population, there have been steady increases among the Black and non-Hispanic White population. The increase of the non-Hispanic White population is especially notable as they are the fastest-growing group in the neighborhood today. While these indicators alone are not enough to show gentrification, they do show a clear and relatively rapid shift in racial demographics that is often associated with gentrification.

In addition to racial turnover, other socioeconomic indicators signal that Chinatown is gentrifying. Chinatown continues to persist as a poor and working-class immigrant community, but this demographic also may be shifting. In 2019, over 71 percent of adult residents were considered poor, and the median household income was $22,417, while Los Angeles County was $55,870. Chinatown is also home to a disproportionate number of Asian adults living in poverty. They make up 42 percent of this population in Chinatown, while Asian Americans make up only 13 percent of this population in the county. The foreign-born population has also decreased by 7 percent and family households by 9 percent from 2000 to 2014, whereas in prior decades these numbers were increasing. These changes, combined with major increases among individuals who hold professional, management, and office and administrative occupations and decreases among those who work in blue collar jobs during the same period, indicate that the neighborhood residential composition may be slowly shifting toward single households that work in professional occupations. It also signals that the residential character of Chinatown may no longer be a primarily working-class immigrant and ethnic community, an identity it has held for its entire history.

In addition to demographic changes, there have also been notable shifts in Chinatown's physical and cultural identity. The most noticeable change was in West Plaza, one of the original New Chinatown Plazas, in the late 1990s.[69] Along Chungking Road in West Plaza, art galleries began to replace the old trinket shops, some of which were already vacant storefronts. This area is now part of the east side art gallery scene in Los Angeles. A few years later in 2003, along the southwestern border of Chinatown and downtown, Geoffrey Palmer, a major, but controversial Los Angeles downtown developer, built the Orsini apartments. These apartments created over one thousand new market-rate housing units in Chinatown. These changes, along

TABLE 2. Socioeconomic Characteristics and Trends of Chinatown Residents, 2000–2019

	2000	2010		2009–2014		2015–2019	
	Number of Residents (% of total pop)	Number of Residents (% of total pop)	% Change from 2000	Number of Residents (% of total pop)	% Change from 2000	Number of Residents (% of total pop)	% Change from 2010
Total population	14,546	15,907	9	15,388	6	18,489	16
RACE							
Asian	9,616 (66.1)	9,773 (61.4)	2	9,283 (60.3)	–3	9,397 (50.8)	–4
Latine	3,969 (27.3)	4,330 (27.2)	9	3,951 (25.7)	0	4,944 (26.7)	14
Non-Hispanic White	439 (3.0)	1,061 (6.7)	142	1,530 (9.9)	249	2,510 (13.6)	136
Black	241 (1.7)	470 (3.0)	95	485 (3.2)	101	980 (5.3)	108
ASIAN ETHNIC GROUPS							
Chinese	7,021 (48.3)	6,783 (42.6)	–3	6,129 (39.8)	–13	6,088 (32.9)	–10
Cambodian	598 (4.1)	730 (4.6)	22	1,163 (7.6)	94	567 (3.1)	–22
Vietnamese	1,030 (7.1)	753 (4.6)	–27	636 (4.1)	4.1	744 (4)	–1

Foreign born	10,139 (69.7)	9,450 (61.4)	-7	9,831 (46.8)	-3
Individuals living 200% below poverty level (poor or struggling)	10,688 (74)	10,892 (71.1)	2		
OCCUPATION					
Production	1,516 (32)	1,101 (17.7)	-27.4	699 (7.9)	-54*
Service (including food service)	1,379 (29.5)	907 (14.6)	-34.2	942 (10.7)	-32
Office and administrative	481 (10.3)	677 (10.9)	40.7	834 (9.4)	73*
Professional and related	428 (9.2)	1,268 (20.3)	196.3	2,201 (24.9)	414*
Management, business, and financial operations	269 (5.8)	566 (9.1)	110.4	1,099 (12.4)	309*

SOURCE: U.S. Census Bureau Decennial Census for 2000 and 2010 and American Community Survey 2009–2014 and 2015–2019 5-Year Estimates prepared by Social Explorer.

*Percentage change was calculated from 2000 due to missing or incomplete data.

with the presence of corporate businesses, such as the Starbucks and the Walmart Neighborhood Market, boutique retail, and trendy restaurants, are in stark contrast to the businesses and low-density multifamily housing that have historically defined Chinatown's commercial and residential character. Many of these changes are also not centering or being led by working-class Chinese immigrants and refugees who have also been integral to defining Chinatown's identity. The contemporary residential and business changes have called into question whether Chinatown is becoming "less Chinese," one of the major narratives about gentrification in Chinatown. The neighborhood culture and history are seen as one of the main assets of the neighborhood that distinguishes it as a specific type of ethnic space compared to the newer settlements in the San Gabriel Valley, which have eclipsed Chinatown as the hub for the Chinese American community. While these changes may be seen as an erasure of Chinatown's culture and local economy by outside forces, entities like the BID, which is managed from within the Chinatown community, are supportive of many of these changes to economically sustain the neighborhood.

These demographic and physical changes occurring in Chinatown today thus raise important questions as to what legacy of Chinatown these changes are a part of. Chinatown is recognized as an important historic neighborhood, a racialized space formed in response to the exclusion of Chinese immigrants and has persisted throughout the history of Los Angeles. Are these changes happening today a part of the legacy of community activism to assert a sense of spatial belonging and political visibility? Or are these changes an evolution of the attempts to spatially exclude and marginalize working-class Asian Americans and other communities of color from the urban landscape?

. . .

Chinatown is a downtown-adjacent neighborhood that has a core purpose to serve the social, cultural, and economic needs of the Chinese American community across the region. While it has consistently been shaped by the ethnic community, immigration and urban policies have also structured its development. These policies also reflect the racialization of Chinese and Asian Americans. Given the restrictive immigration policies during their early formations, Chinatowns should not have sustained. However, contemporary immigration policies have sustained it as an immigrant space, albeit it is not the only immigrant gateway in the region. As these policies also continue to shift based on broader global relations and geopolitical events that prioritize specific countries and professions, or in some cases shift to less open immigration policies, this will also have an impact on whether Chinatown is sustained as an immigrant neighborhood, and specifically, an Asian immigrant neighborhood. They will be especially critical in that the most recent neighborhood changes since the 2000s, both demographic and physical, suggest that Chinatown may be losing this identity, and the city's plans for Chinatown have limited tools to prevent this loss of identity, both cultural and socioeconomic.

Urban policies that have tried to promote economic development in the city and region have shaped Chinatown and led to it being a contested, but precarious site, constantly experiencing the threats and actualities of forced displacement. This history of displacement began with the Chinese Massacre of 1871 and demolishment of Old Chinatown for Union Station when Chinese Americans were explicitly racially excluded. Today, there are growing concerns that the neighborhood, which has historically been driven by the cultural and social needs of Chinese Americans, may now be shifting toward a dominant identity as a downtown-adjacent neighborhood, catering to an upwardly mobile population regardless of race or ethnicity. As Chinese and Asian Americans navigate their position as model minorities that contribute to multicultural urban identities, the question of if and how low-income Chinese and Asian Americans are represented as a part of these changes continues to be a tension in urban politics.

Chinatown has also always been a networked community destination for Chinese Americans across Los Angeles County because of how residential segregation was historically structured for Chinese Americans in Los Angeles. While the early Chinese American community may not have faced hyper-segregation into one area, they still were geographically concentrated in specific sections of the city and county. The regional migration patterns that led to the emergence of Chinese American settlements outside of Chinatown and the growth of the San Gabriel Valley as a region of ethnoburbs was due to the patterns of residential segregation and exclusion against Chinese Americans. The history and residential trends show how Chinese Americans are a geographically dispersed community, but also a community that has had limits to their mobility across space. It is perhaps because of these limits, that Chinese Americans continue to engage in Chinatown, a symbolic geographic anchor for the community, as it is a way to ensure political visibility and to resist the erasure of this history of marginalization. As the subsequent chapters will show, through their political engagement and activism, Chinese Americans have sought to maintain Chinatown as an important center for the community. Yet they also have different ways of defining Chinatown as an ethnic space, which contributes to the community power conflicts over neighborhood development.

TWO

Doing the Work in the Community

I think there's multiple levels [to defining a Chinatown stakeholder]. It's complex! But I would say initially, the first level is people who live and work here. Those to me are the number 1 community stakeholders. I think another level to that, like a little bit more removed, is people who have roots here. For me at one point, before I was working here, I felt like I was a community stakeholder because my family all came through here. It's something that I want to make sure that people who are like my family, who came through here, don't go through the same shit that they did.

—Young community activist

LOS ANGELES CHINATOWN is both a politically underrepresented and overrepresented community. It is underrepresented, like many low-income immigrant communities, as both the residents and workers face many of the common barriers to political and civic engagement, from language to time and knowledge of the political system. Geographically it is also a small neighborhood and has a population size that is under twenty thousand people. Thus, proportionally it does not hold the most political clout within the city and its city council district. Yet, as I found during my fieldwork, Chinatown does not have a lack of individuals who are politically engaged and advocating for the community. As the previous chapter highlighted, Chinatown has historically been a networked neighborhood for Chinese Americans across the region, which has contributed to what the young community activist described as many individuals having "roots" in Chinatown.

These roots have been maintained and nurtured through the various organizations in Chinatown that promote civic engagement in the neighborhood. This civic engagement has also historically been driven by a sense of linked fate based on a shared racialized and ethnic identity. Angie Chung argues that urban ethnic enclaves, especially ones in Los Angeles, have evolved to be institutionally centered neighborhoods whose roles have expanded to serve the ethnic community across geography, and more specifically, have become sites for ethnic political engagement.[1] They provide spaces and opportunities for political activities ranging from traditional modes of politics, such as voting and running for office, to counter-politics and radical organizing.[2] These organizations also serve as critical sites for political gatekeeping to mediate with outsiders and mainstream institutions, especially on community development issues.[3] Many organizations were a home base for the community leaders interviewed during my fieldwork in Chinatown, some of whom have since become political leaders beyond the neighborhood and ethnic community.

This chapter provides an overview of the generations of community organizations that have come to define Los Angeles Chinatown as not just an enduring ethnic space, but a conflicted political space as well. The organizations that are highlighted in this chapter do not capture all the different organizations that have been established throughout the neighborhood's history; however, by showcasing a few key organizations, I show how all the community-based organizations have been critical sites for Chinese Americans to connect to their roots in Chinatown. The organizational landscape has evolved to represent different generations, immigrant cohorts, and interests, mirroring the complexities and layers of history that define Chinese Americans today. The engagement that happens via these sites contributes to a rearticulation of a politicized ethnic community identity, while also responding to the social and material conditions of the neighborhood. Ultimately, these organizations are critical to resisting both material and symbolic displacement of Chinatown. They provide political representation and resources to sustain the neighborhood community, while their presence also signals to others that Chinatown continues to be an important political and cultural center for Chinese and Asian Americans.

Through this overview of the organizational landscape, I also interrogate how community representation is also contested because the organizations have created "multiple levels" of Chinatown stakeholders. While Chinatown may have continued to have an important symbolic meaning for Chinese Americans who did not live there, community leaders also recognized that the primary stakeholders were the people who had a routine, everyday presence in Chinatown, particularly working-class residents and workers who experienced the everyday material impacts of gentrification. Yet, through their involvement in local organizations, nonresidents have also become community stakeholders, with some emerging as important community leaders who represent the neighborhood, especially regarding development issues. The disproportionate political power the organizations and their members held in Chinatown and whether they included local stakeholders in their advocacy and decision-making were points of contention within the community. This issue became especially salient in the post-1965 context as Chinatown became a majority Asian American residential community. The identity politics and civic engagement of Chinese Americans now had to explicitly contend with representing Chinatown as a residential community, not just a space of cultural heritage and economic investment for the ethnic community. Thus, how the leaders and members of long-standing community organizations, as well as relatively newer progressive organizations, were engaging in local concerns and distinguishing themselves as a place-based versus an ethnic community-based organization became a salient issue defining the contemporary political landscape and culture of Chinatown. The definition of community stakeholdership was and continues to be a contentious issue in determining who should represent the Chinatown community, with community leaders often questioning the power and authority of stakeholder claims.

THE "ABUNDANCE" OF
CHINATOWN ORGANIZATIONS

Edmund Soohoo, a community leader who grew up in Chinatown and became politically active in the 1970s, described the Chinatown organizational landscape as diverse, with an "abundance" of organizations for civic engagement. In his interview, he enthusiastically shared that "there's no lack of organizations. . . . And these are all clustered within five blocks from each other. Literally! . . . You would be able to touch each of these organizations. It's that easy." His observation is reflective of his own civic engagement in various community organizations, from his family association to the Los Angeles Chinatown Firecracker Run. While the sheer number of organizations would suggest that Chinatown is an institutionally complete neighborhood in which these organizations maintain a sense of ethnic cohesion,[4] the organizational landscape also physically symbolizes the diverse political interests, backgrounds, and histories within the Chinese American community.

The leaders and members of the various Chinatown organizations have continuously influenced community development in Chinatown, as they represent the different aspects of the neighborhood that make it a whole, from economic and housing development to ethnic heritage and preservation efforts. The organizational landscape shows that Chinatown is not just persisting, but transforming according to the evolving political interests and material needs of both the regional Chinese American community and local Chinatown community. These organizations serve as an important site for civic engagement that raises a political consciousness and creates a sense of belonging among Chinese Americans. However, the establishment of new organizations and the tensions within existing organizations also demonstrate the difficulty of representing not just the different interests of the Chinatown community, but also generational and immigrant cohort differences.

The History and Salience of Ethnic Voluntary Associations

Ethnic organizations are an integral part of the history of Chinese Americans and the formations of Chinatowns, as they were created in response to racial exclusion. While these early organizations can be classified as voluntary organizations in that their capacity is based on the work of volunteer members, the formation of these organizations was not purely by choice. Early Chinese American communities developed these mutualist organizations as a means of survival that helped to create a sense of connection, place, and belonging in the United States, even if it was limited by the laws and policies of the time.[5] These associations pooled resources among their members to provide financial and social support, as well as assisted members with migration and settlement in the United States. While the explicit systemic racism facing Chinese Americans that contributed to the establishment of these mutualist organizations has since been struck down, they still are present in Chinatown and remain important gathering spaces for its members.

The mutualist organizations were often based on shared ancestry, such as family surname and regional origin in China, with some based on political and business interests. Some of the oldest mutualist organizations include the Wong Family Association, Bing Kong Tong Association, Lung Kong Tin Yee Association, and the Hop Sing Tong Association, which were established in the 1870s along with Old Chinatown. The Chinese American Citizens Alliance–Los Angeles Lodge (CACA) was established in 1912 and is part of a national network of CACA lodges that, together, served as one of the first Asian American civil rights organizations. While the mutualist organizations were based on shared ancestry, membership in CACA was based on US citizenship, a requirement that continues today. This requirement of CACA emphasized that there were Chinese Americans who were legal citizens in the early 1900s, and thus they could claim the rights and protections of citizenship. CACA provided a space for that assertion of citizenship and belonging. The Los Angeles Lodge of CACA was notable for their early advocacy beyond the local community. For example, prominent Chinese American lawyer and CACA member, Y. C. Hong, testified to Congress to overturn the 1882 Exclusion Act. Their political advocacy to overturn discriminatory policies continued after World War II, when Chinese Americans were no longer legally an excluded group.[6] CACA and these older organizations were originally located in Old Chinatown and were some of the major institutions to be resettled in New Chinatown after the demolishment of Old Chinatown. As much as the development of Central and West Plazas for New Chinatown helped to relocate businesses and catered to tourism, the resettlement of these associations and organizations also strengthened New Chinatown as the Chinatown created for the Chinese American community, further contrasting it from China City.

In addition to these individual organizations, the Chinese Consolidated Benevolent Association (CCBA) served as an umbrella organization that included CACA and other mutualist associations as members and provided de facto governance to the early Chinese American community.[7] It was originally formed as the Wai Liang Association in 1889 and renamed CCBA in 1910. The organization was housed in the Garnier Building, which community historians often refer to as the "City Hall of Chinatown." CCBA was considered the central authority in Old Chinatown, and this carried over to New Chinatown, where it provided social control in the community that included mediation over legal and business conflicts. They also acted as mediators between the community and mainstream institutions to try to secure protections and rights for Chinese Americans amid anti-Chinese sentiment.[8] In the 1920s, CCBA also began to secure burial plots in East Los Angeles, which eventually led to the development of the first official Chinese cemetery in the city. The organization also maintained ties to China, especially through fundraising efforts in the early 1900s during wartime and political instability. CCBA's transnational scope and connections to global Chinese politics continues today as members debate the organization's relationships with the People's

Republic of China and Taiwan. In the 1950s, they also developed a Confucius Temple which is home to the local Chinese school. They were thus an early form of community development, providing governance and resources to the neighborhood at a time of exclusion. This history also established the importance of local organizations in both ethnic community representation and neighborhood development.

The structure and purpose of these older voluntary associations continue to resonate with the community, especially new immigrants. New mutualist organizations also formed in the 1970s and 1980s, reflecting the contemporary wave of Chinese immigrants and refugees to the United States. These new organizations include the Teo-Chew Association of Southern California, the Southern California Fukienese Association, and the Cà Mau Association of America, all of which are located in Chinatown.[9] The Cà Mau Association is based on a shared ancestry of that area in Vietnam, while the Teo-Chew and Fukienese associations are based on a shared ancestry from the Chaoshan and Fujian regions in China. Members of the Teo-Chew and Fukienese Associations are primarily immigrants and refugees from Southeast Asian countries. This was not unique to their immigration to the United States, as similar mutualist organizations were established in Southeast Asian countries to help the new ethnic Chinese immigrants establish a sense of community and local base of power in these countries.[10] These associations have a structure and intent similar to the older mutualist organizations, which is to help new immigrants and maintain transnational relationships based on a shared ancestry. They also are sustained by the volunteer work and financial capital of its members and are recognized as important community institutions by other community leaders.

The new immigrants and refugees reinforced the salience of ethnic-based mutualist organizations in Chinatown. However, they did not necessarily strengthen the older organizations as the new immigrant mutualist organizations are not a part of CCBA and operate independently from the older community power structure.[11] Community leaders often speak of "cultural differences" based on regional ancestry and migration histories among the different immigrant cohorts to explain these organizational divides. While CCBA provided services to Chinese refugees from Vietnam who arrived in Camp Pendleton following the fall of Saigon, as an institution that is over a century old, it remains a Cantonese-dominated organization. Several community leaders who were active in their family's mutualist associations and CCBA cited this as a limitation, stating that the primary language of communication within CCBA is still Cantonese Chinese, which is a reflection of the early immigration history of Chinese Americans, and it has not evolved to reflect the cultural and generational changes in the community. The linguistic dominance of Cantonese in CCBA and other older mutualist organizations was thus a perceived barrier for other Chinese Americans to become involved, whether new immigrants who speak another Chinese dialect or later-generation Chinese Americans who are less fluent in Cantonese.

Because the neighborhood infrastructure reflected an older Chinese American immigration history, newer immigrants and refugees did not always see these as spaces of community for them. As one first-generation Chinese American business leader who immigrated from Vietnam explained, he was perceived as an "outsider" because he was relatively new to the community despite becoming politically engaged in the older mutualist associations. Thus, he and other business leaders with a similar background were primarily dedicated to the newer mutualist organizations that reflected their experiences of being part of a contemporary global Chinese diaspora. As many of these immigrants and refugees came from Southeast Asian countries, particularly Vietnam and Cambodia, they also were a part of a diaspora shaped by larger geopolitics and US Cold War militarism, in addition to historical political and ethnic tensions between China and other Asian countries. Chinatown today thus has multiple generations of mutualist organizations that represent the different waves of Chinese immigration to the United States, as well as the intracultural diversity within the community.

The Influence of Business Leaders in Chinatown

The Chinatown organizational landscape has historically been dominated by business leaders who have been instrumental in the development of the neighborhood. Even among the older organizations that do not explicitly represent business interests, such as CCBA and CACA, the leaders in these organizations have traditionally been business leaders and property owners of major sites in Chinatown. While formed as a civil rights organization, the Los Angeles Lodge of CACA is recognized by many community leaders, young and old, as a space that has historically been politically conservative and representing business interests in Chinatown, although the membership is currently more diversified across political interests and backgrounds. The current Chinatown began with the development of Central Plaza in

1938, which was developed under the leadership of the Los Angeles Chinatown Project Association (now Los Angeles Chinatown Corporation), a partnership among Chinatown business leaders. A prominent leader of this development who navigated the mainstream politics to develop the plaza was Peter Soohoo Jr., a college-educated US-born Chinese American active in CCBA and CACA. Other members included business leaders such as Soon Don Quon, Wah-Shew Lee, and Ping Yuen Louie, whose families, along with Soohoo's, continue to be involved in the business community and are honored as important founders of Chinatown.

Following World War II, a new generation of business leadership emerged, which included new voluntary organizations that specifically represented their interests. The Chinese Chamber of Commerce formed in 1955, and while their offices are located in Chinatown, they provide support to Chinese American businesses across Los Angeles. They also managed the various cultural events and festivals, including the Golden Dragon Parade and Miss Chinatown pageants. The business leadership also evolved to include Chinese Americans who were not direct descendants of the original founders of New Chinatown. These newer business leaders not only became prominent leaders in organizations like CACA and the Chinese Chamber of Commerce, but also continue to have an important role in community development in Chinatown. Wilbur Woo and George Ching were the cofounders of Cathay Bank, and Jack Lee cofounded First Public Savings Bank and Yee Sing Chong, Chinatown's first major grocery store. Cathay Bank was established in 1962 and was the first Chinese American owned and operated bank in the United States. Cathay Bank, along with First Public Savings Banks and other local Chinese American–owned banks that were in Chinatown, provided Chinese Americans the financial capital to own homes and start businesses in Chinatown, as well as other neighborhoods in Los Angeles that did not have restrictive covenants against Chinese Americans. These banks were integral in further developing Chinatown so that it continued to be an economic and cultural hub for the Chinese American community following World War II. Woo, Ching, and Lee also partnered to develop Mandarin Plaza in 1972, one of Chinatown's major commercial plazas that was home to some of the first Chinese immigrant businesses from Taiwan in the 1970s. The plaza's name not only signified the intracultural differences within the Chinese American community, but also signaled the possibilities of transnational investment to Chinatown during this time. This new generation of business leaders contributed to the development of a more formal infrastructure to provide financial resources for neighborhood development beyond the social support and informal resources provided through the older mutualist organizations.

While the business leadership was evolving, they also struggled in responding to the demographic shifts within the community since the 1970s. The *Los Angeles Times* highlighted the divides and tension between the old and new businesses. One article published in 1996 was candid about the community divides:

> Chinatown is a community divided. A new wave of immigration over the last two decades has created a dual society of scrambling entrepreneurs from Southeast Asia and more assimilated, older merchants whose families emigrated from China more than six decades ago. They ply their wares on the same streets, yet remain miles apart in tradition.[12]

These tensions among business leaders were similar to the experiences with the older mutualist organizations. The cultural differences within the community led to limits in leadership and collaboration within the business sector to promote economic development in Chinatown. They were also often expressed as linguistic divides that made it difficult to develop a unified voice. Chester Chong, who was the president of the Chinese Chamber of Commerce during the time of my fieldwork, explained how, unlike CCBA, the Chamber is a predominantly English organization. This still made it difficult for new immigrants to engage in the organization:

> If you don't speak Cantonese, you have a hard time! And even the Cantonese [speakers], [for] some, [it was] hard to communicate. Not to mention the Mandarin [speakers]. And then as [the] Southeast Asian immigrants [are] coming in, and of course they are culturally different from the ones from China. So, they have their own way of doing business. But of course, most of them, when they come in, they settle in Chinatown. . . . And so pretty soon they more or less form their own organization. . . . We tried to solicit them too but unfortunately the Chamber when they [are] meeting, they talk in English. And those immigrants coming in, their English is limited. . . . They would join the other organizations.

While Chinese immigrants and refugees were integral in sustaining and growing the local business economy following the 1965 Immigration Act, the older leadership and organizational infrastructure of Chinatown did not always provide the support for this new wave of businesses.

Instead, the new immigrants continued to rely on their own organizations. Similar to CCBA and the older mutualist associations, the leadership in the Teo-Chew and Fukienese associations also primarily consisted of immigrant business leaders, some of whom now own prominent Chinese restaurants in Southern California. In the 1980s, Chinese American leaders who have roots in Southeast Asia also formed their own Chamber of Commerce.[13] Despite their increasing economic influence and organizational presence, this newer cohort of Chinese immigrants was still not as actively involved and represented in local politics as representatives for Chinatown during my fieldwork. Representatives from the older Chinese American community power structure, as well as organizations representing later-generation Chinese Americans, continued to have a more visible presence beyond Chinatown.

During my fieldwork, the Business Improvement District (BID) was the most prominent business voice in the neighborhood. As explained in the previous chapter, the BID is supported by state law, but because it follows a public-private structure, it is governed from within the community. It is managed by a nonprofit organization, the Los Angeles Chinatown Business Council, and the board consists of commercial property owners in the area.[14] The BID was created with support from business leaders associated with some major Chinatown institutions, such as Patrick Lee, a former president of the Chinese Chamber of Commerce and board member of Cathay Bank. Cathay Bank also provided the $100,000 seed money to initiate the formation. Some of the business leaders who supported the BID formation included the younger generation of the Old Chinatown families who were beginning to manage the Chinatown family businesses and properties. Other business leaders were relatively newer to the community. Kim Benjamin, a developer from New York, and Peter Woo, a first-generation Chinese American and co-owner of Mega Toys, Inc., represented new outside real estate development interests. They both became active in the Chinatown business community through their participation in the BID and Chinese Chamber of Commerce. The founding and current executive director of the BID, George Yu, a Chinese American who immigrated from Taiwan, is a commercial property owner who owns Far East Plaza, home to many new restaurants that are associated with gentrification and discussed in more detail in chapter 6. During my fieldwork, the BID board roster included representatives from the old Chinatown business families, but many were relatively newer stakeholders, including corporate property owners Forest City and Redcar Properties. Given the composition of the board, the BID primarily represented a new generation of business owners, many of whom had backgrounds in real estate development and were commercial property owners who had an increasing presence in downtown and the northeastern neighborhoods of Los Angeles, areas that are also contested sites of gentrification.[15] Chapter 4 further documents the emerging political dominance of the BID and the tensions this has brought in defining community control.

Throughout Chinatown's history, business leaders have been integral to its development, from their involvement in various organizations to their investment in commercial projects. Their prominent role in the community represents how Chinatown is in many ways still insular and relies on resources from within the ethnic community elite. These business leaders were not just credited for helping with commercial development, but also helping to provide and bring social services to the community. Yet, many of these business leaders also have a personal, economic interest in Chinatown, which may ultimately prioritize economic development and property value increases over the collective interests of the community. They have had several organizational spaces, some of which do not have an explicit mission to promote economic development, where they can engage in ethnic growth machine politics that position Chinatown to try to follow development trends that increase property values and individual profits.[16] Given these limitations of leadership in Chinatown, new voices have also emerged to try to represent other community interests.

Asserting a Politically Progressive Chinese American Identity

In addition to Chinese and Asian immigrants revitalizing the economic, institutional, and residential character of Chinatown in the 1960s and 1970s, young Chinese Americans began to convene in Chinatown, which contributed to a political revitalization of the neighborhood. The New Left movements that focused on anti-imperialism, civil rights, and Ethnic Studies in college campuses were a catalyst for politically activating young Chinese and Asian Americans in ways that nurtured a critical perspective in how they connected to their heritage and community. A new generation of Chinese Americans, many of whom were US-born or 1.5 generation, were developing a politicized panethnic Asian American identity based on a recognition of the shared marginalization and racism facing all Asian ethnic groups. Their activism was informed by radical politics that critiqued racial and class inequalities through an analysis of colonialism and imperialism as well as

interracial solidarity with other communities of color.[17] This new generation of leadership was directly challenging the model minority assumptions
of Chinese and Asian Americans that positioned them as good immigrants
who could assimilate without needing government resources and services.
Their involvement did not simply attempt to rearticulate a new ethnic
community identity, but also reshaped the organizational structure and
leadership for community development to center the specific needs of the
working class in Chinatown rather than the Chinese American community
more broadly.

Deborah Ching, whose father was business leader George Ching, was a
community activist in the early 1970s and became the executive director of
Chinatown Service Center (CSC), a social service organization founded in
1971 that served the new immigrant and refugee population in Chinatown.
She explained that being involved in Chinatown during this time was a way
for young Chinese Americans like herself to try to make sense of how they
fit in with these larger political movements about racial inequities and race
relations. She explained:

> In the Civil Rights Movement, it was always framed as Black/White. Many
> Asian Americans resonated with the issues and tried to find their place in
> the Civil Rights Movement. We also—Chinese American students—were
> trying to find our path in the Civil Rights Movement. Because we knew it
> was a path for us. But we had to define it for ourselves. So, Chinatown was
> the place. There was no San Gabriel Valley at the time, you know, [no] other
> major enclaves. Many Chinese American students from UCLA [University
> of California, Los Angeles], from Cal State LA [California State University,
> Los Angeles], even USC [University of Southern California] and other
> local campuses, came together in Chinatown. . . . We had our study groups.
> We had our women's groups. We had the whole thing. [We were] trying to
> think it through, figure it out. But the Chinese American students were also
> gathering. So, I was part of both. And in Chinatown, you know people like
> [California Congresswoman] Judy Chu and [Asian Americans Advancing
> Justice founder] Stewart Kwoh and [former California State Assembly mem-
> ber] Mike Eng, and others were trying to figure out how do we engage in our
> values in Chinatown? So, we organized.

As Ching also noted, many of these individuals who started in Chinatown, such as Congresswoman Chu, would later become prominent Asian
American political leaders in Southern California. Chinatown became an
important space for that initial politicization and built a sense of community among future Chinese American political leaders. Whereas the older

generation of Chinese American leaders relied on Chinatown to assert a sense of belonging and assimilation to the United States that positioned them as an exceptional group, for this newer generation of activists, Chinatown served as a symbolic and physical site to assert a different type of political visibility. Instead, they advocated for Asian Americans to be included in policy conversations about race relations and inequities that centered solidarities and countered assimilationist assumptions.[18]

Some who grew up working class in Los Angeles and other Chinatowns also drew directly from their lived experience as much as abstract political ideologies to shape their community work. Sharon Lowe, who worked as deputy in former Councilmember Gil Cedillo's office during my research, was a community activist during this time. She grew up in Philadelphia Chinatown and became involved in Los Angeles Chinatown when she attended law school at UCLA in the 1970s. She explained that a sense of community was "ingrained" in her through her upbringing that influenced her activism and professional work:

> I have it from my father. I have his legacy. He worked two jobs, and our door was always open. . . . It used to crack me up when I would go home from college and from law school and I'd go back to visit him and he even after I had my sons, when they were babies, I'd come back to visit him and here he is and he'd go—he'd say, "Ok, give me baby. You go." "Where am I going?" "Oh, you need to take so and so to the social security. You take so and so to immigration. You take so and so to the doctor." . . . I mean I grew up with that. I looked at my father as a stray cat, stray dog, stray people. Somebody was on the outside and asked for a handout and a meal, he'd feed them and then he'd give them a job.

For Lowe and other community activists with a similar working-class immigrant family background, that sense of family and kinship informed a political activism that focused on collective community care.

In contrast to Lowe who displayed an unwavering sense of pride in her family background in motivating her activism, Gay Yuen, another community activist from this time, who later served as president of the Friends of the Chinese American Museum, recalled how, growing up, she believed in traditional assimilation narratives that equated middle-class Whiteness with "American" and felt ashamed of her Chinese heritage. She immigrated to the United States as a child and grew up in Chinatown. She struggled with how her family did not fit the mainstream narrative of White America that she saw on popular media. As a student at UCLA, she became exposed to Asian

American Studies and began to embrace her background as a strength. She explains how her activism in the community was also about instilling that sense of ethnic pride among the Chinatown youth whom she recognized as experiencing similar identity issues:

> My roommate was coaching a girls' basketball team at Alpine playground [the local Chinatown recreation center] and after winning a game, we said, "Ok we'll treat you girls to dim sum." ... So, we walked over, and we sat down and then we ordered. And then one of the girls says, "I need a fork." And I looked at her and I said—and she could barely speak English, right, so I said, "Why do you need a fork?" "I don't eat with chopsticks anymore." I said, "Then you don't need to eat because we're eating with chopsticks." That was me [when I was younger]. That was me, ashamed of being Chinese, wanting to eat with a fork, wanting to throw away the chopsticks. And so, as a role model, right, I think it was really important to engage in these kind of community activities.

These early activists spoke about how their work was to help establish a sense of belonging and self-confidence for the new generation of Chinese Americans who were "feeling outside of the mainstream." They were what Victor Nee and Brett de Bary Nee called "cultural radicals," young activists who were embracing the traditions of everyday culture of Chinese Americans in Chinatown to inform their politics.[19] They embraced their ethnic difference as not just a source of pride, but also as a distinct political voice that mattered in political decision-making. At the same time, through their volunteering, they were directly connecting with and providing services to the local Chinatown working-class community.

These new, young activists were volunteers who did not work with the established organizations. Instead, they organized as informal groups and developed new programs and activities that contributed to community development across various issues, including housing, education, and labor. Phyllis Chiu, another college activist from UCLA, who later taught at the local elementary school, Castelar Elementary School, explained how there was a "push" to strengthen the community-based social service infrastructure in the 1970s because the current infrastructure was still "inadequate" and "bare bones." She bluntly stated that Chinatown "didn't have anything." Despite the past work of community leaders to create a community infrastructure through the mutualist organizations, the population increase and influx of immigrants and refugees created a major need for more social services and spaces in Chinatown to deliver those services. One social service leader shared why he also became involved with CSC in the 1970s, explaining that both the mainstream and older Chinatown community elites simply did not want to highlight how Chinatown was an urban poor community. He shared that "all those folks [new immigrants] are coming in. people don't like to admit that there's poor people. So, there's always that stigma to overcome. I think that was a limitation." The old Chinatown community leaders often took a more assimilationist stance in navigating the mainstream and public perceptions of Chinese Americans, as they wanted to present Chinatown as a presentable community.[20] The social problems facing working-class residents, such as labor exploitation, gang activity, and other issues associated with high levels of poverty, were either minimized or framed more as individual problems than a result of structural problems that led to these conditions in Chinatown.

This service gap provided opportunities for new organizing and organizations. Unlike the mutualist organizations, this new infrastructure would not consist of organizations bound to serving family and kin, but instead focus on serving the most socioeconomically marginalized within the Chinese and Asian American communities. Many local college students in the 1960s and 1970s were involved in youth development activities, including the Chinatown Youth Council (CYC) and the Asian American Tutorial Project, the latter of which still exists at Castelar Elementary School. Along with CSC, another social service organization that was established in the early 1970s was Chinatown Teen Post, which evolved from the volunteer youth development activities. While this organization is no longer active, this was part of the city's larger network of Teen Posts funded through grants created from Johnson's War on Poverty that sought to provide opportunities for at-risk urban youth. The Chinatown Teen Post was the only one in the city that specifically targeted Asian Americans.

Some of these college organizers also were a part of Asian Americans for Equality (AAFE) and Chinese Progressive Association (CPA), which were part of a national network of new left, progressive Asian American groups across the United States that advocated on behalf of working-class Asian American interests. AAFE was particularly active in trying to advocate for Chinatown in the 1970s. They pressured the city to place stop signs in front of Castelar Elementary School after a car accident led to the death of a student (Figure 5). As mentioned in the prior chapter, they also spoke out against the Chinatown Community Redevelopment Agency (CRA) designation, raising concerns about how the CRA was catering to the business

WOMAN EJECTED FROM COUNCIL MEETING

2 Traffic Deaths Spark Protest

By ERWIN BAKER
Times Staff Writer

A leader of a group protesting an alleged lack of traffic safety measures in Chinatown was ejected from the Los Angeles City Council chamber Tuesday.

The young woman, who refused to identify herself, was escorted from the crowded room by two police officers after interrupting testimony on another issue and attempting to address to council.

Sergeants-at-arms John Madras and Anthony Radovich said the woman was not arrested. Outside the chamber, she joined about 20 persons chanting, "Lindsay, we want lights now."

Councilman Gilbert W. Lindsay represents the Chinatown area, where two persons, one a 9-year-old boy, have died in the last 10 weeks in automobile-pedestrian accidents.

Angry residents have demanded installation of traffic signals and other safety measures at two of the busiest intersections—College and Yale streets and Alpine and Yale streets—because of deaths and injuries at the locations during the last few years.

On Nov. 9, after a demonstration by students at Castelar Elementary School, which lies in the middle of the traffic hazard pattern, the community won a partial victory. Stop

Please Turn to Page 4, Col. 3

A woman tries to take over the microphone . . .

FIGURE 5. *Los Angeles Times* article from December 19, 1979, profiling an Asian Americans for Equality member advocating for pedestrian safety at Castelar Elementary School at a City Council meeting. Photo taken by Fitzgerald Whitney. Image courtesy of *Los Angeles Times*.

interests, both in Chinatown and the broader downtown area. Some AAFE members also sat on different community advisory committees during the CRA designation, which is documented more closely in the next chapter.

While AAFE and CPA were no longer active by the end of the 1980s, progressive organizations continue to be established in Chinatown. In the 2000s, the Chinatown Community for Equitable Development (CCED) and the Southeast Asian Community Alliance (SEACA) represent a contemporary young, politically progressive voice that seeks to provide representation for resident and labor interests. These new groups formed in response to the ongoing political invisibility of the Chinatown community. Sissy Trinh founded SEACA in 2009, a group that continues the legacy of youth activism in the 1960s and has provided a critical space in promoting progressive civic engagement among Chinatown youth. SEACA gained prominence in helping to develop the Cornfield-Arroyo Seco Specific Plan (CASP), a plan that includes Chinatown and its northern neighbors that was driven by community input and adopted by the city in 2012. Through

SEACA, youth from Chinatown and neighboring Lincoln Heights were a part of the planning process. In 2012, a group of young Asian American activists also formed CCED. One of the founding members, Daniel Huynh, who is of Chinese Vietnamese descent was a volunteer for Chinatown organizations, including CSC.[21] He and other young Asian Americans who were starting to be engaged in Chinatown wanted to "come together to have a conversation around why is it that there is no real strong progressive voice in Los Angeles Chinatown." They started a reading group to discuss this gap, which also coincided with the proposal for the Walmart market. The Walmart market thus was a flashpoint that led to the establishment of CCED as these young Asian Americans saw the need for an organized progressive voice specific to community development issues to push back on the proposal. Both SEACA and CCED were the most vocal Chinatown-based opponents of Walmart. Since its formation, CCED has become a prominent anti-gentrification voice in Chinatown and has initiated the formation of tenants' rights groups throughout the neighborhood.

The members of both CCED and SEACA have similarities to the Chinese Americans in the 1960s and 1970s who were coming of age and becoming politicized through their involvement in Chinatown. They also were not necessarily joining the older community groups and instead were developing their own groups that represent their politics and experiences in Chinatown. One CCED member who is a second-generation Chinese Vietnamese American and of Chaozhou background explained that before she joined the organization, she only saw Chinatown as a commercial area based on her childhood visits. She spoke about how her view transformed through her organizing work as she now worked more directly with the working-class immigrants in Chinatown. She explained:

> It wasn't until I got involved in CCED and I was in Chinatown a lot more that I saw it as a larger community. In my memory [as a youth], I only remembered certain locations in Chinatown, and it was this vast area. But then once I got involved with CCED, I guess all those pieces connected and I actually saw a community. And I feel like ever since being involved with CCED, like, I'm learning more and more about Chinatown. . . . I really see it as a community now.

Other Chinese American CCED members who never lived in Chinatown also explained that their involvement helped to expand their perceptions of Chinatown that they formed primarily as visitors to the neighborhood.

Through their organizing, they directly engaged with the residents and workers of Chinatown, which provided a counter perspective of Chinatown as a symbolic destination neighborhood for Chinese Americans and tourists. These political groups have helped to continue the political engagement of young Asian Americans through community-based work in Chinatown that mediates how they construct a sense of self and community.

Finding and Preserving Ethnic Heritage through Space

In addition to civic and business groups, the organizational infrastructure of Chinatown also now includes community leaders and organizations with the primary purpose of preserving the history of Chinatown and the Chinese American community. These efforts emerged in the 1960s along with the progressive activism in Chinatown. These leaders also often included young Chinese Americans who became engaged in Chinatown to learn more about their personal and community history, as it was not part of mainstream historical narratives.

The Chinese Historical Society of Southern California (CHSSC) was one such organization. Established in 1975, it is now considered a major community institution in Chinatown. The founding members explained that the original intent of this group was to bring together individuals with an interest in Chinese American history, both personally and professionally, as the public information about the community's history was limited.[22] Suellen Cheng was a UCLA graduate student from Taiwan interested in Chinese American women's history, which led her to the first meetings at CHSSC. She explained that the "Chinese Historical Society was very, directly related to my own interests. It's because I was studying the history, the past, the preservation. And really to me, it's just learning about the communities." Cheng would go on to help to publish several of the foundational community-based publications that document the early history of Chinese Americans in Southern California. Similarly, Eugene Moy was initially interested in historical preservation as an undergraduate student at California State University, Long Beach, which eventually brought him to CHSSC. Through his organizational involvement, he also "became much more familiar with the Chinatown community." Both Cheng and Moy eventually became involved with other organizations, including CACA. This search for history brought young Chinese Americans to Chinatown, and some became politically engaged with the older institutions. It is a pathway to political engagement in the neighborhood that continues for many young Chinese and Asian Americans today.

Institutions like CHSSC, and eventually the Chinese American Museum (CAM) which was established in 2003 in the Garnier Building, ensured that the historical narratives and resources of Chinatown were controlled from within the community. Munson Kwok, another founding member of CHSSC and a leader in establishing CAM, explained that the purpose of these organizations is to protect the local history. He shared that in his discussions with one of the founders of CHSSC, Paul Louie, they saw that the formation was "not based on scholarship" and that "it was formed so we could define enough of our history, to define our identity, so that in turn we can then tell the government, we count. We are here. We are not invisible." This assertion of community control over history continues to resonate as members of CHSSC, past and present, have become important community leaders who represent historical preservation interests in the neighborhood. Because Chinatown is an integral part of understanding Chinese American history, these heritage organizations are seen as legitimate community representatives. While they are not necessarily Chinatown specific, those from within and outside the community defer to them as the local community experts and authoritative voices about Chinese American history. Any new developments that involve the alteration or destruction of an older building are often vetted with CHSSC board members, especially Eugene Moy, who also has a professional background in urban planning. In some cases, CHSSC will ask for community benefits, such as the inclusion of public parking spaces and community meeting spaces.

During the fieldwork, heritage leaders were also actively involved with Survey L.A., a city initiative to document historic resources to ensure that historically significant buildings are identified in Chinatown, buildings whose architecture represents the older history of the city, as well as ones important to Chinese American history, such as movie theaters and those designed by some of the first Chinese American architects. Their advocacy was challenging and expanding the criteria for historical designations to include more than just cursory inclusions of ethnic communities or those purely based on architectural design. Their work considered the social significance of everyday spaces in helping to establish community roots in neighborhoods like Chinatown in the face of continuing racial exclusion.

While the presence of a local heritage organization like CHSSC is critical to ensuring preservation amid gentrification and displacement pressures, there are still limits to what heritage is preserved, both outside and within the history of Chinese Americans. As they engage in these efforts, heritage leaders openly grappled with Chinatown's multiethnic history and the differences across immigrant cohorts within the Chinese American community. The cultural leaders spoke about their responsibilities as stewards who must protect the history of the neighborhood, even when it is not based on their personal ethnic heritage. Many of the older buildings not only are artifacts of the early Chinese immigrant history, but also remnants of the Italian, Croatian, French, and Jewish immigrant history in Los Angeles. As local community historians and heritage leaders recognized the different histories that define their own neighborhoods and communities, they were also positioned as leaders who could potentially advocate beyond their own ethnic communities in their preservation and heritage efforts. Given the cultural shifts and long history of the neighborhood as an immigrant gateway, how the current Chinese American leaders, who are the most politically powerful and visible group in the neighborhood, should advocate to preserve the history of other ethnic groups who settled in Chinatown remains an open question as the concerns of cultural erasure and displacement of the neighborhood continue.

As heritage organizations such as CHSSC and CAM have become important community institutions, there are questions about which histories and experiences are most visible as they represent the community. Several younger individuals who became active in some of the older organizations and whose family history represents the post-1965 immigration history spoke of the limits of the current community control over history. One spoke about the experience volunteering with CHSSC as a learning experience about "gatekeeping" local histories, hinting at how some histories within the community are emphasized less than others. Another younger Chinese American spoke more explicitly about how there seemed to be a limited inclusion of historical activities of Chinese Americans whose roots are in Southeast Asia and that much of the work still focuses on the older history of Chinese Americans that highlights the era of racial exclusion and experiences of systemic racism. While they acknowledge this as an important history, they also expressed a desire for preservation activities that provide insight to the diversity of experiences that define their histories. This is an ongoing tension that heritage leaders must contend with as they continue to define and assert a shared Chinese American history to fight for neighborhood preservation.

The organizational landscape in Chinatown is expansive, representing different generations of Chinese American civic engagement in the neighborhood. New organizations have constantly formed as groups respond to the limitations of older organizations in serving the needs of a growing and diversifying community. Furthermore, many community leaders are associated with different organizations. Through their organizational affiliations, they also act as representatives for the community, especially when mediating with the city and other community outsiders. Yet the organization dynamics have also led to concerns about political representation as these organizations have also provided spaces for nonresidents to become not just neighborhood stakeholders, but vocal community leaders.

These dynamics and characteristics of Chinatown organizations have shaped how community leaders define community stakeholdership. When discussing who is a stakeholder in Chinatown, Deborah Ching, the former executive director of CSC and current commercial property owner through her father's investment in Mandarin Plaza, questioned if all the organizations should have an equal right to represent Chinatown. She explained how some organizations may not be directly concerned with the neighborhood:

> The looser [definition of a stakeholder] is who has traditional ties to Chinatown, [including] members of organizations that are based in Chinatowns— so they have family associations and people come from all over to go to those organizations. But then you have [these organizations] whose interests [are] not in Chinatown even though it's based in [Chinatown] . . . but you know, it's about what is the purpose?

Not all of the organizations in Chinatown focus on neighborhood-specific issues, and the leaders and members of some organizations do not always have a grounded understanding of Chinatown beyond their experiences as organizational members and frequent visitors. However, Eugene Moy, who was born in Chinatown but never lived in Chinatown, has been involved in the community since the 1970s and is recognized as an important community leader today. He explained that given the demographics of Chinatown, nonresident voices like his can still matter, as they can act as mediators for the community:

> Since probably more than 90 percent of the members of these organizations do not live here or do not have a business here, then it begs the question,

what's the connection and how much power, how much of a vote should that person have? . . . A lot of [Chinatown] businesses and residents are just trying to survive. And they're just going to work or they're going to school or they're trying to make ends meet. A lot of those folks are not involved [and] engaged in the public policy issues that many of us [in these organizations] are engaged in. So it's appropriate for those who have through either [knowing the community] history or [are concerned with] economic [development] or just through long-standing involvement in the affairs of the community, [that they] should have the right to participate.

Similarly, Mike Fong, who grew up in Chinatown and is currently involved in local politics, explained how nonresidents were still important for political representation, especially in a low-income, limited-English-proficient community like Chinatown. He explained how sentimental and economic attachments to Chinatown should still be factored in defining a stakeholder:

But the folks who live in the community for many years, a lot of them still probably are monolingual or . . . it's hard to get them to a meeting and express themselves. And at the same time, a lot of folks who are actively engaged in Chinatown, don't live in Chinatown. They live in the San Gabriel Valley and they live elsewhere. But they're vested in Chinatown because they have a lot of memories. They have family who live there. They have a business there.

The varying sentiments demonstrated a tension as to who should and could represent the neighborhood community. While this power conflict over representation is not uncommon in land use conflict, in Chinatown, there was a layer of complexity because of the organizational landscape. While the organizations represented the Chinese American community, they did not always represent the Chinatown community.

As they spoke about community stakeholdership, community leaders often engaged in symbolic boundary work. Through symbolic boundary work, individuals create social categories based on specific characteristics that deem people as either community insiders or outsiders, which can be used as forms of domination to control resources and power.[23] The boundary work of community leaders was a method of asserting their legitimacy and power to speak on behalf of Chinatown. In particular, symbolic attachments to Chinatown that were purely based on ethnic ties and sentiment were constantly questioned as a means to delegitimize specific individuals and organizations. As part of this questioning of their legitimacy, community leaders acknowledged that they did not fall under the primary stakeholder category, but also often demonstrated how their work showed a commitment to helping the local Chinatown community. This boundary work to assert their political legitimacy focused less on claiming ethnic and cultural attachments to Chinatown and more on determining people's knowledge of neighborhood issues and whether they were grounded in lived experiences and, ultimately, if their activism helped to build collective power to sustain Chinatown.

Symbolic Political Power of the Older Organizations

The older organizations, such as CCBA, CACA, and the mutualist organizations, continue to be important stakeholders in Chinatown, but other community leaders also recognize them more as historic institutions that tend to hold symbolic power in the neighborhood. During my fieldwork, CCBA and CACA continued to be spaces for Chinese American political representation and to build political relationships in Chinatown. For example, local elected officials would often visit CACA for endorsements during election time. While some of the politicians included representatives that would represent Chinatown specifically, such as former councilmember Gil Cedilo, other politicians who represented other areas would still visit CACA because it was still seen as a place that showed they had buy-in from the regional Chinese American community. In addition to elected officials seeking endorsements, CCBA would also host fundraising events for Chinese American candidates in the county, reflecting how their political advocacy emphasized the importance of increasing representation of Chinese Americans in local politics. The CCBA and CACA properties were also often used as community and public meeting spaces (Figure 6). The continued use of their spaces for community meetings, even those that are hosted by other organizations, signaled how these organizations were still seen as central spaces for the Chinese American and Chinatown community. It also indicated that Chinatown had few public community gathering spaces.

These organizations thus still held some degree of political power in the neighborhood. The enduring symbolic power of these older institutions was due to their legacy in establishing Chinatown and representing the ethnic community, especially during the time of explicit racial exclusion. They also were important Chinatown stakeholders in a material sense as property owners of their buildings. Because of how they now have come to symbolize the ethnic heritage of Chinese Americans and their status as property owners, many community leaders identified these older mutualist organizations

FIGURE 6. Council District 1 Candidate Forum held at the Chinese Consolidated Benevolent Association, May 2017. Photo courtesy of Rick Eng.

as the institutions most likely to be preserved in Chinatown. They felt that their presence would help to sustain the neighborhood as a Chinatown that honors the history of Chinese Americans.

While people acknowledged that these organizations will probably continue to physically stay in Chinatown, some doubted that the older organizations will be more than symbolic and historic markers for future generations. Many community leaders, including some who were involved with the older mutualist associations, expressed skepticism about these organizations' ability to continuously attract members and provide political representation on behalf of Chinatown. They noted that they were no longer as consistently active in Chinatown as they were in the past. One community leader who was born in the United States and became involved with their family's mutualist association as an adult explained how the traditional mutualist organizations no longer have the same sense of urgency in helping their members since their mission and establishment was in response to the era of racial exclusion. He stated, "That kind of survival need was no longer there. . . . Many of the members have assimilated [and] gotten jobs. . . . There's not a need for those kind of legal protections." He reasoned that this has led to the associations losing purpose for the younger generation, including his family association, which experienced a decline in membership among US-born Chinese Americans. Another community leader, who was also a member of his family's mutualist association, critiqued how the organization membership requirements were old fashioned, still based on a shared family last name, which no longer holds the same sense of community that it did for early Chinese immigrants. While CCBA was an umbrella organization and originally formed as a group that provided social control across the community, today they primarily represent and assert control over the twenty-seven organizations that are a part of CCBA, which is not the entirety of Chinatown community organizations or of Chinese American organizations in the region. They have not had a new member organization for several decades, and thus they too are limited in whom they represent in Chinatown.

These older organizations, as well as the newer mutualist organizations, remain important symbolic leaders in the community, but as ethnic organizations, their mission is not necessarily dedicated to neighborhood issues. Hence, their activities reflect that gap. For example, at CACA meetings, sporadic debates about the future of Chinatown sometimes occurred, as members debated the current changes in Chinatown, especially business turnover, which they saw as critical to maintaining the ethnic identity of the neighborhood. CACA's involvement in Chinatown-specific issues was dependent on individual members' interests in these matters and whether they had a prominent leadership role within the organization to mobilize other members. CCBA members also confirmed that they do not consistently discuss neighborhood development issues during their meetings. This may be changing, as the current CCBA leadership has shown an increased interest in these issues when attending other community meetings. Toward the end of the fieldwork, CCBA connected with CHSSC and newer progressive groups, including CCED and SEACA, to try to create a cultural center to sustain Chinatown. While this shows an effort to still be a part of Chinatown and to arguably assert a presence in the neighborhood, it also symbolizes how the main purpose of these older organizations is to assert and maintain the ethnic heritage of Chinatown that is specific to a Chinese American identity.

Positioning Progressive Voices as "Outsiders" and Business Voices as "Insiders"

While many questioned the salience of the older organizations, the boundary work around stakeholdership tended to be most prominent among progressive activists and business leaders in the community. This was especially apparent during the conflict over the Walmart Neighborhood Market in which business leaders and other long-term community leaders questioned the progressive organizers. Many were especially critical of CCED, accusing the organization of not being representative of Chinatown. They argued that most of the members not only were new to the community, but also were not Chinatown residents or workers. One long-time resident of Chinatown indicated that some of the Asian American student protestors of the Walmart "had a cause . . . but they didn't know the whole thing," hinting at how the community had planned for a grocery store in that space for over twenty years. Many saw how Chinatown had become a conflicted site for what they saw as outside interests who were not historically engaged in Chinatown and provided no viable alternatives to address community needs.

The contentious presence of CCED and other progressive organizers in Chinatown throughout its history is aligned with the tensions and dynamics in many urban social justice movements. Peter Marcuse explains that the composition of these movements includes those who are directly oppressed as well as those who may not be directly oppressed but are motivated by their political ideologies to address social injustices.[24] These movements may sometimes experience disconnects in their activism due to a lack of shared lived experiences among the activists and communities they are often fighting for. This tension is present in Los Angeles Chinatown. The progressive activism in Chinatown continues to resist assimilationist representations of Chinese and Asian Americans by highlighting the inequitable conditions facing the poor and working class.

Yet the class, educational, and political differences among community activists and the Chinatown residents and workers can also lead to challenges in creating a sense of solidarity for political mobilization.[25] For example, the language of anti-gentrification in progressive activist circles that draws from anti-capitalist and anti-imperialist frameworks did not always resonate with other community leaders or the residents and workers whom they sought to represent. In their interview, one community leader working in cultural heritage efforts even suggested that using the term *gentrification* might be "elitist" as it is a term often used by academics and college-educated individuals. The adoption of socialist and communist values has also been controversial in Chinese, Vietnamese, and other Southeast Asian communities because these ideologies are associated with the political instability in their home countries. These ideological differences, along with the fact that much of the progressive activism has stemmed from individuals with limited material attachments to Chinatown, have led some community leaders to have a critical view of their community work in Chinatown. The residential interests have mainly been voiced by politically left formations steered by younger Chinese and Asian Americans who were often driven by both social justice concerns and a shared sense of ethnic identity. But the lack of material stakeholder claims often situates these groups at a disadvantage, as other community leaders and the city tend to view them as not being legitimate representatives of the community.

However, these critiques tend to erase how the progressive organizing in Chinatown since the 1960s has helped to expand the political representation of the neighborhood. The progressive presence challenged the older elite who were primarily business leaders active in various Chinatown organizations. Some of the activists were from working-class families in Chinatown but politicized through their college education and the social movements of that time. Don Toy, who was a community activist in the 1970s and director for the Teen Post, became a prominent community leader by the 1980s through his involvement in the Chinatown Community Advisory Committee (CCAC), despite having no past political connections to mainstream institutions or the old Chinatown power structure. Toy and another activist who was also raised in Chinatown, Edmund Soohoo, often spoke of how their childhood experiences of providing everyday translations for their parents and family members laid the foundation for their activism to advocate for the Chinatown community, which often included language accessibility. Leaders like Toy and Soohoo, and others who were raised in Chinatown but not specifically part of the older Chinatown elite, ushered in a new type of leadership that could potentially provide a more grounded perspective of the lived experience of Chinatown residents.

This new generation of leadership also included women, who further challenged the older male-dominated ethnic power structure. While men still make up much of the Chinatown power structure today, the contemporary changes in Chinatown's organizational infrastructure provided spaces for women to influence community development. There were notable women in the progressive groups in Chinatown who have sustained their involvement in Chinatown and local politics since then. Phyllis Chiu, Sharon Lowe, and Diane Tan were prominent members of AAFE who continued to be involved in political advocacy for Chinatown during my fieldwork. Lowe has since worked with the city, including the city councilmember's office, and is considered an ally for some Chinatown community leaders, while Tan and Chiu continue their commitment as grassroots community organizers in CCED. These female leaders spoke about having to navigate the male-dominated power structure and gender expectations. Lowe explained that her law degree granted her legitimacy and deference in the community, but she still had to be cautious of gender norms:

> I'd be representing somebody in a hearing and it's like one of the seniors would tell me cause I raised [my voice] . . . that out of respect you [don't raise your voice because you're] young. "*A-nui*!" [Cantonese for *girl* and a term elders use when referring to a young woman.] You know, yeah [they] scold me in Chinese not to raise my voice, that I'm being disrespectful to the hearing officer or whatever. And I'm [thinking], "Really?" You know, but that's the culture! . . . It's knowledge of our own culture, recognizing that you know them at the same time. I'm always very appreciative. But I raise my voice, so I get scolded!

As a progressive activist, Lowe engaged in methods of conflict and resistance as a part of her activism, which challenged the older generation's expectations of the role of women and youth in the community. By the 2020s, Sissy Trinh, who founded SEACA, had also became a prominent community leader for equitable development in the neighborhood. Chinese American women were also holding more leadership roles in the older organizations in Chinatown. While women volunteered for CACA, organizational membership was exclusively male until 1977. The CACA Los Angeles Lodge would have its first female president, Daisy Ma, in 2009, followed by Suellen Cheng in 2013. During my fieldwork, CACA had voted in its third female president, Annie Yee.

Furthermore, some of the older generation progressive activists sought external financial support through government and foundation grants that helped to formalize and legitimize their presence in the community and beyond. For some, this was necessary to sustain the services in Chinatown. As one community activist who became involved in the 1960s explained:

> To me, if I were to read our generation of Asian American activists, I think somehow, we made a decision that we're going to fight it from the inside. We're going to learn the rules and we're going to fight it legally with the mainstream and learn how to play with the rules. . . . We fought [for our issues] from the inside and not bashing our heads against the wall.

For some of these activists, they saw that it was necessary to work within mainstream institutions to bring resources to Chinatown. CSC received their first city grant in 1975, which allowed them to incorporate as a nonprofit organization, and they have since received major private and public grants, including a federally qualified health center designation. These organizations in Chinatown that have emerged since the 1960s are aligned with the trends among community-based nonprofit organizations, which often rely on external funding for sustainability and legitimacy.[26] Some of these organizations, like CSC, were originally seen as outside of the community power structure but now are recognized as important institutions that formally brought mainstream resources to the community. Yen Le Espiritu observed that through the professionalization of social work, Asian Americans working in social service organizations have become de facto community leaders.[27] This same argument can be applied to the organizational leadership in Chinatown. Joyce Law and Irene Chu were professional social workers who were instrumental to the establishment of CSC. Deborah Ching, who was the executive director of CSC throughout the 1980s and 1990s also had ties to the broader Asian American community. She was able to create partnerships with Little Tokyo Service Center. Bill Watanabe, a community leader in Little Tokyo, cited his personal relationship with Ching as one of the reasons why the two communities had successful collaborations, including the development of an affordable housing complex in Chinatown, Cesar Chavez Gardens. While Ching had a family legacy, she made a name of her own through her community leadership in contemporary Chinatown organizations throughout the 1980s and 1990s.

While some groups obtained nonprofit organization legal status in Chinatown, other organizers have resisted this formalization. As previously mentioned, AAFE and CPA had both dissolved by the 1980s. Los Angeles stands in contrast to other urban Chinatowns that have sustained these organizations. In the case of AAFE in New York, it is no longer on the political fringe and has evolved to become a part of the Chinatown power structure.[28] When I asked former members and current activists about why these groups dissolved, some who followed more radical politics were critical of institutionalizing progressive groups in Chinatown. They spoke of contributing to a "nonprofit industrial complex" in which they would be pressured to respond to funding demands rather than community needs. This sentiment is aligned with neo-institutional scholars who have argued that organizations that seek out external legitimacy ultimately face pressures to conform to mainstream social values and norms to secure financial and political security.[29] Soo Ah Kwon further argues that this professionalization of ethnic organizations and the state's adoption of the term *Asian American*, a political identity that originated from student activists Yuji Ichioka and Emma Gee in the 1960s, is emblematic of the state attempting to control more radical interests, leading to the further depoliticization of the Asian American identity in a competition over resources.[30] Many radical activists have thus resisted engaging in these formal and mainstream structures in order to have more freedom and control in their community work.[31] This tradition continues with organizations like CCED, which at the time of the fieldwork did not have any plans to incorporate as a nonprofit organization. While not having this legal nonprofit status allowed for CCED to not be constrained in their political work, it was also a limitation, as other community leaders often used their lack of incorporation status to question their legitimacy as community stakeholders and representatives for Chinatown.

Despite the contributions of progressive activists, business leaders, particularly those involved with the BID, often questioned their right to represent Chinatown, especially if they were not formal nonprofit organizations. They asserted a narrow definition of stakeholdership that valued material or economic attachments to Chinatown more than sentimental and political attachments. As one individual associated with the BID explained:

> My definition of a stakeholder is skin in the game, right, whether you live there or work there or own property there. And for a stakeholder to be just anybody that cares about Chinatown, that can be anyone. That can be anyone. Not that it's wrong to care about Chinatown. I think it's great. You know the more people that care about Chinatown the more attention and voices that we're going to have for it. And that's great. But not when you're coming in and telling me I need to do this for my house and my community that I spend more time in than you.

This criticism was extended to new organizations, such as CCED, as well as older organizations, such as CCBA and CACA. Those who took this stance explained that individuals associated with these organizations tend to have less direct connections to the neighborhood and should not be prioritized over property owners, whom the BID primarily represents, along with those who live and work in the neighborhood. For example, during one public meeting about the development of a new neighborhood park, George Yu, the BID executive director, openly criticized the utility of the park for the residents. He did so by highlighting how one of his staff, Xiayi Zhang, was a resident of Chinatown who did not support the park. Zhang was a former Miss Chinatown and had just purchased one of the few condominiums available in the neighborhood. While she fit the narrow definition of a stakeholder, she also represented a newer resident that was a young professional and homeowner, contrasting with average Chinatown residents who were primarily renters.

The BID also critiqued established community stakeholders to assert their legitimacy. Many members of the BID expressed a shared narrative that the BID formation and purpose was a response to disengagement and neglect, from both the city and Chinese Americans. This perceived neglect of Chinatown created a "burden" on property owners, especially the ones active in the BID, to address neighborhood issues, including public safety and general upkeep of the neighborhood. One of the founding board members explained how there were persistent gaps in government provision of services to Chinatown:

> Chinatown was neglected, and [when] I say neglected, I mean in terms of public services. And there was a sense that it wasn't going to get any better. I mean, there's the iconic view from Chinatown of City Hall. And it's so close and yet so far.... So, once again, we have to do it ourselves. And the way to get an infusion of money is the BID structure.

Other board members bluntly stated that the BID exists because of the "failure of government" in providing services. One board member explained that through the BID, the "city's responsibility in [ensuring] a clean and safe community" is now on the property owners, who pay the extra assessment. This criticism about responsibility and neglect was also extended to some longtime stakeholders of the Chinatown community. Most community leaders recall the BID formation as a response by local business leaders to the perceived economic decline in Chinatown that began in the 1980s. Several current and former members of the BID board explained that some of the older business organizations, such as the Chinese Chamber of Commerce, were becoming less focused on Chinatown as the San Gabriel Valley became the new economic center for Chinese Americans. Some business leaders, especially those with commercial property interests, felt it was important to have a group that specifically focused on economic development in Chinatown rather than the broader economic interests of the ethnic community across the region to compete with these changes. They also justified the BID's purpose in the community by criticizing longtime Chinese American property owners for being "absentee" and "not stepping up" to take care of their properties, as well as shared public spaces. This positioned the BID as a necessary entity in Chinatown to ensure that the ongoing provision of local services once provided through informal community relationships are continued today, albeit in a more formalized manner.

Because they perceived a disinvestment from Chinese Americans, especially in relation to the investment that has gone into the San Gabriel Valley, many BID board members and staff openly supported non-Chinese investment coming into the neighborhood. They reasoned that they are doing more to revitalize the neighborhood than some Chinese Americans, including the older property owners they often criticized. As one BID staff member explained:

> These restaurants or merchants aren't Chinese American, but they create a space that people—including Chinese Americans—would enjoy and that ultimately bring more Chinese Americans back to the community. . . . I like to use General Lee's [an older restaurant in Central Plaza] as an example, where none of the [current] partners for General Lee's are Chinese. But they are very respectful to that history that General Lee's had in Chinatown. And instead of doing modern renovations, they actually renovated it back to what it looked like in the '70s. And I [think] that counts. They're not Chinese Americans, but they are respectful of the Chinese American story in Chinatown. So why should we have any opposition to it? And especially in the absence of Chinese Americans being interested or investing in this space.

This sentiment legitimized business leaders and business owners as cultural preservationists doing the work that would normally be left to heritage groups such as CHSSC and the older organizations that have evolved to represent Chinese American heritage, such as CCBA and the older mutualist associations. It has also openly challenged the idea that only Chinese Americans cared about Chinatown, acknowledging how new property and business owners were helping to both preserve and "activate" the neighborhood despite not being Chinese Americans or having prior ties to Chinatown.

Some of the newer property owners that sit on the BID board also claim that they were trying to protect the neighborhood from speculators, thus distancing themselves from other new property owners that may not care for the neighborhood. Alexis Readinger was one such newcomer to the neighborhood. She was the owner of Preen, a design and architectural firm, and owns a property in West Plaza, noting that she was attracted to the live-work design of the building and the unique character of Chinatown. She explained her motivation for joining the BID board:

> There's a lot of hungry wolves trying to work their way in. Finally, the perception has fallen away that [Chinatown is] impenetrable. So there's a lot of people that are—we call them carpetbaggers. [laughs] [They] want to come in and scam and make money off brokering deals and don't have vested interest.

Readinger and other BID board members saw themselves as important gatekeepers who were keeping the "kind of people with their sort of cursory interest out [of Chinatown] and really make it attractive and powerful for people that really want to invest and be in the community." The BID provided a legitimate space for newcomers like Readinger to show that they were engaged with the Chinatown community.

However, there was still uneasiness—and for activists involved with CCED, a complete resistance—about how the BID represented the neighborhood and acted as gatekeepers. Progressive activists, new and old, were the most critical of these stakeholder claims that the BID asserted. While the BID board members were all property owners, an important stakeholder group, they also supported new businesses who had limited relationships with other organizations in Chinatown. One older community leader who started as a youth organizer in the 1970s was openly critical of the BID, their governance, and how they tried to rationalize their decisions as "insiders" that represent the community. He stated:

> You get these people who come from [outside] the Chinatown community who say they grew up in Chinatown or they did this in Chinatown or they do that in Chinatown. But . . . they don't realize that helping out the community means to help people help themselves. Without that element, I think you're actually hurting the community. [They're] thinking that, "Okay well, I'll just be active in taking care of their needs, it would waste too much of my time to get them involved. I can do this myself for them." Which is a prevailing type of attitude that a lot of people have.

While he acknowledged that the BID provided services to the community, he critiqued their governance, which tends to keep decision-making power within the property owners who are a part of the BID board. As explained in chapter 4, the governance of the BID often did not include input from other community stakeholders who were not commercial property owners. It was still seen as an exclusionary space that was not structured to represent the diverse interests of the broader community.

More Than "Doing Good in the Community"

The members of the different Chinatown organizations appeared to be cognizant and, in some cases, self-reflective about the limits of their claims as community stakeholders. Many community leaders, especially those involved with organizations like CACA and CHSSC, acknowledged that they and their members were not residents and were, at times, hesitant to take public stances on behalf of the neighborhood. When they did openly speak on development issues in the neighborhood, their definition of forced displacement was often expansive. In their advocacy and discussion of gentrification, they often centered the potential displacement of the Chinese American historical and cultural identity that has defined Chinatown. This expansive definition of forced displacement thus justified the involvement of the broader ethnic community, not just those living and working in these ethnic neighborhoods.

However, most community leaders I met in my fieldwork openly grappled with this tension rather than shying away from doing place-based community work in the neighborhood. This was especially true of those working in tenant organizing. While a few college-aged CCED members would try to assert their stakeholdership by moving to Chinatown, this also brought up implications about their role in gentrification. Instead, it became more important to center and unpack the motivations for their community work with the current Chinatown residents. Phyllis Chiu, who continued to be involved with CCED after her time in AAFE, explained that she felt that the legitimacy of the community work was not about a nonprofit status or where the members lived, but what the work entails. She explained that organizations and their members should be thinking about "who you're working for. And are you still helping the community and are you there?" With this philosophy regarding community work, there were distinctions about who was centered in community work, as the activism should not just be about a vague sense of community, but should specifically center those who historically have been politically marginalized. Gilbert Hom was also an activist since the 1970s. His activism started with the Chinatown Youth Council and Teen Post in the 1970s and became involved with CHSSC and CACA in his later years. In his interview, he similarly observed this tension and noted how it had been an issue since his time as a community organizer in the 1970s. He reflected on that time, stating, "I think what became a challenge is . . . to develop a philosophy [that] we're trying to organize a community to help themselves, not so much a missionary group that is just doing good in the community." Volunteers, both old and new to Chinatown, spoke about a similar goal of trying to do political work that went beyond self-interest and would build community capacity.

Many CCED members were aware that they were not the primary stake-holders of Chinatown, cautiously stating their role as "supportive" to the residents and immigrant small business owners. CCED member Craig Wong, who was also an activist with the Los Angeles branch of CPA in the 1980s, explained that the CCED philosophy continues the traditions of "serving the people" and local empowerment that began with the social movements in the 1960s and 1970s:

> When we go into these like different situations where we're working with people, they will say, "Oh well why don't you just do it for us." We don't ever do that. We'll say, "We'll help you, we'll work with you, but you have to decide what you want to do. You have to decide your strategy. . . . When we walk away from this, we want to leave you more empowered than when we came. If that doesn't happen, then we haven't really accomplished very much.

CCED has tried to exemplify these principles through a number of activities. In addition to organizing with residents and creating tenant-based advocacy groups for different developments, they have also provided community forums and social gatherings for residents (Figure 7). At their community events, many residents have openly talked about their precarious housing situation, eviction and rent-increase letters, landlords ignoring repair requests, and rumors about property ownership changes. At one tenant outreach meeting in 2015, the group developed a map of all the different developments in the pipeline for Chinatown and held discussions about rent increases and the legal rights of tenants. During another CCED community meeting in 2017, the group designed a quick icebreaker introduction, which included over fifty people in the room. Rather than providing a short introduction, the first few people began to speak about their housing concerns in detail. While this unexpectedly prolonged the introduction activity, it also highlighted how residents needed a space to share their concerns.

CCED members shared that they deliberately design their activities to try to create spaces of dialogue and community building so that their work represents the experiences of residents and empowers the residents themselves to become politically engaged. Sophat Phea, a Chinatown resident, explained that he learned about community organizing through SEACA and CCED and that he would not have received this knowledge in other community spaces. He recognized how the neighborhood is still an isolated community and spoke about how his organizational involvement helped

FIGURE 7. Chinatown Community for Equitable Development Tenant Rights Workshop, July 2015. Photo courtesy of Chinatown Community for Equitable Development.

him build connections to other Asian Americans who helped him mature politically, "I feel so invested in CCED. And then the people I work with, I find them really inspiring."

CCED and younger generation community activists have also questioned the identity politics and ethnic solidarity that has historically defined Chinatown politics. CCED member Craig Wong continued to explain that their philosophy of community work puts less emphasis on ethnic ties and more emphasis on addressing broader issues of systemic racism, classism, and exclusion that transcend the Chinese American community. He spoke about "a particular obligation to the Chinese American movement, the Chinese American communities in general [because] it's historically a Chinese community." However, he also noted that CCED "will work with anyone who really wants to improve the conditions." Thus, their organizing is driven around ideological principles that can involve individuals who do not always identify as Chinese American. This was further articulated as Wong shared CCED's stance on the 2015 conviction of Chinese American police officer Peter Liang for the shooting of Akai Gurley in New York City in 2014. This conviction divided the Chinese American community, as some saw Liang as a scapegoat for the ongoing police brutality against Black communities since White police officers were not convicted in the past. Other Chinese American progressive organizers, including CCED, questioned the identity politics of immediately sympathizing with Liang and saw the conviction as a necessary step toward addressing systemic anti-Black racism, particularly in the criminal justice system. Wong explained that CCED had a responsibility to educate the Chinatown community about cross-racial solidarity during Liang's conviction: "There's a large number of Chinese Americans in CCED. So that's why with the Peter Liang thing, we took that on because even though we're a Chinese American organization, we have some obligation there, right?"

This work was arguably a double-edged sword for CCED, especially as they were seen by other community leaders as formed by outsiders. While still driven by young Chinese and Asian Americans, the impact of CCED's work was not necessarily exclusive to the Asian American community. They also worked toward cross-racial solidarities that could possibly raise critical consciousness within the community about gentrification and race relations. This approach in place-based progressive political organizing is becoming more commonplace among Asian American communities as issues of labor and immigration become more defining characteristics of political solidarity.[32] Simultaneously, it also can further question belonging in places like Chinatown, as this type of advocacy does not always reflect traditional identity politics—that the goals of political engagement among the ethnic community is to ultimately raise the visibility, power, and belonging of Chinese Americans, which is what has historically defined Chinatown politics.

· · ·

Los Angeles Chinatown continues to be a place of symbolic and material importance to Chinese Americans across the region. In particular, the neighborhood's organizational landscape has evolved to serve the different interests and segments of the Chinese American community. Through these organizations, whether old or new, Chinatown persists as an important ethnic space because it remains an important political center for Chinese and Asian Americans. Chinatown continues to provide spaces where generations of Chinese and Asian Americans can be politically engaged in a way that provides a sense of community and belonging based on their heritage and interests. While civic engagement in Chinatown can be seen as a part of ongoing identity politics, the experiences and work of community leaders who are involved in the different organizations demonstrate that community work is more complicated than simply fighting for and on behalf of the ethnic community. The community work in Chinatown also necessitates a place-based approach that supports the working-class families and individuals who live and work in Chinatown.

Because of these tensions of doing place-based community work in a neighborhood that holds symbolic meaning for an ethnic community across the region, community leaders have engaged in symbolic boundary work to regulate community stakeholdership. This boundary work is a defining part of the community politics of Chinatown, with community leaders asserting and legitimizing their political power while also minimizing the power of others. This internal conflict can be situated as a response to the legacy of racialized marginalization and how Chinatown has served as a site of political belonging for generations of Chinese Americans to resist that marginalization. They were asserting both a right to represent Chinatown as well as a sense of political belonging in the city. The different organizations and the claims around political legitimacy are constantly being challenged and are changing over time, reflecting the demographic, cultural, and political complexities of the Chinese American community. Through their boundary work, community leaders were not just regulating each other, but were also centering the voices they believed mattered the most in Chinatown, whether residents, business owners, or property owners. As Chinatown continues to experience gentrification and displacement pressures, how community leaders continue to speak on behalf of and directly work with these specific stakeholders will have implications for how community control is defined and practiced in sustaining the neighborhood.

THREE

The Limits of Legitimizing Community Control

> I'm trying to find out more about the different projects going on
> and what buildings are being bought out [in Chinatown]. For
> me, it seems that it's going really fast. But I know that for a lot
> of other folks that aren't as aware of it, because [the process is]
> not that transparent, it's really low-key.... They might not even
> identify it as gentrification and displacing folks.
>
> —Chinatown Community for Equitable Development member

> It occurs to me that there are a number of groups in Chinatown
> that really don't have a voice as far as what's going on in our com-
> munity.... How do you manage that? How do you bring the
> community together?
>
> —DAVID LOUIE, community leader

AS LOS ANGELES CHINATOWN continued to evolve as a space for political
engagement for Chinese and Asian Americans, local government has also
provided more opportunities for community representation and control in
neighborhood development. State and local policies established mechanisms
and spaces for communities to be formally involved in the development
process, such as advising on decision-making and having direct control over
public funds. However, these new forms of governance have also complicated
the political landscape of places such as Chinatown which have a preexisting community power structure with organizations that provides resources,
political representation, and informal governance. Chapter 2 detailed some
of these organizations and how they represented diverse interests and different segments of the Chinese American and Chinatown communities. In
contrast, these new formal spaces, backed by public polices and deliberately
designed for place-based representation, are meant to provide a platform
for different community voices to be heard and, in some cases, for the community to come together as a unified voice. During my fieldwork, I found

that despite the presence of these spaces, community leaders across different interests expressed a common sentiment that they have yet to bridge the disparate voices of Chinatown, nor have they led to more transparency in the decision-making processes that shape local development.

This chapter examines how these mechanisms that promoted and legitimized community control in local government have had a paradoxical effect in building community power in Chinatown. I highlight three specific spaces that were established in Chinatown through city and state policies and have been contested spaces of power since the 1970s: the Chinatown Project Area Committee (PAC), which later became the Chinatown Community Advisory Committee (CCAC); the Historic Cultural Neighborhood Council (HCNC); and the Business Improvement District (BID).[1] Chinatown community leaders had to navigate these new city structures that formalized neighborhood governance and local control outside of the informal work of community organizations. These new formations provided avenues to build relationships and influence elected officials, city staff, and developers. They also provided access to public resources and the power to determine how they would be distributed to the community. They thus became important spaces of power in the neighborhood, but also conflicted and controversial spaces.

Asserting dominance and control in these spaces became a part of the larger politics of governance in Chinatown. In the PAC/CCAC and HCNC, which were city-initiated spaces of citizen participation, the power of business leaders, which represented the traditional community elite, was challenged by politically progressive community leaders who engaged in methods of resistance and conflict in these spaces. Business leaders responded by disengaging and initiating other legitimate political spaces and groups to reassert community control in Chinatown, including the creation of the BID. The BID was recognized as a form of local control and considered to be one of the most politically powerful spaces in the community. But the BID also represented the increasing neoliberalism of local governance that privatizes the provision of public goods and services, which often supports economic growth and profits at the expense of other social needs of the community.

These spaces contributed to political displacement and restructuring of power to a new generation of community leaders in Chinatown. However, they also did not necessarily contribute to a transformation of community power. Instead, together, they were perpetuating power imbalances within the neighborhood. The trends of hyper-engagement and disengagement of community leaders across these different spaces indicate that while there is and has been community control in Chinatown, that political power was limited and has yet to be democratized. Instead, community control has been narrowed to specific individuals and groups in the neighborhood. The community engagement that emerged from these spaces magnified community conflict beyond these spaces and challenged romantic assumptions that community engagement is both inherently progressive and representative of the entire community.[2] At times, these platforms facilitated in amplifying community voices to maintain a status quo or to promote self-interest. These tensions in Chinatown underscore the difficulties in how we define and practice community in all neighborhoods, which has implications for how local government tries to institutionalize community engagement to ensure equitable development.

"MORE THAN A RUBBER STAMP": CITIZEN PARTICIPATION IN CHINATOWN

Since the 1970s, the city has established various participatory governance structures that have impacted the political landscape of Chinatown. In response to the political organizing and demands of the Modern Civil Rights Movement, local government and urban planners have developed and implemented spaces of citizen participation to promote racial and social equity.[3] These are intermediary spaces that establish formal linkages between communities and local government and facilitate in bringing diverse political actors to engage and deliberate on information and to make decisions on behalf of the community.[4] These deliberative spaces provide forums where information about the neighborhood and the planning process is shared, discussed, and negotiated. Depending on how these spaces are structured and what practices occur in them, they may encourage more political participation and empower communities. But they also may lead to the reproduction of power, and communities may continue to feel politically tokenized and disempowered.[5]

In Chinatown, these spaces of citizen participation provided legitimate community representation within the broader city political structure. Because they were also purposely designed as advisory spaces to the city and were never meant to be a decision-making body, they were also purposely limited in community power. However, progressive activists pushed against these limits, which contributed to the emergence of a new generation of community leadership in Chinatown that sought to center residential interests in these platforms. Historically, the community was represented by community elites who owned property and represented business interests, and these spaces provided a forum for non-elites to represent the community. While this contributed to a political restructuring that uplifted historically underrepresented voices in Chinatown, it also led to intense conflict among community leaders and, ultimately, disengagement in these spaces.

Resistance through the CRA?
The Chinatown Advisory Committees

The first spaces of citizen participation in Chinatown were established when the neighborhood was designated a CRA project area. Through the CRA designation, Chinatown had two different advisory committees, a Project Area Committee (PAC) and the Chinatown Community Advisory Committee (CCAC) (Figure 8). These committees were a response to past criticisms of redevelopment practices that excluded communities from providing political input in the city's redevelopment projects, especially when there was a potential use of eminent domain. Through their participation in these committees, community members advised the CRA and the City Council on all local land use issues in the project area, regardless whether the proposed development received CRA funding. These committee meetings were also open to the public to promote transparency in decision-making processes. Combined, the PAC and CCAC served as the formal space for community representation to the city for over thirty years. Both sought to provide a holistic representation of Chinatown with stakeholders representing different interests, as it required business, residential, and institutional representatives. But these spaces were also subject to policy changes and internal conflict that limited community representation and power.

The Chinatown PAC formed in 1978 during the designation process to approve the project area plan and to mediate the use of eminent domain, which ultimately was never used in Chinatown. When the PAC formed, community representatives quickly called attention to the limits of community power within the space and sought to change it. In an excerpt from the PAC meeting minutes on March 2, 1978, which was a meeting to advise the CRA on the designation process, some committee members advocated for the PAC to be more than an advisory space for the CRA and city. The minutes state:

FIGURE 8. Chinatown Community Advisory Committee with Community Redevelopment Agency staff in the late 1980s. Image from the Chinatown CRA Biennial Report, 1988–1990.

There was some discussion over the role of the PAC. Some felt it was to be an advisory committee with powers to review and revise the plans developed by the city planners. Others felt the PAC should be more inclined to initiate the wants and needs of the community. Marianne Yee [the CRA community liaison] explained that the PAC's role is advisory in nature, [and] that [the] PAC serves as the formal means through which people participate in all stages with CRA during the formulation and execution of a redevelopment plan. [The] PAC participates in the decision-making process *before* final decisions are made by CRA and City Council.[6]

Since the formation of these advisory bodies, Chinatown community leaders were already pushing back and making demands to ensure that they would not be politically tokenized. Those community representatives were young progressive activists who were politicized in Chinatown in the 1960s and 1970s, including Gilbert Hom, Sharon Lowe, Chi Mui, Don Toy, and Edmund Soohoo, and were active in Asian Americans for Equality (AAFE), Teen Post, and the Chinatown Youth Council. They approached the PAC, and the CCAC later on, as an actively engaged space where community demands could be made to the CRA and the city. These activists also challenged the economic interests that both the city and business elites had for Chinatown.

The limits and tensions of community control in the PAC contributed to its dissolution and subsequent multiple restructurings. The PAC was originally designed as an elected body decided by the community. In 1984, City Councilmember Gilbert Lindsay dissolved the PAC and restructured the committee to the CCAC, which consisted of half elected and half city councilmember appointments. By changing the PAC to a CCAC, the councilmember would be able to decide who would participate in this space. This was a key distinction that could potentially restructure representation and power relations. CCAC representatives had to have some relationship with the councilmember's office to be appointed, whereas the PAC representatives would have to build relationships and campaign in the community to be elected to the committee. The CCAC was again restructured in 1985 when it became a fully appointed body and in 2006 as part of larger citywide efforts to standardize CRA advisory councils throughout the city. The multiple restructurings throughout time indicated that while these were spaces of citizen participation and community control, ultimately, they were always advisory spaces controlled by the city, which could limit who and what was being represented on behalf of Chinatown.

Many community leaders and former CRA staff saw the restructurings of the PAC/CCAC as a way to temper the conflicts among community leaders representing residential and business interests and, more specifically, the increasing influence of specific progressive voices in Chinatown. Representatives from both interests led the PAC/CCAC at some point. The first chair of the PAC was business leader David Lee, whose family owned one of Chinatown's well-known restaurants, General Lee, while the longest-running CCAC chair was Don Toy, who grew up in a working-class family in Chinatown and became involved in the community through AAFE and Teen Post. However, Toy and other activists who represented residential interests emerged as the most visible and vocal actors in the PAC/CCAC. Speaking to the media after the PAC dissolution in 1984, Sharon Lowe, a former PAC member who was a part of AAFE, argued that the dissolution was the city's attempt to specifically dilute the voice of residents and residential interests. She shared to the press that Councilmember Lindsay "wants to do for Chinatown what he did for Little Tokyo. We don't want our community displaced and replaced completely by business with empty streets at night and nobody around."[7] Lowe was referring to developments like the

New Otani Hotel, which was backed by international Japanese investors but displaced Japanese American seniors living in the current buildings. Chinatown community activists who were elected to the PAC were aware of this history, and some know the activists who were trying to resist redevelopment in Little Tokyo, the Little Tokyo peoples Rights Organization (LTPRO). They also saw similar pressures of Asian investment and flight capital arriving in Chinatown in the 1970s. This concern contributed to their activism to not just advocate for affordable housing, but also to oppose most commercial development throughout Chinatown's CRA designation.

Because of their stances, they were often described as "resistant" to the city, CRA staff, and other community leaders. In both the interviews and archival research of past CCAC meeting minutes, there were multiple instances of CCAC members yelling at each other, questioning the accuracy of meeting minutes and translations, and walkouts before a vote to break a quorum and delay decision-making. People interpreted their actions as purposeful conflict to create barriers for other members to participate, disrupting the ability for the committee to "conduct business" at meetings.

One event cited by individuals as an example of the resistance of the CCAC and their perceived power to "slow down" processes, and by extension development, was the community review process of Blossom Plaza, a mixed-use, mixed-income development that opened in 2016. The development discussions began in the early 2000s as it was being proposed next to the newly opened Chinatown Metro Station. The development was envisioned as a major entrance to Chinatown, but because it was proposed by an outside developer and potentially receiving public funding, community leaders, especially progressive activists in the CCAC, were monitoring the progress closely and constantly questioning the review process. One CCAC member, Gilbert Hom, walked out on the first call for a vote on the project. He recalled how he saw the process as "undemocratic" and not transparent to the community:

GILBERT: The first or second meeting where Blossom Plaza was brought up, there wasn't even a set public hearing for the project. So, one of the members of the advisory board, as soon as it came up on the agenda, said, "I propose that we recommend that the project be moved forward." And I said, "Where is the hearing?" You know? How can you even vote on a project that we haven't even heard what's being proposed or anything, you know?

LAUREEN: How did he respond? Did the person respond in any way? What was their justification?

GILBERT: Well, it was fairly clear that there was a group of people with the intent on moving forward the Blossom Plaza project. And that they had met, and they had gotten all their people to their advisory committee meeting and actually had the majority [to approve the project].

LAUREEN: Within the advisory [committee]?

GILBERT: [nods head] They had the majority of the advisory council. If there was a vote held that day, as proposed, they would've won the vote. But what happened was I raised that this was totally undemocratic and if that we [were] to have a vote at this time, it'd be a total farce. And then a couple of other people stood up and said that. That this is not a vote. And they stood up and everybody walked out of the meeting. Not everybody, but the opposition [to Blossom Plaza] walked out of the meeting. So, they were left with no quorum. So, they said, "Well we can't discuss this."

There was eventually an open discussion about Blossom Plaza at the May 6, 2004, CCAC meeting. This meeting was chaired by Don Toy, the CCAC chair at the time, and it lasted three hours. The Blossom Plaza proposal was the only agenda item discussed. While other CCAC meetings were primarily attended by board members and CRA staff, the meeting minutes stated that it also included the councilmember at the time, Ed Reyes, and his staff, as well as "over 150 community members 'standing room only' in attendance for the meeting. Community members including senior citizens, youth, adults, residents, businesses, benevolent groups, family associations, social service groups, businesspeople, philanthropic groups, nonprofit groups, etc. from Chinatown."[8] After a ten-minute presentation from Larry Bond, the developer, a Q&A session was convened that took up most of the three-hour meeting. CCAC members and community members questioned both Councilmember Reyes and Bond about the community benefits, including affordable housing, parking, and a cultural center, all benefits that have been demands from the community for decades. In response to the critiques, they explained their vision for this project as a distinct landmark project and an eastern gateway for Chinatown to attract more visitors. The meeting minutes showed that community members were not supportive. There was one statement that summarized several public comments:

> Developers invest in Chinatown to make a profit and leave, never caring about the community. Most Chinatown residents only make minimum wage and struggle hard to make a living. Chinatown's funding should only be spent to benefit Chinatown community members, not to subsidize private developers and victimize the community with higher housing and living costs.[9]

The resistance to this project also displayed the tenuous history that the community had with outside developers and the community's skepticism about whether they would indeed provide benefits beyond their promises in the proposal stage.

Through the involvement of progressive activists like Gilbert Hom in the CCAC, it was not simply a space to challenge developments; it was a space to challenge assumptions about the participatory structure. Other members who were highly engaged in the CCAC explained that they did not want to become a token participatory entity, or just part of a "rubber stamp" process. Edmund Soohoo, another former CCAC member representing residential interests, explained that his and others' engagement defied expectations that advisory boards were simply passive entities:

> People expect you to be advisory, therefore just advise and get out of the way. But [we were] more of an action-oriented advisory board. If we didn't like something, we were likely to pull a press conference. We were likely to demonstrate or if we supported something we were likely to come out strong in support of it. I think that was a little difficult for some people.

These new community leaders in the CCAC were also part of the newer cohort of leadership that emerged through the Asian American activism that began in the late 1960s in Chinatown. They brought in a specific style of political engagement that used methods of conflict to advance issues and mobilize others for their causes. This conflict approach was also antithetical to the consensus model of deliberative democratic practices. However, these activists explained that it was imperative to communicate a strong residential voice that was specific to the Chinatown context. They wanted to challenge norms to ensure a more precise definition of affordable housing that was aligned with the median income of the neighborhood, not the county, as well as translations that recognized the dialect differences within the Chinese American immigrant community. The inclusion of the residential perspective was critical in ensuring that the development through the CRA would not lead to residential gentrification and displacement in Chinatown. Their activism was also not simply about resisting outsiders and new development, but steering and tailoring resources to address the specific needs of Chinatown.

As leaders like Don Toy, Edmund Soohoo, Gilbert Hom, and others from progressive organizing backgrounds became the dominant voices in the PAC/CCAC, many business leaders appeared disinterested in participating in the CRA advisory committees by the 1990s. Munson Kwok, who initially became involved in Chinatown because of his interest in culture and heritage, was an active member of the CCAC since the mid-1980s and throughout the early 2000s. While not a business leader or a progressive activist, he also shared that he, at times, had conflicted exchanges with other CCAC members as the culture of the space was often strained. He was passionate about being a part of the committee and believed in its intentions, but also observed how the business leaders in the CCAC lost influence, explaining, "I must say, the progressives were all dedicated. . . . Frankly, I think the business element became somewhat therefore vulnerable. They were never able to press their issues successfully as maybe they should have." Another former CCAC member explained that the business leaders did recognize that the resistance from CCAC members was about the process, but they felt that most of the time it focused too much on "governance minutia," such as "correcting typos in meeting minutes," which they saw as ineffective. He explained that "after non-productivity you can imagine that those people that were in the business [community], 'I've got better use of my time than just sit there and waste it.' So, they didn't stay involved." Many business leaders also criticized the CRA as being too bureaucratic and that the community resistance added to the layers of city bureaucracy. One business leader explained that the CRA "ignored" them, while another business leader pointed out that this slowed down economic development in Chinatown, stating that "the city councilperson [was] looking to the CCAC to give their recommendations and . . . sending any developer to the CCAC to seek their recommendation, their approval. That was how nothing happened." Even though business leaders were the most vocal advocates for the CRA designation, the CCAC was ultimately not a space for business interests nor a space that could bridge different groups together to provide a collective voice of Chinatown.

Reproducing Conflict: Chinatown and the Neighborhood Council System

The CCAC has been inactive since the statewide dissolution of the CRA in 2011, and the neighborhood council system is now the formal mechanism for citizen participation in Los Angeles. In 1999, the city reformed its charter to address growing alienation from communities who were threatening to secede from the city. The city established a neighborhood council system with

FIGURE 9. Historic Cultural Neighborhood Council General Board Meeting held at the Chinese American Citizens Alliance–Los Angeles Lodge, February 2015. Photo courtesy of Rick Eng.

the intent to increase local representation. Unlike the CCAC, the neighborhood councils are an elected body from stakeholders in the neighborhood. This elected body includes business, residential, and nonprofit organization representatives.

From 2003 to 2018, Chinatown was part of the Historic Cultural Neighborhood Council (HCNC) (Figure 9). Despite being a council directly elected from neighborhood stakeholders, the HCNC was not a council specific to Chinatown because of how it was designed. The HCNC included six downtown adjacent neighborhoods: Little Tokyo, El Pueblo, the Arts District, Solano Canyon, Victor Heights, and Chinatown. The small population size in each of these communities disqualified them from being independent neighborhood councils, and thus they came together to form one neighborhood council. In addition to the HCNC representing multiple neighborhoods, Chinatown was split into two neighborhoods. Victor Heights was the residential area of Chinatown, and is in reference to a street within that area, while Chinatown only represented the historic commercial core. Although this arrangement provided Chinatown more representation, as each neighborhood acquired a set number of representatives, it also contributed to fragmentation within Chinatown by positioning these spaces as separate neighborhoods with separate interests. Thus, similar to the PAC/CCAC, the HCNC was also designed as an imperfect space of representation for Chinatown.

The neighborhood council system in Los Angeles provided another formal space of citizen participation for Chinatown, but it was also a highly conflicted space. While similar conflicts that happened in the PAC/CCAC also occurred in the HCNC, there were also differences because Chinatown was one of six neighborhoods, and each neighborhood had their own distinct development needs and issues. There were not just concerns about how the HCNC structured representation for Chinatown and the power struggles to secure that representation within the community, but also contentiousness across the neighborhoods as they sought to find a collective voice. This tension across the neighborhoods was apparent in how development projects were vetted through the HCNC. The major subcommittee of the HCNC during the time of my fieldwork was the Urban Design and Land Use Committee (UDLUC), which was similar to the PAC/CCAC in that it played an advisory role on development matters for the neighborhoods. The UDLUC was a committee that consisted of select board members from each of the HCNC neighborhoods. At the UDLUC meetings, developers would present their projects, and board members who were present would vote to recommend to the rest of the HCNC board whether to write a letter of support for the project to the city. Most of the projects presented to the UDLUC needed discretionary approval, as they were proposing developments not currently zoned for that specific use or density. Securing community support was seen as a critical part of this process, even if they were not the final decision-makers on approving the project. Some by-right projects, which were developments that were within the current zoning laws, did not require formal community support, but their presence at these meetings was a way for the developer to show that they were doing community outreach.

During my fieldwork, a majority of the projects presented at the UDLUC directly impacted the Arts District, which reflected the rapid pace of development that area of the city was experiencing at the time. A few Chinatown and Victor Heights projects were presented at the UDLUC monthly meetings, but no representatives from these neighborhoods were present. The absences of Chinatown and Victor Heights representatives at the UDLUC meetings were possibly due to the meetings being located outside of the neighborhood and the committee not requiring that board members attend the meetings, an issue that was debated at several board meetings but never resolved. Because of an absence of Chinatown representation at the UDLUC, representatives from the Arts District and Little Tokyo would cautiously provide input. It was not until after the 2016 HCNC election that Angelica Lopez Moyes, who was the newly elected Chinatown nonprofit organization representative, began to attend meetings more consistently. However, as a newcomer, she expressed discomfort in making a decision without conferring with more community groups. She also openly questioned the process, stating that she needed to review the projects in advance of the meetings so that she could do appropriate outreach to others in Chinatown. The limited representation from Chinatown and Victor Heights community leaders at the UDLUC meetings situated the HCNC as a weak representative voice of the Chinatown community, but one that had to exist because of the city charter. Furthermore, the HCNC neighborhoods had different local elected representatives, which made it even more difficult to collectively provide input on developments. Chinatown was part of City Council District 1 and the Central City North Planning Area, while the Arts District and Little Tokyo were part of City Council District 14 and the Central City Planning Area.

The structure was not the only limitation of the HCNC in providing a representative or effective voice for Chinatown. Similar to the CCAC, there were issues about the HCNC's ability to "conduct business" as an advisory council that stemmed from the business versus residential conflicts in Chinatown. Kim Benjamin and George Yu, commercial property owners who established the Business Improvement District (BID) around the same time as the HCNC, were founding members of the HCNC. This would suggest that the original intent of the HCNC was to be a space to support business interests. Yet those who were activists in the PAC/CCAC, particularly Don Toy and Edmund Soohoo, also became active members of the HCNC, thus carrying over some of the same tensions to this newer space of citizen participation. Many noted the power struggles when recalling the first HCNC elections as they saw both sides bringing in different people to vote for them to be placed on the board. This "election fraud" was documented in an *LA Weekly* article and described as part of an ongoing power struggle within Chinatown:

> Some blame the tension on two factions fighting for control of Chinatown: one led by [Don] Toy, a well-known player in Chinatown politics; and the other led by Interim Council president [George] Yu, the recently elected executive director of the Chinatown Business Improvement District and former property manager of Chinatown's Far East Plaza, and members of the business community, including Kim Benjamin, a newly elected business representative of Chinatown. "It is simply a matter of two different groups in Chinatown that haven't had a great love for each other," said Dominic Ehrler, former treasurer of the HCNC's interim board and newly elected business representative for Victor Heights.[10]

Since its formation, the HCNC was already an extension of the conflicts that began with the PAC/CCAC, albeit with a new generation of business leaders.

During HCNC meetings, multiple tense exchanges about the lack of quorum at meetings occurred between board members from different neighborhoods, which members consistently expressed as a major issue throughout the existence of the HCNC. During my fieldwork, language access was also a major source of conflict that often halted the decision-making processes. Don Toy constantly insisted on Chinese dialect translations at meetings for community representatives and meeting attendees, a demand he also had in the CCAC. He, as well as other CCAC and HCNC members who advocated for these translations, also fought for different Chinese dialects beyond Mandarin and Cantonese, the common dialects that are provided for translations. As they advocated for translations, they often resisted or delayed meeting procedures and votes, citing the lack of accurate and consistent translations. For example, during my fieldwork, the HCNC board had discussions at multiple monthly board meetings about changing the bylaws and creating standing rules to address these quorum issues. Victor Heights and Chinatown representatives often questioned these attempts to change the bylaws by pointing out inadequacies in these changes to account for the needs of immigrant communities, especially the older monolingual Chinese American seniors participating as HCNC representatives. They argued that more effort needed to be made to accommodate this segment of the community so that they could be full participants. As Edmund Soohoo, the Chinatown nonprofit representative for HCNC, explained, it looked like they were "asking for too much. But if you understand an immigrant community, you realize it's not. We take it for granted that, yeah, I got the minutes. I was able to read it online."

However, as this has become a recurring argument for the past four decades spanning two spaces of citizen participation, community leaders began to question what this fight for translations and other resistant practices mean for Chinatown today. For some, the ongoing resistance has had a negative impact on how the HCNC board members work together, which unlike the PAC/CCAC is not just different representatives of Chinatown, but now includes other communities that do not have the same demographics and needs as Chinatown. Little Tokyo, another historic Asian American neighborhood did not display the same internal ethnic community tensions. The perceived cohesion among Japanese Americans may be due to the community not experiencing the same large contemporary influx of immigrants as the Chinese American community experienced since the 1970s. Thus, language and translations were not as contentious for the Little Tokyo representatives as it was for the Victor Heights and Chinatown representatives. Still, one HCNC Chinatown representative shared that it was "embarrassing" that the "different Chinatown factions hold up legitimate HCNC business, which is advising the city on projects." Some in the community who were not involved in the HCNC but were aware of the conflicts have even expressed that requiring different Chinese dialects beyond Mandarin and Cantonese is an unreasonable request. A few of those who were skeptical of these requests also said that they had heard rumors that those requesting the services may have had enough English-language skills, and in some cases Cantonese and Mandarin skills, to understand the different translators. They felt that resistance to these translation attempts were just power plays within the HCNC. What would appear to be an issue that should potentially unite the community, language accessibility, has instead become a source of internal fighting. Regardless of whether these claims were true, the accusations and suspicions speak to how these spaces of citizen participation have contributed to tensions as community leaders vie for power in these spaces. Ultimately, the conflicts perpetuate the barriers of civic engagement and representation for the monolingual, limited-English-proficient Chinatown residents and workers.

The tensions within and across the neighborhoods in the HCNC came to a head in 2018 when Chinatown community leaders, including some in the HCNC, proposed to subdivide the council. The proposed subdivision would divide the HCNC and create the Historic Cultural North Neighborhood Council (HCNNC), which would include Chinatown, Victor Heights, Solano Canyon, and El Pueblo. Little Tokyo and Arts District would remain as the HCNC. On the surface, this subdivision meant that Chinatown would be fully represented; this new neighborhood council included both residential and commercial areas, as well as the historic area, since the remaining structures of Old Chinatown are located in El Pueblo. However, not everyone was supportive of this proposal, which was voiced in both public and community organization meetings, as well as on social media. An independent website created by Solano Canyon stakeholders to promote the neighborhood, added a subpage during this time called, "Save Solano Canyon from Chinatown." The webpage claimed that Chinatown leaders in the HCNC were planning the subdivision in secrecy as a possible power grab. These concerns raised by Solano Canyon stakeholders highlighted the precarious relationship Chinatown has with other communities. While the boundaries of the neighborhood are porous, Solano

Canyon is also home to the remnants of Chavez Ravine. Given this history of forced displacement, Chinatown should not overshadow this community in a neighborhood council and honor that history. Some Chinatown leaders who did not support the subdivision also expressed that having the other neighborhood representatives in the original HCNC helped to mitigate the dominance of other community leaders even if it meant that Chinatown representation was diluted. The subdivision was ultimately approved by stakeholder vote with the rule that existing representatives could not sit on the newly formed board. However, within a few years some board members returned, including Don Toy. The HCNNC is the only space of citizen participation in Chinatown today, and it continues to be a contentious space in the community.

CENTERING PROPERTY OWNER INTERESTS AS "COMMUNITY" INTERESTS: THE BUSINESS IMPROVEMENT DISTRICT

While Chinatown has a space of citizen participation and different types of organizations that provide community representation, most community leaders and city staff cite the Business Improvement District (BID) as the most prominent political gatekeeper in Chinatown, especially to community outsiders. Originating in the 1970s, BIDs have since become popular urban governance tools that promote public-private partnerships to encourage economic growth. They have become mechanisms for local actors, specifically those who have economic interests in a neighborhood, to manage public money to steer economic development. In Chinatown, the BID is managed by a local nonprofit organization, and thus the city, developers, and even other community leaders spoke of the BID as a legitimate community group and representative. Yet the democratic nature of BIDs and how inclusive they were beyond one stakeholder group, the commercial property owners, was and continues to be a major concern within the community.[11] As Sharon Zukin argues, the growing popularity of BIDs are a part of increasing neoliberal governance that contributes to gentrification.[12] They serve as mechanisms to privatize the responsibility of managing public spaces to local elites, while also contributing to the upscaling of neighborhoods. During my fieldwork, they overshadowed the HCNC, as well as other community organizations, as a space of local representation for issues of land use and development.

Their representation also uplifted a specific segment of the community, commercial property owners, and their economic interests in Chinatown.

The BID was not required to have a representative board or participatory governance structure like the CCAC or HCNC.[13] It was a property-based BID, and thus the board of directors were property owners within the BID boundaries, which was primarily the commercial area of Chinatown. Any property owner within the BID boundaries, including nonprofit organizations, could potentially sit on the board if they were elected in by the other property owners. For example, the Chinatown Service Center (CSC) and Chinese Consolidated Benevolent Association (CCBA) had representatives on the BID board, although CCBA no longer sat on the board during my fieldwork. Nonprofit organization property owners in Chinatown have always been a minority voice, and the majority of the board were commercial property owners. The board, and specifically the executive director, George Yu, who owned Far East Plaza, a commercial property, controlled the governance and decision-making of the BID. Consequently, the BID activities, including their representation of the community, ultimately reflected their interests.

As a quasi-public entity managed by a nonprofit organization, the BID was obligated to have public meetings and publicly share their documents. During my fieldwork, the BID was the only community group that held public meetings that routinely provided presentations and updates about proposed developments and new businesses in Chinatown. Thus, it became an invaluable source of information, as through my attendance, I was up-to-date with local development. All the information about the changes in the neighborhood, including information that was not yet shared with or discussed in other community organizations, was centralized in this one space. The bimonthly board meetings included presentations and updates on upcoming developments in Chinatown, and similar to the HCNC UDLUC, it was also a space that developers, city staff, and elected officials often visited to elicit feedback from "the community." The BID in Chinatown was not just a major resource for information about development, but George Yu also had noticeably close relationships with the City Council and other various city and county agencies. Staff from the City Council to the Department of City Planning, as well as outside developers, were often present at the meetings. At the BID board meetings, Yu would also relay information from his private meetings with other city agencies, including different elected officials, the Los Angeles Police Department, and the Department of City Planning, among others.

BID staff member, Xiayi Zhang, explained that the BID was one of the more "legitimate" organizations in Chinatown and that because they "are always open to the public, [their meetings] should be used as a forum." She, as well as others in the community, recognized that while not within the specific purpose of the BID, it had a potential to be a space for the community to learn about and discuss neighborhood development. During my fieldwork, the same projects presented at the UDLUC were also presented at the BID board meetings. However, the BID also included presentations for speculative and smaller projects that were not presented to the HCNC UDLUC, including a proposed condominium development and multiple conditional-use permit (CUP) applications for new restaurants to serve alcohol. The CUPs were an indicator of the small-scale business changes that were happening in Chinatown. In addition, the BID meetings included regular updates and check-ins about in-process developments. For example, Forest Cities, which owns and manages Blossom Plaza, a mixed-use development that opened in 2016, held a position on the BID board and would send representatives to provide continuous updates at each meeting from construction progress to the affordable housing application process, which included over 2,300 applications for fifty-three units. During the January 2017 BID meeting, there was a presentation for a mixed-use development proposed along New High Street that would potentially demolish the King Hing Theater, a movie theater designed by Chinese American architect Gilbert Leong. Community leaders outside of the BID expressed that they did not become aware of the development until a few months later when a demolition notice was posted on the building. While one property owner and one business owner came back to provide updates on their projects to ensure that they received a letter of support from the HCNC, in general, these updates and check-ins did not occur at the HCNC UDLUC meeting. The abundance of information at the BID meetings compared to the HCNC UDLUC is due not just to the mission of the BID to improve economic development, but primarily to the composition of the BID board. As major commercial property owners in Chinatown, they have firsthand and insider knowledge of the progress of new developments and changes.

The BID staff and board members supported discussions during meetings, but also explicitly stated that the BID was not a "regulatory" space like the HCNC and PAC/CCAC. Those who attended their meetings had opportunities to directly engage with developers, property owners, elected officials, and city staff. However, the meetings were structured to also not require any type of decision-making, as very few items on the agenda were action items. The presentations and updates at the BID tended to be informational for board members and guests. When decision-making occurred, it stayed with George Yu and to a lesser extent the board.

Because the BID tended to represent commercial property owner interests, almost all community leaders, regardless of their personal involvement with the BID, viewed it as a "pro-development" space within Chinatown. The BID was an integral part of the growth machine politics of Chinatown as it acted as both a speculative and structural place entrepreneur.[14] It became a local space accessible for developers who wanted to show that they had received support from the community, as well as one where property owners and developers could develop plans for Chinatown to maximize economic gains. Most individuals associated with the BID were open in their support for most of the new developments being proposed for Chinatown, which were primarily mixed-use market-rate housing and retail spaces. At meetings, board members asked questions to property owners and developers, including displacement issues and time frames for project completion, but often there was no follow-up to find anti-displacement solutions. Overall, most have received very little resistance. These proposed developments and businesses presented at the BID meetings were primarily viewed as benefits, as they would activate spaces that were vacant or replace places in the community that they deemed as attracting external negative influences to Chinatown, such as graffiti and marijuana dispensaries that were illegal at the time. As fellow property owners, many BID board members often asserted their rights as property owners to develop and use their spaces according to their needs and tastes, and they extended that sentiment to those proposing changes in their own properties.

The BID's approach toward new development had ripple effects to other spaces, particularly the HCNC. As previously noted, the UDLUC did not have consistent or adequate representation from Chinatown and Victor Heights representatives until the 2016 election. Other neighborhood representatives would still try to vet projects on their behalf. However, rather than asking specific questions and demands about how it would benefit the Chinatown community, as they did with projects for their neighborhood, they would instead try to determine if the developer did appropriate outreach. In the meetings I observed, all developers indicated that they had already met with the BID, and in most cases, they were the only community representatives they had contacted. Both George Yu and Xiayi Zhang were HCNC board members at the time, but did not regularly attend the

UDLUC meetings. Upon mentioning the BID, the UDLUC members often did not question the developer further about their outreach. Visiting the BID was a way for developers to show that they had visited a community space, but one that was intentionally supportive of their interests. However, at one meeting, the Little Tokyo representative encouraged one developer to actively go to other organizations in Chinatown and seek approval, stating that "a good developer" would do this regardless of what they needed from the community for project approval. Thus, even those outside of Chinatown were uneasy about how developers overly relied on the BID.

The conflict that characterized the CCAC and HCNC did not routinely occur at the BID board meetings during my fieldwork. The only notable resistance at the BID board meetings came in the form of questioning local government. They were often critical of public projects, such as the improvements being made to Union Station, because of the lack of communication to property owners about disruptions and impacts on their properties. At several meetings, the BID board members also expressed that several county- and city-owned properties that were used as parking lots and public transportation resting spots were not the "best and highest use" of land in Chinatown, accusing the city and county of contributing to blight in the neighborhood. Many BID board members were concerned with an increased homeless presence that they saw as spreading from neighboring El Pueblo and downtown. When government staff were present, they would often express the city's ineffectiveness in addressing the increasing unhoused population and questioned how they planned to resolve this issue for Chinatown and the city. Additionally, the BID was active in monitoring the disability lawsuits against Chinatown business owners, who were often in older buildings that were built before the Americans with Disability Act (ADA) compliance regulations. George Yu expressed that these lawsuits were abusive of the system and disproportionately targeted immigrant communities who are receiving limited city assistance. Similar to the PAC/CCAC, the BID members demonstrated resistance to the city, but the resistance was focused on asserting the shortcomings of local government to show how they were negatively impacting Chinatown's economic growth and property values.

The resistance and questioning of elected officials and city staff also reflected how BIDs are part of the neoliberal logics and practices shaping urban governance. In neoliberal governance, private actors, and specifically for-profit developers and commercial property owners, are increasingly providing resources and services that should be public goods provided by local government. As the BID board and staff often highlighted the neglect from the city and how they were fulfilling those gaps, George Yu also openly stated during meetings that, regardless, these public services were better off privatized, and specifically within the control of an entity like the BID. While this sentiment may not be shared by everyone associated with the BID, Yu is the most prominent figure of the BID. He viewed this as a form of community control over development in Chinatown. While the BID was managed by a local organization, it is one that primarily represents for-profit interests among commercial property owners. There is limited representation from other community organizations and other types of stakeholders who also contribute to and have a stake in the Chinatown economy. The BID structure thus centralizes community representation and power to this narrow interest, while claiming that it can represent the entire Chinatown community.

Community leaders recognize the BID's importance as a powerful and active community voice, but also critiqued its accountability to the community. Almost all community leaders praised the BID for providing more services, such as frequent street cleaning and visible security in the neighborhood, which some argued created a sense of safety for businesses and property owners. Other community leaders and property owners, however, have expressed concerns that some areas within the BID boundaries received these services more than others. The BID assessment structure was tiered, with some property owners paying less assessments than others depending on their location, which has led to accusations that there is an inequitable distribution of services. In particular, the area with more community-serving businesses in the southeastern end of Chinatown did not appear to receive as much services as the Central Plaza area to the north, which is the major site of tourism for the neighborhood. These property owners of the plazas in the northern area of Chinatown were also represented on the board.

Additionally, there have been criticisms across the community that the BID is intentionally not transparent and is exclusionary in their governance practices, which facilitates gentrification. While their meetings are public, other community leaders very rarely attend the meetings, if at all. Some noted that it was an inconvenient time, as they were scheduled on a weekday during work hours, while others noted that they felt uneasy being in the space, given who was in the room and the pro-development culture of the BID. The Chinatown Community for Equitable Development (CCED) has consistently and publicly challenged the BID. While they primarily viewed themselves as a tenant organizing group, they also were vocal about economic development concerns and the need to protect the immigrant small businesses which were not always seen as a priority for the BID. In both private and public meetings, as well as through their social media, CCED explicitly called out the BID for promoting gentrification and harassing community members. In 2020, the BID was up for renewal, which coincided with the increasing visibility of the Black Lives Matter movement that called for defunding the police. CCED linked their resistance to the BID to this broader messaging of racial and economic justice, calling for a defunding of the BID. To CCED, the BID represented not just an over-policing of specific community members in Chinatown that George Yu and some others in the BID deemed did not belong, but that it was also a privatization of policing. As mentioned in the previous chapter, the BID has responded by actively delegitimizing CCED as a true voice of the community because of the lack of residents—and property owners—as the most vocal leadership and a lack of being formalized as a legal nonprofit organization. In many ways, the tension between CCED and the BID was perpetuating the business versus residential conflicts that visibly played out in the PAC/CCAC and part of the ongoing challenge to the long-standing political dominance of a business elite in Chinatown leadership.

Given the composition of the BID board and its purpose, it ultimately provided a new space for local business leaders to further assert their power, albeit a different generation of community business leaders. One older community leader who has been active in several community groups in Chinatown, including the CCAC and BID, explained that while he saw the BID as an important part of Chinatown's governance, it should not be seen as representing the entire community:

> The problem with that voice [the BID], strong as it is, for a good pole in the storm as it is, it's not adequate because it does not [as a] whole reflect the needs [of the entire community]. It concentrates on the needs of the business sector creating greater land value, better developments, but it doesn't reflect social needs of the people. It doesn't reflect the educational needs of the people because it is not their mission. It does not reflect, for example, issues like affordable housing, job training. It cannot because it is not their mission. There is still something that is terribly missing here in defining a wholeness of community.

While the composition of the BID board may include a new generation of leadership, as George Yu and many of the other board members do not have direct ties to the older business elites in Chinatown, it still perpetuated the legacy of business leaders, and specifically property owners, as the most powerful representatives of Chinatown. Despite hesitations to renew the BID in 2020, the BID received enough support for renewal, and it remains a politically powerful group in Chinatown that asserts a pro-development stance. In their work about urban Chinatowns and the Chinese American community, Peter Kwong describes the dual oppression that low-income and working-poor residents of Chinatown face in which both mainstream institutions outside of Chinatown and the community elite within the neighborhood simultaneously contribute to their ongoing political and economic marginalization.[15] The neoliberal governance trends that support BIDs reinforce and legitimize this dual oppression through the promotion of public-private governance structures. These structures do not necessarily lead to transformative changes in community power and are instead reproducing power imbalances with a new generation of economic elites.

CHALLENGING THE FAMILY AND VILLAGE DYNAMIC OF CHINATOWN

While they may differ in intent and purpose, the establishment of the PAC/CCAC, HCNC, and BID are all part of a contemporary restructuring in urban governance to promote local control and public-private partnerships in neighborhood development, especially in communities that have been historically underrepresented. However, as Karen Umemoto argues, there are cultural norms and social relationships within ethnic communities that must be considered when designing these community engagement strategies.[16] Policymakers and planners have an ethical and moral role in how they address these dynamics, especially as they implement participatory governance structures and mechanisms that promote community control. If done with little sensitivity to the community context, these participatory practices have the potential to reinforce hierarchies and power differentials not just across communities, but within the community as well. This tension was evident in Chinatown. The engagement and disengagement of community leaders in the PAC/CCAC, HCNC, and BID were embedded and shaped by personal relationships and power relations within Chinatown, which appeared to clash with expectations of the community and their political engagement. As community leaders vied for power in and across these spaces, the sense of community was reshaped, challenging the social and political relationships within the neighborhood.

In a small community like Chinatown, especially among those who have become leaders in the various organizations, participating in these highly politicized spaces can also reshape personal relationships and the informal bonds of trust. For some, having a close relationship with others was a positive experience because there was already a shared understanding and knowledge of how to work together. The interconnectedness of many of the older community leaders was described as a "family" and "village" dynamic. One community leader explained that many outsiders and city government did not recognize or understand these "deep and long relationships" in Chinatown prior to the CRA being established in Chinatown. With these close relationships came an understanding that they could disagree on issues, but would be able to eventually overcome those differences. Several people who were in conflict when they first became involved in the community, which included being on "opposing sides" on the PAC/CCAC, shared that after thirty years of working together they now have positive working relationships. One business leader described the relationships between the current older leaders, "So there's been a lot of good relationships and hard-fought disagreements. . . . Just that we had serious philosophical differences, but we sucked it up and we put aside the differences to do this together."

While the personal relationships allowed for an ease among people to work together, there were also instances where individuals with these close relationships engaged in conflict as they represented the community. Some described the conflicts as "personal attacks." A few shared stories about knowing others since their youth and developing friendships, but their perceptions of those individuals and relationships became strained over time through this political engagement. For example, through the CCAC, individuals who had personal and familial relationships publicly criticized each other on how they maintained their properties. These discussions that would normally be private matters within a family, or at most, community gossip, were now sometimes discussed in public forums and mediated through the city. It was easy for those who worked in the city and not familiar with community relationships to overlook the personal relationships or community context that was underlying the actions in these public meetings or what was written in documents, making Chinatown community representatives appear especially fractured, contradictory, and emotional. They were not acting in an ideal, rational manner of decision-making for the community.

As both Miranda Joseph and Mae Shaw argue, as much as a sense of community provides resources and belonging through social relations, it also can obscure power differentials for the sake of appearing unified.[17] Some community leaders, especially those who grew up in Chinatown and from working-class families, did not have romantic views of community relationships and were transparent in wanting to challenge these social hierarchies. The PAC/CCAC and HCNC attempted to bring segments of the Chinatown community that not only represented different interest groups, but were of vastly different backgrounds. Edmund Soohoo, who grew up in Chinatown in a working-class family and was involved in both the CCAC and HCNC, explained how this was a new experience for him as he was interacting with people who were not just part of the elite in Chinatown, but were also transnational leaders in the global Chinese community, such as Wilbur Woo. He explained the stark differences between their lives and what that meant for their representation of Chinatown:

> Our worlds are very different. A Wilbur Woo's world and Edmund Soohoo's world, at that time, light years away! He actually held a post in Taiwan government. I mean he was an advisor while he was still here. And so, he had dual roles, and he was very enlightened in that way as a leader.... [He founded] Cathay Bank.... And all that is well known. So I can't say that I saw what he saw.... I only saw what I saw walking the streets from Chinatown.

These different life experiences shaped the business versus residential divides in Chinatown. Business leaders may have focused on economic growth, but leaders such as Woo, provided a more global perspective to transform Chinatown, which was critical as Chinatown was positioned to facilitate overseas Asian investment. Woo's experiences and knowledge also differed from other business leaders in the community who may not have been involved in global politics. Residential leaders, like Soohoo, provided a local, working-class perspective of Chinatown and were politicized by socialist and anti-imperialist ideologies that informed their approach in these spaces to engage in conflict and challenge both the city and community power structures.

Edmund Soohoo further explained that these differences that contributed to a community hierarchy were often intimidating and a barrier to participation in the PAC/CCAC and HCNC for himself and others:

> And they [the community] don't go and complain unless someone teaches them you have a right to complain. You have a right to be at the table. And

you know that's hard for people. Because that's conflict. Who likes to be in conflict? Who likes to go to walk in the [bank] and the manager that's sitting there was the person you were fighting against the night before? Doesn't make sense! . . . . And that's hard for people! That's hard for me!

His observation raised an important consideration as to how these participatory initiatives such as the PAC/CCAC and HCNC attempt to build consensus and a unified voice by bringing "everyone to the table." The presence of diverse voices in one space does not inherently flatten power differences. The social relationships and standings that transcend these spaces may prohibit individuals from being empowered to participate, as an individual may be designated as an equal in one space but, outside of that space, is no longer equal.

Yet the PAC/CCAC did contribute to a shift in political power where a segment of progressive activists, especially Don Toy, emerged as powerful leaders that overshadowed the older elite and business leaders. This was arguably a critical political shift in a place like Chinatown, which historically is known for a social structure of class hierarchies, with business leaders and the older organizations often in control of not just the land, but political representation. This power shift led to tension within the community because the city used the PAC/CCAC as their primary mechanism for community representation, and this had ripple effects for business interests in both the HCNC and BID. When recalling both the HCNC and BID formations, which occurred within a few years of each other, several community leaders saw these entities as an attempt by business leaders, both old and new, to find another legitimate space of representation outside of the CCAC, which they saw as dominated by Toy. But the formation of new spaces by business leaders was ultimately met with criticism and resistance, especially in the HCNC. One individual who worked on cultural efforts and had relationships with past HCNC board members explained that "it was wrong for these business interests to be representing communities for the HCNC, when that's what's supposed to be the [formal] pipeline to the city." While many in the community recognized the CCAC as an imperfect space of representation for business interests, they still did not support that business leaders dominate the HCNC as it was also supposed to provide holistic representation of the neighborhood. Through these new spaces of community representation and control, new leadership emerged that was often a powerful, vocal advocate for residential interests. However, this shift also led to visible power struggles within the community, as a new generation of business leaders, most notably represented through the BID, were also vying for control in Chinatown.

While the public narrative of Chinatown often centered the conflict between business and residential interest, the community engagement in these spaces also notably impacted the relationships between progressive activists. These activists have had varied trajectories in their activism; some remained grassroots organizers, some institutionalized their work as local nonprofit organizations, and others worked in local government. Regardless, all of them had the same intent to possibly bring change to the community. Several of the older progressive activists spoke about distancing themselves from the CCAC, and as a result, the political power it provided, despite it being dominated by fellow progressive activists, some of whom were former close friends and allies. One former social services leader explained how the space became less about addressing community need and more about a fight for power, "The whole process was just way too complicated. And too many people had their hands in the pot. . . . So, we were just like, is there any reason why we really need to be a part of this?" Other progressive activists who never engaged with the CCAC were critical of its role in the community. They felt that regardless of their political orientation and interests, CCAC members were influenced by the power that this position provided them, from information on proposed developments to direct access to developers and the City Council. These spaces of local representation and control thus also became spaces representing corruption, regardless of whether it was for business or residential interests. As one older community activist suggested about some of the rumors of community corruption and power grabs that characterized the PAC/CCAC, "Being involved in the CRA you start to see all the different opportunities that are available."

The PAC/CCAC was not simply transforming the physical environment of the neighborhood. It was instrumental in transforming the political structure and was often seen as a major factor contributing to strained relationships within the community. Despite being a voice for residential interests in the past, rumors of Don Toy and the political and financial power he gained through his leadership in the PAC/CCAC, and by extension the HCNC, circulated among different community leaders, both progressive and business leaders, for decades. During my fieldwork, CCED began to organize against Toy for mismanaging Cathay Manor, Chinatown's first affordable housing complex developed during the CRA designation. Cathay Manor was owned and managed by the Chinatown Committee on Aging (CCOA), an organization that was led by Toy. These rumors became public in 2021 when local media began to report about the issues in Cathay Manor. The city filed sixteen criminal counts against CCOA and Toy for failing to maintain the building, placing the safety of the senior citizen residents at risk.[18] By July 2023, Toy had sold Cathay Manor to an outside affordable housing developer, Capital Realty Group.[19]

The questionable governance of the BID has also been in the public spotlight. George Yu has been openly critiqued from within and outside the community for his lack of transparency in his management and leadership with the BID. In 2020, a bench warrant was issued for Yu for violating California's Public Records Act for failing to turn over BID emails from 2017 and 2018.[20] These emails allegedly showed how he and other BID leaders in the downtown area, as well as major commercial developers such as Atlas Capital and Tom Gilmore, who were also purchasing properties in Chinatown, were purposely suppressing the formation of a Skid Row neighborhood council, which would provide more visibility to the growing unhoused community in both downtown and the city. These efforts from Yu and others are aligned with critiques of BIDs as hostile toward unhoused individuals because they are viewed as antithetical to the image of a "clean" and "safe" neighborhood to outside investors.[21] The accusation against Yu also reinforced the criticisms from within the community that the management of the BID had not been transparent and thus not accountable to the broader Chinatown community.

These allegations against both Don Toy and George Yu may not be surprising. They have become the most visible community leaders in Chinatown in the past decades through their involvement in local politics and these formal spaces of community control and representation in Los Angeles. They were also the most controversial leaders and subject to public scrutiny because of the power they obtained through their leadership in these spaces. As these criminal charges levied against both illustrate, there is pressure from within and outside the community for local leaders to be as transparent and accountable to their communities as would any other political leader representing Chinatown. These corruption scandals also show how state and city structures of local control were flawed. They ultimately transformed and legitimized the power of individuals rather than transforming the community power structure to be more inclusive.

The community tensions have not gone unnoticed, as the media, city staff, and even community leaders themselves all described Chinatown as an especially conflicted neighborhood these past decades. One former CRA staff member described the PAC/CCAC meetings as "very emotional. In many cases just at one another's throats." Another former CRA staff member recalled some of the tensions as generational, explaining that the older community leaders "weren't used to being in public and being yelled at" by the younger activists. The behavior and interactions of community leaders in Chinatown seemed especially shocking as there was an expectation that as representatives they would be more "neutral." Reflecting about her involvement with the CCAC, one former member realized that she may have been approached by the city councilmember at the time because she did not have the same level of attachment to Chinatown or the same types of relationships as other members did and thus could be a "neutral voice." Several younger individuals who were learning about the conflict in the community also spoke about the need for "neutral" spaces to do community-based planning, as they were aware of the politics and conflicts among the older generation. However, in places like Chinatown that have a long-established ethnic community power structure, connecting with community gatekeepers is often critical to becoming involved in the neighborhood. Remaining neutral may not even be possible, and the perspectives and tensions from the older generation can be passed on to the next generation of leadership.

The sentiments about neutrality also highlight a paradox about local control and representation. These spaces were intended to include disparate voices, some historically unheard, that could potentially transform political decision-making to be more inclusive. But there were also assumptions that representatives would be able to put aside their relationships to engage in rational decision-making to make objective, unemotional decisions for the entire community.[22] These expectations have led to a valuing of consensus building over conflict, which discount how conflict can often be generative and necessary, especially in challenging current power regimes.[23] Community engagement can become emotional, but the practices and approaches that appear irrational and emotionally charged can convey the authenticity of the issues being debated and contest the underlying values that might be harmful to communities.[24] In many cases it was the long-standing structural and power inequalities that contributed to conflict in these spaces and engendered the responses of anger and resistance.

These assumptions about neutrality and rational decision-making are also often racialized. As Rick Bonus also observed among the Filipino American community, the forms of democracy practiced in these spaces could challenge the norms of racialized political behaviors based on Western democratic principles.[25] This same argument could be extended to the framing of Chinatown politics since the creation of the PAC. Chinatown community leaders did not always fit into the image of Asian Americans as politically passive model minorities. They were publicly challenging the city and each other in these public spaces, and through their engagement, they also expressed the complexities of their community. Consequently, they were often dismissed as "messy" and lacking political control. Yet it was the way these spaces were structured, as well as the assumptions of elected officials, city planners, and developers about what constitutes proper engagement that set the conditions for these dynamics and perceptions to occur. Spaces that are meant to build community power can still be limited, as they tend to conform to the norms and expectations of planners and policymakers, thus perpetuating power imbalances both between the city and community and within the community itself.[26]

The breakdown of relationships and continued strained relationships in Chinatown counters assumptions that mechanisms for local control and citizen participation are always beneficial for communities.[27] In Chinatown, these policies and programs have provided a platform for representation and local control, but they also have contributed to the breakdown of social relationships in the community. This breakdown is not necessarily because of the physical separation of a tight-knit community, often documented as a result of inequitable development and gentrification.[28] Instead, in Chinatown, this has also happened because of the governance structures that are placed upon communities, creating power conflicts while the community continually struggles to be recognized by the city and mainstream institutions. These spaces of local control have evolved to become another node in the local Chinatown power structure that facilitates the uplifting of a specific interest group, and in some cases, individuals.

RETURNING TO THE GRASSROOTS: CONFLICT AND
CONSENSUS WITH COMMUNITY CONTROL

The possibility of having a space that provides community representation that is inclusive of the diverse interests and backgrounds of the stakeholders but also provides a cohesive voice remains an open question for Chinatown.

The creation of these legitimate spaces of community representation and control through the CRA, neighborhood council system, and BID programs in Los Angeles were imperfect and ultimately did not appear to empower the community to collectively work together in Chinatown. Community leaders acknowledged that these spaces had to exist because they were part of the formal governance structures of the city, but they did not necessarily rely on them to represent the community. Instead, Chinatown's leaders were still attempting to establish more meaningful spaces of community power.

Several community leaders, both from the older and younger generations, expressed a desire for a more effective neighborhood-based advisory council that does not perpetuate the political power struggles from the PAC/CCAC and HCNC/HCNNC. When discussing the neighborhood council system, community leaders consistently stated that they did not see it as providing a true community voice. Some expressed that Chinatown has to constantly fight for representation within this structure, whether with the other communities or even within the community itself. As one older progressive activist explained:

> The neighborhood council is a great step in that direction [for community empowerment]. But the way it was configured for the Chinatown community, it's been very much a distortion of what a neighborhood council should be. It should be like a small city council. Sort of what you would have in a small town and be a mechanism for bringing that town together. But instead [the HCNC], it's another political turf fighting situation.

Several others also expressed that to be a part of the neighborhood council was a fight for power rather than a fight for the community. As the HCNC included both Don Toy and George Yu throughout most of its time, it was probably not surprising that this was a deeply contested space that other community leaders actively avoided. The plans to subdivide the HCNC and the outreach within the community to educate community members about the subdivision led to further contentiousness within Chinatown and across the different HCNC neighborhoods about corruption and power grabs within the Chinatown community. The HCNNC is the remaining space of citizen participation in Chinatown today, but other than Don Toy, many community leaders remained disengaged with the space, as they were with the original HCNC and PAC/CCAC over time. The disengagement and resistance to this space is a critique of the city's efforts to encourage citizen participation and, for some, their disengagement is a purposeful resistance against the ongoing power conflicts within the community.

Yet Chinatown community leaders also acknowledge that conflict has been generative for their community, especially given the diversity of the Chinese American community, as well as the need to have different interest groups to represent the different parts of the Chinatown neighborhood. They wanted a space that would still allow for diverse voices to be represented, which was a major limitation of the BID. One longtime community leader who was a former member of the CCAC explained how the BID was an important "anchor" for Chinatown but criticized the lack of contentiousness within the group, hinting at the lack of not just diverse stakeholders on the board, but even a diversity of types of property owners. The BID was ultimately a homogenous organization, representing a narrow interest, which can be misleading if it is presented as either the sole or most powerful advisory voice for Chinatown. This concern reiterates how the BID was not a space that could provide a comprehensive voice of the community and should not be treated as such. He went on to state that there was still a need for "healthy conflict" in the community. He explained, "You want contentiousness. . . . So, you need a forum [today], where there can be enough give and take where you can get the contentiousness to materialize into finally a consensus." He realized that while there were strong voices in the community who could provide leadership, there was currently a lack of dialogue and spaces for this vision of "healthy conflict" among the different leaders to collectively lead Chinatown.

Chinatown community leaders have thus continued to look inward, sidestepping the local government structures, to establish new spaces that support broad-based coalition building and to provide a more holistic representation of the community and build community power. Toward the end of my fieldwork, several community leaders representing CACA, CCBA, CCED, the Chinese Historical Society of Southern California (CHSSC), Organization of Chinese Americans–Greater Los Angeles, and Friends and Alumni of Castelar Elementary School (FACES) formed the Chinatown Sustainability Dialogue Group (CSDG) with the goal of directly addressing neighborhood issues. The intent of the CSDG was to create a space akin to a grassroots community council, something that Chinatown lacked despite different community leaders' efforts to initiate it since the 1970s. As a new group, they experienced growing pains when trying to identify who should be invited to be a part of the group. Given the contentiousness of past spaces, members were hesitant to include everyone in the initial meetings. As one CCED member stated, "The thing is, if you're going to start a group, you have to start a group with people that believe in why you're doing it," expressing concern that if they were too inclusive of disparate voices in the community, including Don Toy and George Yu, the group would reproduce the unhealthy conflict and not be able to find a common ground to develop a collective voice for Chinatown.

Despite representation from established organizations, as well as residents, the CSDG still had to earn their legitimacy as community representatives. City staff, including representatives from the Department of City Planning, the City Council, and Department of Neighborhood Empowerment, have visited this new group, but developers have been more hesitant. During public outreach for a proposed mixed-use development, the representative for the developer was invited to present at a CSDG meeting. Because he saw this group as informal, he chose to present at a CACA meeting and the BID Board meeting twice, the latter of which he invited the CSDG members to attend since those are public. At that meeting, when asked about his outreach efforts, the representative noted that in addition to visiting the BID, HCNC, and CACA, he would be open to visiting any "legitimate community organization" in Chinatown. Even as members of respected organizations collaborate to improve political representation, their legitimacy is not assumed and can still be constrained by the validation of external actors.

· · ·

Community control is essential for resisting gentrification and preventing forced displacement. Los Angeles Chinatown has had many different spaces and mechanisms that are forms of local control, whether through informal means of community organizations or more formal mechanisms such as the different neighborhood advisory councils and BID. Yet all of these spaces have varied in how they provide community representation, as specific voices were magnified more than others. The organizations mentioned in the prior chapter were often working separately, and at times, were in conflict with one another. In formal spaces of local control, such as the PAC/CCAC, HCNC, and BID, where these organizations could potentially work together, these conflicts were, instead, especially heightened. Unlike the community organizations, these spaces provided access to resources and relationships with elected officials, developers, and other community out-siders because they were a part of the city governance structure. The conflicts represented a power struggle over representation of Chinatown beyond the local community.

These power struggles have contributed to the ongoing criticism and skepticism about how community control, and the concept of community in general, has become institutionalized in governance practices. Chinatown may now have formal, legitimate platforms in the city's governance struc-ture that provide a voice to the city and developers, but they were spaces where people began to advance their self-interest rather than make decisions based on the collective good of the neighborhood. There were expected norms and rules of engagement that Chinatown community leaders chal-lenged through their participation. But they did not just challenge the struc-ture and nature of these spaces; they also sought to dominate them. In some ways, the tensions can be interpreted as an empowering political shift for certain groups that have historically lacked a voice in the neighborhood. The PAC/CCAC was characterized as being "dominated" by progressives who fought for affordable housing, which challenged the older business elites in the neighborhood. However, this also led business leaders to try to find other mechanisms to reassert their power, including the HCNC and the BID, the latter of which helped to strengthen this presence in Chinatown, albeit with a new generation of business leaders. While the BID is a type of community control, as a "pro-development" space, the BID contributes to neoliberal governance that prioritizes gentrification and for-profit develop-ment by trying to keep community power in the hands of business leaders, specifically commercial property owners. As community leaders navigated these spaces, their relationships with each other also changed, which also contributed to changes in Chinatown beyond physical developments. These spaces facilitated in a political displacement and restructuring that rein-forced power differentials in the community, which can make Chinatown more vulnerable for development that may threaten the neighborhood's cul-tural heritage and the working poor who rely on the neighborhood.

While these internal conflicts have come to define Chinatown politics, the ongoing creation of spaces to try to provide holistic representation of the neighborhood is also a defining part of Chinatown politics. Generations of community leaders have continuously sought to find and establish spaces of community, through both formal and informal means. The formation of the CSDG at the time of my fieldwork, as well as the continued ebbs and flows of the relationships between community leaders in Chinatown, high-light how grassroots formations are still necessary and fundamental to enact community control. As mechanisms to promote community control are becoming more commonplace in local policy and urban planning practices, ensuring accountability of these spaces in representing and serving local communities also becomes increasingly critical. As the political conflicts in Los Angeles Chinatown demonstrate, these spaces may still have limitations in equitable political representation and resource distribution. Grassroots formations help not just to address those gaps, but also to continue to pressure the city and mainstream institutions to create more meaningful political inclusion. They also continue the legacy of organizing in Chinatown that has been integral to defining and sustaining the neighborhood.

FOUR

Aspirations for a Balanced and Diverse Community

As the representative from Redcar Properties provides updates about the rehabilitation of their newly acquired buildings along Spring Street, there are questions about the possibility of displacement of the current tenants, which are primarily swap meet vendors. In defense of these changes, George Yu, the Executive Director of the Business Improvement District, says that they need to find a "balance" in the neighborhood as some of these older vendors can make the neighborhood "vibrant" but not all of them.

—Excerpt from author's fieldnotes for the Chinatown Business Improvement District Board of Directors Meeting in March 2015

King Cheung, a longtime community activist, provides some opening remarks about the changes in Chinatown. He states that "luxury apartments" are being built right now. He goes onto say that he is not against these luxury apartments but that there needs to be a "balance" so more attention is given to affordable housing and current residents. He then mentions another example of how the vendors on Spring Street were recently displaced to build an "upscale" office building.

—Excerpt from author's fieldnotes for a Chinatown Community for Equitable Development Community Film Screening in April 2016

AS URBAN CHINATOWNS face the pressures of gentrification, cities are also simultaneously embracing diversity in policymaking and urban planning practices.[1] The rhetoric and practices of diversity refer to both the physical diversity of the neighborhood, such as building types and uses, and the social diversity, which is the unique mix of demographic characteristics of the people living and working in the neighborhood. These two types of diversity mutually inform one another to create a neighborhood identity. This goal of achieving diversity, particularly socioeconomic diversity, has informed urban revitalization policies and strategies, especially in the post–Civil Rights Era. To combat concentrated poverty in areas that cities deemed as disinvested and slums, urban policies focused on efforts that would encourage diversity and social mixing to improve neighborhood conditions, de-concentrate poverty, and discourage segregation.[2] This logic guiding these policies draws from neighborhood effects research, which argues that the physical and social conditions of low-income neighborhoods contribute to ongoing poverty and poor life outcomes.[3] These policies that promote social mixing and diversity have also been linked to gentrification and displacement pressures.[4] However, stakeholders may still welcome these changes as they see it as neighborhood improvements after prolonged disinvestment from the city and outsiders.[5]

The rhetoric and practices of diversity in urban development has had tremendous impacts on Los Angeles Chinatown, as the neighborhood has been integral to asserting a multicultural identity of the city while also being shaped by the socioeconomic and cultural diversity that defines the Chinese American community. This chapter examines how an aspiration for a diverse neighborhood informed the gentrification narratives among all community leaders in Chinatown. Rather than defining or discussing gentrification directly, many spoke about the need to strike a "balance" in the neighborhood to support "diversity." I deconstruct and map these narratives to illustrate how this rhetoric showed peoples' stances on housing and economic development for Chinatown and whom these changes should benefit. Community leaders framed this need for balance and diversity in relation to Chinatown's history as a former Community Redevelopment Agency (CRA) project area from 1980 to 2011 and the development pressures it faced in relationship to the in- and out-migration from other spaces in the region, specifically downtown and the San Gabriel Valley. The understanding of diversity for many Chinatown community leaders also extended to their recognition of the diversity within the Chinese American community today and how Chinatown could and should support it.

The various narratives about what defines a balanced and diverse neighborhood ultimately revealed how Chinatown community leaders centered specific stakeholders as integral to sustaining Chinatown. They also show the limits of contemporary rhetoric and practices of diversity for spatial justice frameworks. Sarah Ahmed has notably critiqued how diversity work has become apolitical, as it has been integrated into the bureaucratic practices of public institutions, increasingly becoming detached from the goals of achieving social justice and equity.[6] Susan Fainstein has also argued that this embrace of diversity has been especially contradictory within urban planning.[7] Some conceive of diversity as a way to stimulate economic growth, while for others it is meant as a mechanism to achieve social equity. The rhetoric of diversity in gentrifying historic Black and Latine neighborhoods may also depoliticize past and current historical struggles of racialized communities, contributing to the ongoing erasure and marginalization of communities already vulnerable to displacement.[8] In Chinatown, these narratives showed how community leaders were grappling with the neighborhood's persistent residential identity as a poor, working-class immigrant neighborhood. Some were embracing the logic of social mixing to upscale the neighborhood in a way that would purposely bring in an upwardly mobile population, specifically an upwardly mobile Chinese American community "back to Chinatown." These narratives often justified the power of business leaders in Chinatown and the forced displacement of what they deemed as undesirable characteristics in the neighborhood to improve its economic conditions. While others, especially those working in housing advocacy and other types of community work with residents, used the narrative of balance to emphasize resident power and to counter forced displacement, specifically protecting the low-income immigrant residents and workers in Chinatown who have historically defined the local culture and identity of the neighborhood.

Building from the symbolic boundary work discussed in chapter 2, these narratives further underscore how framing is an integral part of the politics of placemaking and gentrification in Chinatown. Framings of place can selectively draw on specific histories and demographics of the community to advance specific interests and issues.[9] In neighborhoods that are experiencing gentrification, stakeholders may reconstruct the neighborhood identity and community boundaries in a way that legitimizes specific claims while excluding others.[10] The framing of a place and its changes thus is a method of asserting community control and addressing gentrification even if the word is not explicitly stated.

QUESTIONING GENTRIFICATION AND FINDING A "GOOD MIX" FOR CHINATOWN

Chinatown has navigated the threats and pressures of gentrification throughout its history. Some of these threats have led to a direct physical displacement of people and buildings. But more recently, because of its proximity to downtown and other gentrifying neighborhoods in Los Angeles, such as Echo Park and Boyle Heights, the neighborhood has experienced both economic and cultural displacement pressures. This concern about displacement pressures was especially heightened during my fieldwork, as Los Angeles was facing a major affordable housing crisis that contributed to an increasing unhoused population. However, the term *gentrification* was still a politically contested term about how new people, developments, and investments were impacting historically low-income communities and perpetuating urban inequalities and segregation. Throughout my interactions with Chinatown community leaders and our discussions about gentrification in the neighborhood, I experienced this lack of consensus in the use and meaning of this term.

Those who used the term *gentrification* without hesitation were often working in housing advocacy and tenants' rights, such as the organizers in Chinatown Community for Equitable Development (CCED). One of the older CCED organizers explained his perspective of gentrification as those who already "have a great deal of money . . . and power . . . decide that they're going to transform the community . . . without consulting the people and the businesses and the traditional folks who are related to that community." He saw the changes in the neighborhood as dictated by those who already held economic and political power rather than empowering those who have been historically disenfranchised. Another older community activist explained in her definition of *gentrification* that historical and cultural erasure were also integral to the term, especially in urban Chinatowns. She explained, "It's a type of development that tries to erase the historical and cultural integrity of the community and then change the composition of it from low- or very low- or extremely low-income families to richer communities." These organizers not only recognized the physical and economic displacement that occurred in Chinatown, but also acknowledged the cultural and political dimensions that led to the forced displacement of low-income communities.

However, other community leaders had conflicting definitions, openly expressed confusion, and, at times, resistance to using the term *gentrification*. When directly asked about gentrification during interviews, a few individuals who worked for business interests searched for an online definition and read the dictionary definition out loud, a performative response that indicated how they did not take the term seriously. These individuals, as well as others who were reluctant to identify gentrification in Chinatown, were not denying that certain changes were happening in the neighborhood, but they were questioning the use of this term to define the changes. Some openly said that they did not use the term anymore because it had become meaningless and was often used to simply mean "neighborhood change," which everyone agreed was both inevitable and necessary.

In contrast to the activists working for tenant's rights, some business leaders used *gentrification* to support what they perceived as positive changes that would displace "bad" aspects of the neighborhood, such as empty lots and undesirable businesses. As one younger business leader explained:

> Am I afraid that Chinatown will be gentrified? I mean no doubt it will. . . . You know I think change is inevitable. It's inevitable. . . . Somebody's going to come in and change it, you know. Whether it's to improve it, like what they say to gentrify it, or to make the way of life better. Anything is better than nothing. Cause if you don't do anything it's just sitting there and doing nothing.

This business leader, as well as other community leaders, depoliticized the term gentrification and reframed it as a positive neighborhood change. As CCED and other progressive activists spoke negatively about gentrification, these leaders saw them as simply resistant to any type of change, and at times, were impeding the possibility of improving Chinatown. In particular, the presence of vacant lots and storefronts often made it hard to concretely pinpoint gentrification, as these sites primarily provided market-rate apartments but were not directly displacing affordable housing units. One community leader who was a member of the Chinese Historical Society of Southern California (CHSSC) and Chinese American Citizens Alliance (CACA) explained that they saw gentrification occurring when developers "tear [housing] down and then build a new one on the same place" but that building market-rate apartments in these empty lots was not gentrification; it was "just change." Many in the community had a similar sentiment, as they also only associated gentrification with direct physical displacement and did not consider the various forms of indirect displacement and displacement pressures that also occur with this type of new-build gentrification.[11]

As many community leaders valued individual property owner rights, it was also difficult for them to fully critique the socioeconomic changes that came with rising land values associated with gentrification. Yet they also acknowledged that there should still be a sense of collective responsibility in ensuring that the character of Chinatown does not disappear. One community leader who was active in the BID explained, "Maybe a different way [to look at gentrification] is how do you allow evolution of the property and still keep some of the original stakeholders or the current stakeholders satisfied that their way of living is preserved?" A community leader expressed a similar sentiment, despite his past advocacy to bring affordable housing to Chinatown during its time as a CRA project area:

> I think gentrification, it's just a word. . . . On one hand, if gentrification or change means I can charge more for whatever I own, that's a good thing. The bad thing is if you're starting out and you're a new family and you want to live in this area, maybe you can't. Now is that my fault you can't? Not necessarily. Because it's not my job to have affordable housing for you. Not really.

Chinatown community leaders openly struggled with honoring individual property owner rights, especially the long-term Chinese American property owners, and their responsibility to the larger community in Chinatown. This apprehension was not simply a tension over individual rights versus collective responsibilities, but also spoke to the history of how first-generation Chinese and Asian Americans were excluded from property ownership prior to the mid-twentieth century. This history arguably was a reason why there was much emphasis on the importance of respecting these property owners in Chinatown—it was a part of recognizing that history and the rights that they did not always have.

Community leaders, especially those who were active in the business community, were also critical of people who were resistant to change because of their nostalgia for the neighborhood as they saw this as stifling economic development. One community leader who was relatively newer to the community echoed this sentiment. He explained that he felt that this was his "Golden Age" in Chinatown and appreciated the mix of people and places in the neighborhood. His sentiment recalled how older community leaders framed the "Golden Age" of Chinatown in the 1950s to the 1970s when the neighborhood was predominantly Cantonese-based businesses and organizations, had a lively nightlife, and was still considered the major center of Chinese American community life in the region. Thus each generation had a different frame of reference for what defined Chinatown for them and, relatedly, the changes that constituted threats to their ideal Chinatown.

There was also a questioning and resistance to the traditional racial turnover arguments associated with gentrification—that Chinatown was becoming a relatively wealthier White neighborhood. While there were some who advocated for Chinatown "to stay Chinese," many saw this as a simplistic argument. Some explained that the cultural tourism that catered to outsiders was always a part of the neighborhood identity. They also acknowledged the neighborhood history, as it was an immigrant enclave for European immigrants before it was an official Chinatown. In the previous chapters, business leaders have highlighted several non-Chinese Americans moving into the neighborhood and acting as cultural preservationists. Furthermore, as explained in the next chapter, young Asian American entrepreneurs were opening restaurants, retail spaces, and art galleries in Chinatown, which signaled for some that the neighborhood still had a Chinese and Asian American base, albeit a different one than what is traditionally assumed about Chinatowns. Thus, these racial turnover arguments often did not help bring clarity to the community in defining gentrification.

Despite the varying responses to gentrification, there was a common theme in which many spoke of the need to obtain a balance of people and uses to create a diverse neighborhood. These narratives spoke to a historic tension of how both policymakers and communities grapple with gentrification beyond abstract definitions and attempt to rectify the history of economic, social, and political marginalization in these communities. There appeared to be a consensus that most community leaders did not want Chinatown to be a disinvested area, either from the city or the Chinese American community. Instead of preventing change, they were trying to navigate neighborhood changes by expressing their understandings of Chinatown's redevelopment history and its current relationship with other spaces to justify specific types of diversity and to achieve balance in the neighborhood.

BALANCING THE PAST: REFLECTIONS ON THE CRA AND AFFORDABLE HOUSING DEVELOPMENT

The Community Redevelopment Area (CRA) designation was a crucial policy tool that shaped the contemporary development of Chinatown, setting the stage for the gentrification debates during my fieldwork. While the CRA was a controversial institution that devastated many poor and working-class communities of color in Los Angeles in the post–World War II era, community leaders also acknowledged that Chinatown infrastructure needed to improve in the 1970s. Chinatown had poor housing conditions and a lack of appropriate housing stock to support the growing population. Real estate values were also increasing due to Asian flight capital, placing low-income individuals and families in a vulnerable position to be displaced. As explained in previous chapters, there was community mobilization to address these needs, but community leaders also recognized the need to draw from city and outside resources. Some business and social service leaders supported the CRA designation as one of the responses to improve the neighborhood infrastructure for both housing and economic development. Progressive activists who resisted the designation knew that it had the potential to be a force of gentrification by prioritizing economic development that was aligned with visions of revitalizing the broader downtown area, as it did in neighboring areas of Chavez Ravine, Bunker Hill, and Little Tokyo.[12] This concern shaped the activism as explained in the previous chapter. But during my fieldwork, community leaders, as well as those working in local government, spoke of the CRA as critical to affordable rental housing development in Chinatown, especially for low-income immigrant seniors and families.

The CRA was not just a mechanism for redevelopment in Chinatown; it served as the primary policy mechanism that supported housing development, especially affordable housing. By the time Chinatown was designated as a CRA project area, redevelopment policies also had an inclusionary housing mechanism.[13] Chinatown's redevelopment plan required that a minimum of 20 percent of the revenue generated from tax increments was reserved for housing development. Furthermore, at least 15 percent of the units in new housing construction were reserved for affordable housing, 40 percent of which was for very low-income households. If new or substantially rehabilitated housing received CRA financing, this percentage of units reserved for affordable housing increased to 30 percent. Ultimately, twelve affordable housing developments were built during its time as a project area, primarily with CRA funding, and for ten of these developments, all the housing were affordable units.[14] These twelve housing developments provided over fifteen hundred new affordable housing units over the course of three decades.

The CRA affordable housing developments specifically targeted senior citizens and families, two groups that community leaders often highlighted in their advocacy. Senior housing was necessary for the aging immigrant population who were living in substandard housing, including the single resident occupancy units in the older Chinatown buildings. These plans were already set in motion before the CRA designation. In the 1970s, community leaders, which included both progressive activists and business leaders, mobilized to provide senior citizen services, and a part of their activism included a plan to develop new housing for senior citizens. This carried over to the CRA designation, as the very first project completed as a CRA project area was Cathay Manor, a 280-single-unit affordable-housing apartment complex for seniors that was completed in 1984, followed by Grand Plaza in 1992. These developments were also mixed-use developments with the intention to provide social services and amenities for the senior residents who were less physically mobile. The ground floor of Cathay Manor would eventually house the Chinatown Service Center (CSC), Chinatown Teen Post, and the Chinese Committee on Aging, which was the nonprofit organization that managed Cathay Manor. Prior to Cathay Manor, these organizations did not have permanent spaces. When it first started, CSC used a space in the Chinese United Methodist Church in Chinatown. As CSC began to grow, they eventually secured a larger space outside of Cathay Manor. These housing developments were thus important for overall community development as they also provided spaces for social service organizations.

Affordable housing for families was also a major demand, especially family housing that was culturally specific. CCAC members explained that many Chinese immigrant family households were multigenerational. Their advocacy in the CCAC included demands that the new housing reflect this family structure. Gay Yuen, a former CCAC member, emphatically spoke about Yale Terrace, an affordable family housing development built in 2009 near the Thien Hau Temple and Chinatown Branch Library, as one of their major accomplishments:

> I think we were proudest of what I call the multigenerational apartments that were built on Yale Street.... And I still use that as an example of appropriate awareness for cultural needs because some of those apartments have four and five bedrooms. If you look at the cultural habits of Chinese Americans, a family is not mom and pop, two kids, and a dog. A family is grandma, grandpa, and unmarried children [including] aunts and uncles [that is] in addition to mom and pop, and the kids. And so, to think, to develop neighborhood housing and set aside below-market housing to reflect the awareness for the different cultural habits of what a family is? That's really not just giving lip service [that] families come in all shapes and sizes. This is really saying, "Hey, we're building units because we know what your needs are." And then to have a courtyard where grandma can sit and keep an eye on the little kids that she ... is babysitting. I'm so proud of that project.

This advocacy for affordable family housing that considered intergenerational households was an important contribution from the CCAC. Their activism showed how public policies defined housing and households based on heteronormative and Eurocentric family structures. They were challenging assumptions that households were defined by a traditional nuclear family, which forced housing developers and the city to rethink how they planned and designed housing for Chinatown, and by extension other immigrant neighborhoods. They also challenged the idea that these households were simply overcrowded, a perception about Chinatown households since its early history. The current housing advocacy in the neighborhood, as well as other urban Chinatowns, continues to emphasize that new developments must consider multigenerational family structures.

All community leaders acknowledged that the housing construction was an important accomplishment of the CRA designation, especially as the city was facing an affordable housing crisis. There was not just an increase in new housing developments, but the housing was designed to be culturally appropriate to the needs of the Chinatown community. As Gilbert Hom, another former member of the CCAC, explained, "I really feel that [the CRA] was able to bring a lot of additional housing to Chinatown. It stabilized Chinatown as a community." The construction of affordable housing in Chinatown was also arguably a surprising legacy of the CRA, given its history and criticism of displacing other communities, such as Little Tokyo, to prioritize economic development less than a decade prior to Chinatown's designation.

Yet the current housing trends that emerged by the mid-2010s, especially after the dissolution of the CRA in 2011, suggested that Chinatown was rapidly shifting away from affordable housing development. Table 3 shows the number of housing developments from 1980 to 2016. A majority were affordable housing developments as ten of the seventeen developments were 100 percent affordable units and two were mixed-income developments. It was not until the early 2000s, with the construction of the Orsini Apartments, that a 100 percent market-rate housing development was constructed in Chinatown, albeit on the neighborhood border. This was followed by Jia Apartments in 2013 and Blossom Plaza, which was a CRA-funded mixed-income development, in 2016. While there are fewer market-rate and mixed-income developments, these developments had more overall housing units. When examining the number of housing units constructed from 1980 to the opening of Blossom Plaza in 2016, the last CRA-funded project, there

TABLE 3. New Rental Housing Development by Type, 1980–2016

	Number of Affordable Housing Developments (%)	Number of Mixed-Income Housing Developments (%)	Number of Market-Rate Housing Developments (%)
1980–1989	4	0	1
1990–1999	2	0	0
2000–2011	2	1	3
2012–2016	2	1	1
Total	10 (59%)	2 (12%)	5 (29%)

SOURCES: CRA Implementation Plan, 2011–2014; City of Los Angeles Housing and Community Investment Department Redevelopment Affordable Housing Roster, August 2016.

TABLE 4. New Rental Housing Units by Decade, 1980–2016

	Number of Affordable Housing Units (% of total units)	Number of Market-Rate Housing Units (% of total units)	Total Housing Units
1980–1989	740 (94)	45 (6)	785
1990–1999	328 (100)	0 (0)	328
2000–2011	196 (15)	1080 (85)	1276
2012–2016	236 (33)	464 (67)	700
	1500 (49)	**1589 (51)**	**3089**

SOURCES: CRA Implementation Plan, 2011–2014; City of Los Angeles Housing and Community Investment Department Redevelopment Affordable Housing Roster, August 2016.

was almost an even mix of affordable and market-rate housing development. Table 4 shows that approximately 49 percent of the total new housing units constructed from 1980 to 2016 were affordable housing units and 51 percent market-rate housing units. By the end of 2016, however, housing development in Chinatown appeared to be shifting away from being dominated by affordable housing as predominantly market-rate housing was being proposed for the area.

Despite this trend toward more market-rate housing development in Chinatown, not all community leaders agreed that there should be more affordable housing in the neighborhood. Community leaders acknowledged that affordable housing was still a need in the city, but business leaders, in particular, also often spoke about how the CRA overemphasized affordable housing development and expressed reluctance to support more affordable housing in the neighborhood. Some business leaders even stated that there needed to be at the very least a "50–50 balance" of affordable and market-rate housing in Chinatown, not realizing that the numerical balance had already been achieved, at least among new housing developments. As they spoke about the CRA, they were concerned that the designation resulted in a lack of market-rate housing and commercial development to "balance" the neighborhood. In addition to housing, the CRA provided funding for street beautification and loans for small business rehabilitation, but they did not financially support major commercial development in Chinatown apart from Bamboo Plaza in 1989, a mixed-use parking and retail space developed by a prominent business family in Chinatown. As explained in the previous chapter, this frustration also led to the formation of new spaces of community control in the 2000s, including the Business Improvement District (BID), where business leaders could reassert their power over development in the community that could counter the CRA and CCAC.

Business leaders, especially those associated with the BID, were thus not just supporting more market-rate housing, but also pushing back on affordable housing, justifying their stances by arguing that Chinatown needed demographic diversity to sustain the neighborhood, which the CRA failed at providing for the community. One business leader who became involved in Chinatown in the 1990s noted this criticism:

> We went through two real estate cycles and there was no market-rate development in Chinatown.... And I mean there's an argument to be made that what Chinatown needs is not more affordable housing. The community needs housing that has people that [have] disposable income and [are] able to spend in the community.

They saw Chinatown as an area of concentrated poverty with residents who could not support the neighborhood economy. A BID staff member further argued how the commercial occupancy rates were due to the lack of market-rate housing:

> We don't have enough disposable income in the community to support our businesses. So until the commercial vacancy is on par with the residential vacancy rate that's when we're balanced. Then that's where we could talk about, okay, let's build more affordable housing at the same time we build market-rate housing. But right now, I think there's a catch-up that we need to do.

Another commercial property owner, while not currently involved with the BID, also expressed similar support for the new market-rate housing projects, explaining that a "healthy neighborhood is diverse." He explained his vision of Chinatown as a "cool community" with a mix of seniors, kids, and professionals, and unique shops and restaurants for everyone in the neighborhood.

Additionally, business leaders stressed that Chinatown should not continue to bear the burden of addressing the housing affordability crisis in the city. From their perspective, the crisis was due to overall scarcity of housing of all types and levels of affordability across the city, not just Chinatown. As one person who worked with several Chinatown business leaders simply stated, "You just need to build." While these arguments show that business leaders and developers were attuned to the demand for affordable housing, they also espoused neoliberal principles in which individual, for-profit private developers should be given the freedom to meet those demands. These arguments are also aligned with fiscally conservative, libertarian perspectives that favor the free market and deregulation on development. Business and real estate interests have criticized California, in particular, for having regulations that are inhibiting housing production, such as those imposed by the California Environmental Quality Act (CEQA). CEQA includes an environmental review that is integrated into the local development public review process to identify and mitigate any potential environmental impacts, which are subject to public review and hearing. Critics accuse these policies of slowing down development and increasing overall housing costs, both in Chinatown and across the city. A person who worked in local government explained that this tension about regulation was a major factor as to why affordable housing is often not desirable as they had to consider the interests of both the developer and the community, "If the City Council puts in an ordinance saying, 'Hey, 100 percent affordable housing!' would that fly with the developer that eventually develops the project? Would the community want that? And so, it's very much a delicate balance."

Developers were also adopting this messaging of bringing balance and diversity to Chinatown to justify their proposals that included market-rate housing. This included the outreach for College Station, a mixed-use development with all market-rate housing that was proposed to be built across from the Chinatown Metro Station. A representative for the project stated at several public meetings that they were bringing "balance" to the community. They further defended College Station by explicitly sharing that they were responding to Chinatown business leaders' concerns, specifically from the BID, about the CRA overemphasizing affordable housing development and the need to support Chinatown retail by bringing in residents with disposable incomes. In response to some initial criticism of the lack of affordable housing, they offered to do off-site construction of affordable housing elsewhere in Los Angeles, although it was uncertain where that would be.

While it may not be surprising that current business leaders supported more market-rate housing in Chinatown to promote more economic and social diversity, there were others in the community who also supported a mix of housing. Many of the former CCAC members who were vocal advocates for affordable housing during the CRA designation were also expressing their support to diversify Chinatown. One former CCAC member who was a vocal advocate for residential interests saw gentrification as a possible positive change that would make Chinatown "both ethnically diverse and economically diverse" and could create "mutual benefits." He explained:

> I think that the so-called gentrification of [the] downtown area—Chinatown, in particular—doesn't necessarily have to be a negative thing. I think that there's a lot of advantages to having a more diverse neighborhood. That diversity includes economic diversity. I think though that the city is creating a two-tiered city if they keep separating so-called market-rate housing from affordable housing.

He perceived the benefits of diversity from both a community and city perspective. The social mixing in Chinatown would be a benefit for the current residents in accessing different kinds of resources and creating local opportunity structures, but that it also would create a less stratified city that had areas of concentrated wealth and concentrated poverty.

While this framing of diversity may at first appear that those who had more progressive interests in the CCAC shifted their stances on affordable housing, their sentiments reveal their experiences in successfully asserting community control on behalf of the neighborhood. A former CCAC member who was another advocate for affordable housing also explained that the community needs to be politically active and mobilized to create a "nice mix" in the neighborhood that is defined on their own terms, "We want the vitality of the immigrant spirit, of the immigrant families. . . . So, you have to plan accordingly. Now who does that planning? So, is that planning up to the community? Well, then you have to train your communities. . . . You have to be vocal." Similarly, another former CCAC member who was also a community activist in the 1970s expressed confidence that the community would be able to protect the most vulnerable in Chinatown:

> With gentrification, the fear is that we push out the labor class or the elderly. I don't think it's either/or. Unfortunately, I think that with the CRA, we were able to, maybe, provide more long-term income and services. But I think, we're [the community] smart. We can think about ways of taking care of our elderly and of taking care of our low-income people without cutting off our nose to say we don't want to gentrify. Let's [have] Chinatown continue to deteriorate and close its door at sundown and have people three blocks from here not wanting to come here to spend money to eat. I think that's a very narrow-minded [outlook]. You want gentrified people coming in. You want the balance. . . . You don't want to shoot yourself in the foot.

These CCAC members have been a part of the leadership and grassroots organizing that provided community-based resources since the 1970s. They were also involved in ones that became more formalized organizations representing Chinatown. Thus, they recognized the political strength they have built over time. Because of the history, it is perhaps not surprising that those who participated in the CCAC did not see the community taking a backseat to developers and believed that they would be able to bring more diversity to Chinatown without it leading to displacement.

AMENITIES FOR WHOM?
BALANCING "DOWNTOWN LIVING"

Chinatown is not an isolated community, and community leaders were cognizant that the neighborhood was and continues to be intrinsically linked to other areas in the city, especially to downtown, its neighbor to the south. As one community leader who worked in heritage efforts stated matter-of-factly, "Unfortunately or fortunately Chinatown is part of that downtown community. We have to be mindful of that." During my fieldwork, the city was updating their plan for the downtown area, which included Chinatown, and it projected that the area would absorb much of the city's population growth through 2040, including the creation of over one hundred thousand new housing units. Within these plans though, there was no inclusionary mechanism that requires a certain percentage of affordable housing units for these new developments. Since the CRA dissolution, downtown-adjacent neighborhoods like Chinatown that relied on the CRA designation for affordable housing were now more vulnerable to developments that reflected trends shaping the downtown core. Thus, community leaders were trying to balance the pressures of being part of the larger downtown area. Within the spatial perspective of balance, they acknowledged that these new investments brought changes to Chinatown that could contribute to residential and business diversity, but also questioned whether those who were attracted to Chinatown's proximity to downtown had a long-term commitment to the community.

During my fieldwork, most of the new housing developments that were proposed and in construction primarily had market-rate apartment units. They also primarily consisted of studio and one-bedroom apartments, with a few developments proposing micro units, studio units that are usually less than three hundred square feet. The unit types were similar to what was being proposed in the larger downtown area. This trend signaled that these new developments, both in Chinatown and downtown, were marketed to primarily young professionals, whether single or married with no children. An older community leader expressed that catering to this population would shift the type of amenities in Chinatown, making it an "extension of downtown." He further explained:

> Chinatown [will become] the backside of the ultra-development that is going on in downtown [that will] accommodate the young singles, anticipating people earning as much [as] an average of $100,000 a year for high-tech and excellent jobs down here. No need for good schools because they don't have any kids. There is a need now for nightclubs and upscale restaurants and things like that. But that doesn't speak of what Chinatown should be.

Those who worked in housing advocacy, social services, and cultural heritage were concerned that new developments were designed for this downtown demographic and creating displacement pressures, including rent increases in unsubsidized affordable housing and new amenities that were disrupting the identity of Chinatown as an immigrant and intergenerational family-based community. This tension was exemplified along the ground floor of Blossom Plaza in which empty storefront windows showcased advertisements for the development by stating that the plaza was "A New Era in Downtown Living" with two young women taking selfies in the open area of the development (Figure 10). When discussing the presence of Blossom Plaza in the neighborhood, one young activist who recently became involved in social service work, argued, "It's $2,000 for one-bedroom for a month. So, I feel

FIGURE 10. Advertisement on the ground floor of Blossom Plaza advertising "downtown living" in Chinatown, 2023. Photo taken by author.

like there needs to be balance right now. I feel like it's not a balance." Despite Blossom Plaza providing a few affordable units, many in the community, as well as the property owner of the plaza, still saw this development as part of the trends since the 2000s to attract young, upwardly mobile professionals to downtown, a stark contrast to the CRA housing development in Chinatown, which focused on promoting residential stability through affordable housing for families and seniors.[15]

New retail trends in Chinatown also appeared to primarily appeal to a broader downtown community and tourists, not necessarily the local residential community. As further explained in the next chapter, many of these new businesses included restaurants and boutique businesses that appealed to the tastes of what many in the community deemed as "hipsters," a primarily young, upwardly mobile population in creative professions who were increasingly moving to downtown and downtown-adjacent neighborhoods. In response to these criticisms, several BID board members and staff asserted that the changes in Chinatown were unique to the neighborhood, balancing the broader downtown retail mix rather than replicating it. George Yu, the executive director of the BID, explained, "For the longest time when all those things were being built downtown—where are you going to eat? You can't eat at Roy's every night or the Palm [two upscale restaurants]. I mean [you need] real places." One new property owner and BID board member similarly shared how he saw Chinatown as an important space to provide everyday amenities for the broader downtown community, "It could be great though. You can have a lot of these like little corner groceries stores and things like that. If it really embraces the Broadway downtown community, it could be the place where people drive in from the Arts District and from Echo Park and everything to shop." From this perspective, Chinatown's economy should be serving not just the neighborhood residents and Chinese American community, but the downtown residential community. Moreover, Chinatown's authenticity as a "real community" balanced the chain stores and the more expensive retail in the downtown core.

There were also arguments that the new businesses were balancing the Chinatown retail mix that made the neighborhood appealing to a diverse consumer base without contributing to competition to the current businesses. These new restaurants and retail were not just maintaining the small business character that defined the local economy of Chinatown, but were also diversifying the offerings available in the neighborhood. One older community leader involved with heritage efforts shared his conversation with an owner of one of the new restaurants, Little Jewel, which served New Orleans–inspired cuisine. He explained how the owner felt welcomed by his neighbors:

> The owner of Little Jewel of New Orleans has said several times, . . . "The neighbors around me, the other Chinese restaurants, they said they were glad that I was not Chinese, not opening a Chinese restaurant because they didn't need that competition." Because there's 1, 2, 3, 4 [Chinese restaurants] immediately either across the street or on the same block. . . . And then another block away there's more.

These business owners, and the community leaders supporting them, situated themselves as helping to diversify the small business character, and specifically the restaurant landscape of Chinatown. They were not in direct competition with the older businesses and could possibly coexist together. Yet, as the next chapter will illustrate, these new businesses were contributing to the transformation of the neighborhood culture that appealed to a young, creative-class population, which can still contribute to displacement pressures for these older businesses.

Not all the business changes in Chinatown were necessarily catering to the relatively affluent population moving to downtown. As mentioned in previous chapters, one of the most notable new businesses was the Walmart Neighborhood Market. The origins of the Walmart market date back to when Chinatown was designated a CRA project area. Donald Spivack, the former deputy director of operations and policy at the CRA, explained that there was a need to develop amenities to anticipate a growing downtown residential community:

> Chinatown, Little Tokyo, and Bunker Hill, the rest of downtown, were all considered to be a part of downtown for the community redevelopment purposes, understanding [that] they had discrete needs and desires of their own. But in terms of trying to provide services, CRA's perspective was if we're trying to market downtown as a mixed-use, mixed-income residential community, it needs a certain amenity base. And a fairly common amenity is a supermarket.

Grand Plaza, the CRA-funded affordable senior housing complex, was selected as the site for the market. This complex was located on the southwestern border of Chinatown and was seen as optimal to serve several communities in the downtown area.

The presence of the Walmart Neighborhood Market brought up questions similar to those that the other new businesses in Chinatown engendered: would the market provide retail diversity or competition to the existing small businesses? The Southeast Asian Community Alliance (SEACA) and CCED saw it as competition, explaining that the assertions that Chinatown lacked grocery store options and was a food desert were misleading. They argued that this narrative overlooked the smaller produce markets that have historically served the local and ethnic community. To them, the Walmart market was a form of commercial gentrification that would not just displace these small businesses but would also be the start of more big-box and chain stores opening, which included the Starbucks that had recently opened in the neighborhood. This was a commercial trend that was also happening across the downtown area. However, other community leaders stressed that the Walmart market could provide choices for residents in addition to the existing markets. One older community leader shared his conversation with some Chinatown residents about the Walmart market. They saw it as not necessarily in competition with the existing Chinatown businesses since, like the new non-Asian restaurants and retail in Chinatown, it provided different products:

> It's a transitional learning experience. In other words, they saw it as beneficial and educational. It was their opportunity to just not go necessarily to the same old place and buy the least expensive item. But then they could see, "Oh gosh, here are these other choices and they can learn about that." So, it was probably educational for them.

Yet he also noted that while Chinatown residents frequented the Walmart market, it didn't "necessarily shift enough customer loyalty to them—to the Walmart—to make it worthwhile" for the corporation.

This is perhaps the overarching takeaway from Walmart's brief and tenuous presence in Chinatown, regardless of the conflicting positions and stances within the community. While it was providing an amenity, especially for the low-income senior citizen community in Chinatown, in the end, the corporation was also looking for opportunities to test its new model of small-scale grocery stores in the urban market. It did not matter whether it was providing a needed amenity for the community or was potential competition for the other small businesses; Walmart's concern was simply with their overall company profits, which did not hinge specifically on their success in Chinatown. Chinatown was one of many test markets across the nation, and when it left, both those in support of and opposition to the Walmart were surprised, as it was closed just a few days after the public announcement in January 2016 (Figure 11). As one community leader who supported the Walmart explained, this was ultimately out of the control of anyone in the community, despite the community being impacted the most:

> Walmart came in because they had a new concept going, come hell and high water, to try it. And they didn't leave because it didn't work here. They left because suddenly Benton, Arkansas, [location of the Walmart headquarters] decided that they had taken the wrong direction, and they withdrew the idea of the line of smaller markets, actually, all over the country. It was a national action, which was very deplorable.

The conflict over the Walmart Neighborhood Market was an internal community conflict between residential and business interests, as well as senior and younger community leaders. However, the tensions ultimately spoke to how Chinatown community leaders must balance the interests of outside

FIGURE 11. Grand Plaza after the closing of the Walmart Neighborhood Market, 2016. Photo taken by author.

developers and investors who may only see an economic opportunity in the downtown market, which may not translate into long-term benefits for the community.

Furthermore, in 2019, Chinatown's remaining major supermarket, Ai-Hoa market, shut down. The owners of the market faced rent increases when Tom Gilmore, a major Los Angeles real estate developer, bought the property. This created an even bigger amenity gap since Ai-Hoa was the largest grocery store in Chinatown. Whether a new supermarket would take the place of Ai Hoa market remained a question at the time of writing this book. Undoubtedly the tenuous conversations about these new businesses will continue. Will they actively center the needs of Chinatown residents, or is Chinatown a footnote concern as they aim to capitalize on the potential growth of downtown?

The concern about the growing downtown residential community and its impact on Chinatown was not simply reflected in discussions of businesses. It was also evident in the struggle over public education. Chinatown's local school, Castelar Elementary School, is a community asset recognized beyond the community. In addition to its positive academic reputation, it is considered a community school, as the curriculum and activities were tailored for Chinatown residents. It has also served as a hub for social services for the entire neighborhood community beyond its students, including adult education programs. The past principals and teachers of Castelar Elementary were respected community leaders who were not just educators, but also advocates for the families and children in Chinatown. Most notable was Dr. William Chun-Hoon, the first Chinese American principal in Los Angeles, who was Castelar's principal in the 1970s and 1980s. He was instrumental in promoting bilingual education in response to the increasing diversity of Asian immigrants and refugees in the neighborhood during this time.

The school also has served as an important community space. Under Chun-Hoon's leadership the school became a space for local organizations to meet and hold events, as there were no other accessible community spaces in the neighborhood. During my fieldwork, I attended multiple community meetings at Castelar hosted by both the city and community groups.[16] Chun-Hoon and other Castelar educators also led the activism to establish a Los Angeles public library branch in Chinatown, which was originally a part of Castelar but is now located a few blocks away from the school. The library serves as an important community space for the local youth and families, including an active Chinatown Teen Council. Castelar was not simply a school. It was a community institution that was a homebase for many community leaders and supported other Chinatown organizations.

As the downtown residential community was growing, there were initial assumptions that Castelar could possibly support and benefit from this growth because of its good reputation that extended beyond the local community. As George Yu of the BID explained, Chinatown was a "real community with services" and "as downtown matures, where are those kids going to go to school? Castelar [has] incredible API [Academic Performance Index] scores." Instead, in 2016, Castelar Elementary School, was subject to a possible co-location with a downtown charter school. Because of Proposition 239, local public schools that had empty classrooms could be used for charter schools. The school district identified Castelar as having excessive empty classrooms despite the fact that they were being used for extracurricular activities. The policy required that a district teacher had to be formally assigned to those rooms to count as a space that was actively used. The empty classrooms were also a marker of demographic changes as the number of family households and youth residents in the neighborhood had been decreasing since 2000.[17] The proposed co-location from the downtown charter school showed that those who were moving and attracted to downtown were not necessarily trying to strengthen the current amenities of Chinatown, but instead creating their own.

The threat of co-location became a major moment of community activism during my fieldwork. In addition to its academic reputation and important role in providing services to the local community, Castelar also had a Mandarin Immersion Program that attracted Asian Americans who chose to enroll their children in Castelar rather than in their neighborhood schools. Many of these Asian Americans never lived in Chinatown or had any prior history of civic engagement in the neighborhood. Similar to older community leaders who came to Chinatown in search of their history, they saw this program as a cultural and educational opportunity for their children to learn both Chinese language and Chinese American heritage. It was these young Asian American parents who also emerged as new leaders in the community to resist the co-location.

Martin Wong and Wendy Lau were two young parents who became members of the Friends and Alumni of Castelar Elementary School (FACES). Through FACES, they helped mobilize other parents and community groups, including CACA and CCED, against the co-location. While Wong and Lau did not live in Chinatown, they still had deep concerns about how co-location would be disruptive to the Castelar students and their families who lived in Chinatown. They questioned the rhetoric of diversity that the charter school used to justify the co-location and instead highlighted the socioeconomic exclusion it would have created:

MARTIN: [The students wear] clothes from the swap meet over there [on Broadway], like bootlegged Mickey Mouse shirts and it's not fancy that way. You see the two-striped Adidas shoes and Ultraman backpacks. And I think that's cool. I love it. But you know that other kids from other demographics [from the downtown charter school], you know that's not the [norm] for them.

WENDY: That's not to say that their school [the downtown charter school] is not diverse because you know that was one of their arguments. It's like, "Oh no, our school is very diverse. We have this many Title I [students]."[18]

MARTIN: But those kids are not going to come to Chinatown.

WENDY: The problem is they [the low-income Charter School students] were located far enough away [from downtown and Chinatown]. I'm like, "Well when they come here, are they going to bring those low-income kids? How are those kids going to get here?" Those kids are going to be forgotten over there and they're going to pick up a new set of low-income kids from our community, which would then take funding from our school.

Thus there were possibilities of resource competition between the schools that would weaken Castelar. Furthermore, if the co-location occurred, the schools would operate separately in the same space, and some likened this agreement to a "separate but equal" policy that would treat the current students who were from Chinatown as "second-class citizens." They acknowledged that the charter school would bring in more resources from families with higher incomes, but because it would remain a separate school, the local students from working families could see these resources, but not have access to them despite sharing the same space.

Additionally, Wong and Lau expressed concerns that the co-location would have ripple effects beyond the students because Castelar had multiple purposes for the community. Wong further explained:

> One of the things we pointed out [is that Castelar] serves the parents, the families. Not just the kids. Because if you go there in the morning, you'll see [a Castelar volunteer], she'll be outside, translating bills and letters or notices for parents. They'll give clinics, free flu shots, all these different things. Nutrition. CPR. All these things for the community as well. I think across the street with Alpine [Recreation Center], you drive by there, you always see adults there. There's always seniors. It's not like other parks and schools. I feel like it's a real hub for the people to live there. And the resources are used. So, to slice it up and weaken it with outside forces that may suck even more out of it? It is really sad.

They and other community leaders involved in resisting the co-location did not simply recognize Castelar as the local elementary school, but they also honored its history as a community institution.

The possible co-location of Castelar showed that the changes from downtown were placing pressures onto Chinatown that could have a negative impact on the community infrastructure. While some newcomers, such as Wong and Lau, became embedded with the community, other newcomers were contributing to diversity by creating their own amenities rather than trying to strengthen the current ones. As a means to not promote exclusion and separation between the downtown and Chinatown communities, Wong, Lau, and other Castelar advocates encouraged the downtown charter parents to instead enroll in Castelar. Ultimately, the co-location did not occur. Despite this victory, community leaders noted that Castelar will continue to be vulnerable for possible co-location because of the empty classrooms and possibility of declining enrollment due to fewer family households and youth in Chinatown.

These new developments, businesses, and institutions aimed to serve a broader downtown community and theoretically help to diversify Chinatown—and, in the examples of Walmart and Castelar, to fill "empty" spaces. However, community leaders, especially those representing residential and cultural interests, observed that many of these newcomers simply saw opportunity rather than a sense of community, heritage, or social equity in Chinatown. A former CCAC member shared his observations "that [the] balance is once again tilted" but in the opposite way to when Chinatown was a CRA project area. He went on to say that these new developers and property owners are "making lots of money [by] turning it over. But that doesn't mean people would want to invest in the community anymore here. Because they come in and they leave. . . . So that's no good!" Another older community activist shared similar sentiments, but more bluntly stated, "I think [we should] not let downtown take over Chinatown and turn it into like some hipster [area] . . . [with] people who have no roots. Just moving around whenever you get a different job and go somewhere else." In contrast to the business owners who saw these changes as helping to diversify and activate the neighborhood, these community leaders felt that the current changes did not necessarily mean that investors, residents, and other newcomers would build an emotional connection to the neighborhood that would help sustain the neighborhood as a Chinatown.

BALANCING THE SAN GABRIEL VALLEY AND THE SOCIOECONOMIC DIVERSITY OF THE CHINESE AMERICAN COMMUNITY

While the post-1965 population growth solidified Chinatown as a majority Asian American neighborhood, the suburbs in the San Gabriel Valley were also emerging as new centers for Asian Americans, and specifically for Chinese American community life. By the 1990s, suburbs and smaller cities in the western San Gabriel Valley, including Monterey Park, Alhambra, and San Gabriel, eclipsed Chinatown as the major residential and economic centers for Chinese Americans. As described in chapter 1, the San Gabriel Valley was developing from a rural to a suburban area, which included the construction of single-family homes, and it was marketed as a space for upwardly mobile Chinese Americans.[19] Rick Eng, who was involved in CACA, CHSSC, and his family's mutualist association during the time of the fieldwork, grew up in Monterey Park in the 1970s and 1980s. He often visited Chinatown, as his father was also active in organizations. Eng recalled the real estate marketing of the San Gabriel Valley during this time:

> One of the big events or phenomena was the migration of long-time residents [in Chinatown] into San Gabriel Valley, and when Monterey Park and Alhambra and some of the other cities became magnets for the Chinese. And I just remember—because it happened right after I graduated from high school, I started to see a lot of [Chinese Americans in the area]. And I would ask my dad, I said, "Why are Chinese coming here?" And so, he was reading a Chinese newspaper and he showed me this ad. And it had like a home—pictures of homes and what they were offering. And he said, "They're basically telling people that are from overseas that Monterey Park is like the Beverly Hills for the Chinese." [laughs] My god! Talk about false advertisement! And boy, if I had a chance to talk to these people, [I would] say how they were being snowballed! But that was it. That was the appeal.

His facetious comment about how the San Gabriel Valley was being labeled as "Beverly Hills for the Chinese" highlighted how the area was promoted in ways to appeal to the aspirations of middle-class Chinese Americans that masked the area's socioeconomic and racial diversity.[20]

Yet this image of a "Beverly Hills for the Chinese" continues to characterize the San Gabriel Valley. When discussing the relationship between the San Gabriel Valley and Chinatown, community leaders spoke of spatialized class differences within the Chinese American community. Despite the socioeconomic and racial diversity of the San Gabriel Valley, community leaders often framed this area as the center for middle-class Chinese Americans, especially in relation to Chinatown, which was home to poor and working-class Chinese American families and senior citizens. These perceptions of a spatial imbalance of the ethnic community based on class led to concerns about residential and economic competition with the San Gabriel Valley for the middle-class Chinese American community. This issue was specific to class and socioeconomic differences, as other low-income urban areas with a noticeable Chinese American presence, such as Lincoln Heights, were not perceived as residential or economic competition to Chinatown. These perceptions of the spatial sorting of the ethnic middle-class contributed to debates as to whether Chinatown can and should be a mixed-income community, and the role of the Chinese American community in contributing to that identity.

Community leaders acknowledged that for many middle-class Chinese American families, Chinatown was a less desirable place to live compared to the San Gabriel Valley. They spoke about how Chinatown did not have the amenities to compete for the attention and investment of middle- and upper-class Chinese American families that the suburbs and cities in the San Gabriel Valley had and could quickly develop. One older business leader, who saw the economic growth and decline of Chinatown since the 1970s, explained that these economic trends were intrinsically linked to Chinese American families wanting single-family homes:

> Chinatown has no [single-family] housing. It mainly is multiple housing apartments. So, some of these immigrants when [they arrive] here, they may work in Chinatown, but they get housing outside, like Monterey Park, Alhambra. And then as time goes on, people are gradually moving out. So, in the late '80s or early '90s, Chinatown started going downhill.

Besides the San Gabriel Valley having more single-family homes, Chinatown was also slowly losing this housing type during this time, especially because of redevelopment. While it is currently a neighborhood with predominantly multifamily homes, Chinatown was previously a neighborhood primarily of single-family homes. The 1960 Census indicated that 52 percent of the Chinatown area was single-family homes. However, many of these homes were redeveloped or converted to multifamily homes, most likely in response to the population growth and shifts. Between 1970 and 1980, there was a net increase of 469 multifamily units with a net reduction of 21 single-family units in the residential area of Chinatown.[21] Furthermore, the CRA primarily focused on developing affordable rental units. While this helped to develop and maintain spaces in Chinatown for low-income renters, it also limited home ownership opportunities, as only one condominium complex, Angelina Terrace, was built during this time. By the mid-2010s, over 80 percent of Chinatown's housing stock consisted of multifamily housing units. This goal of owning a single-family home continued to be a symbol of upward mobility and a part of the American Dream for many immigrant communities, including Chinese Americans. But it was a symbol that was difficult to obtain in Chinatown. As a predominantly multifamily and rental housing neighborhood, Chinatown was physically antithetical to the American Dream.

The lack of opportunities to own single-family homes was cited as a reason why many middle-class Chinese American families eventually left or bypassed Chinatown. Several younger individuals spoke of their parents temporarily residing in Chinatown before moving to the San Gabriel Valley to buy a home. As one person who grew up in Chinatown explained about the changing demographics, "I have to wonder whether or not for most families that start out in Chinatown, mine included, Chinatown is just a steppingstone. Like you come, you settle, you do what you need to do, and then when you can you move on to the San Gabriel Valley." She further explained that Chinatown's housing stock did not fit her family's expectations for home ownership once they had built enough financial capital to own property, "They want a single-family home. They don't want a condo." Another individual who recently became involved with the Chinatown community also echoed these sentiments by sharing that her parents' generation were not as involved in Chinatown because "they were part of the generation of 'learn the language, move to the suburbs, go to college.' It was a different mentality back then." Several community leaders noted that Chinatown has historically been seen as a "ghetto" and that those who were raised in the neighborhood did not romanticize the local conditions as some community leaders may inadvertently do when they advocate for the community. They shared the difficulties and struggles of living in the neighborhood and stated that for a long time Chinatown was not necessarily a source of pride but a place that you wanted to eventually leave, with little reason to come back. This perception that Chinese Americans were leaving Chinatown and moving to the San Gabriel Valley was reflective of the dominance of spatial assimilationist perspectives that contributed to the devaluing of Chinatown for the community, especially later generations. It also spoke to the history of Chinatown being subject to subpar conditions due to ongoing neglect from the city and mainstream institutions, positioning it as an unappealing place, especially compared to the smaller cities and suburbs in the San Gabriel Valley.

The growth of the San Gabriel Valley has also impacted the local economy of Chinatown. Many business and heritage leaders indicated that Chinatown has been losing its major consumer base, the Chinese American community, because of competition from the San Gabriel Valley. As mentioned in chapter 1, the neighborhood has historically been a destination for Chinese Americans across Los Angeles, as much as it has been a home for Chinese Americans. However, both new Asian immigration and global investment throughout the San Gabriel Valley led to a flourishing of Chinese restaurants and retail in this area, which has challenged Chinatown's role as the primary destination for ethnic-specific goods and services for the Chinese American community.[22] Even those concerned with the revitalization of Chinatown acknowledged that they were part of this problem. As one Chinese American who owned a business in Chinatown explained, "You don't have to drive to Chinatown and have Chinese food. I live out that way, so I go to San Gabriel area, and I don't come to Chinatown to eat."

Furthermore, similar to the housing development, the San Gabriel Valley was also more favorable for commercial development, which further contributed to these shifts. One former president of the Chinese Chamber of Commerce explained that the businesses could easily follow the migration to the San Gabriel Valley because of this:

> Economic activity moved with the residents.... More Chinese immigrants are residing over in San Gabriel Valley and more businesses are developing over there. You have better potential of developing business there because you have emptier [land]. Ample supply of land and parking. That marked the beginning of the, as you say, downfall, [or] less significance of Chinatown.

Chinatown, as a developed urban neighborhood, was an area that did not have as many opportunities to be built out further, placing limits on how much the neighborhood could compete with the San Gabriel Valley. The policies and governance, as well as the growing Asian American presence in the different San Gabriel Valley cities and suburbs, also made it relatively easier for Asian-initiated development to flourish there than in Chinatown and, by extension, the rest of the city of Los Angeles.[23]

The loss of this Chinese American consumer base and investment has led to the closing of several major businesses in Chinatown. Business leaders referred to the closing of Empress Pavilion, a major banquet hall and dim sum restaurant that opened in 1989, as an example that not only signified the economic decline of Chinatown, but also the competition it faced with the San Gabriel Valley. During its first decade of operation, it was a bustling restaurant and a major dining destination in Chinatown. By the time of my fieldwork, it had become a catering company for special events with no daily operations. One individual, who was a second-generation commercial property owner in Chinatown, explained how the shutting down of Empress Pavilion was an "interesting milestone" for Chinatown:

> Sometimes people would hear that Empress Pavilion would close down, and they say, "I'm surprised! I'm surprised! The last time I was there for dim sum, the place was packed." ... But then as Monterey Park and the San Gabriel Valley opened up, and more and more banquets moved to the San Gabriel Valley, that took away that source of money from a lot of the restaurants in Chinatown that used to have kind of a captive audience for three or four months' worth of Chinese New Year's banquets. And that the guarantee

that almost every night that those restaurants were going to have Chinese New Year's banquets made a big difference to the restaurant owners. You take that away, then that undermines the whole cultural rule of Chinatown as the place that you go for good Chinese food.

As Chinatown was no longer the only place for banquet halls to host various celebrations, the restaurants were also losing their core Chinese American consumer base. Similarly, Wing Hop Fung, a major Chinese American department store that first opened in Chinatown, closed in 2016. Yet the other locations in the San Gabriel Valley remained open. A young business leader explained their business decision:

> I'm really sad that they're gone, but is that because of how Chinatown is changing? [Or] is that because of how San Gabriel Valley is changing which is outside of our control? Like they're going to follow their customers. . . . It wasn't because of how Chinatown was changing. It was just because of how other places were changing.

Business leaders saw places such as Wing Hop Fung and other similar businesses that catered to Chinese Americans leave Chinatown and thrive in the San Gabriel Valley; thus they were able to reason that not all business closures were a form of displacement. This observation strengthened their arguments that because the neighborhood persisted as a low-income residential community with limited "disposable incomes" and "buying power," businesses could not sustain themselves in Chinatown, especially as the San Gabriel Valley became a place of potential Chinese American consumers with that buying power.

The areas in the San Gabriel Valley have also begun to overshadow Chinatown because it has quickly developed to represent the post-1965 Chinese American community diversity, while Chinatown is still predominantly linked to an older history of Chinese Americans. Chinatown remains a Cantonese-dominated space, appealing to that segment of the community. One older heritage leader explained how this lack of diversity has impacted Chinatown because it does not have the "larger scales of varieties of [Chinese] food," referring to how the Chinese restaurants still tend to be Cantonese restaurants. Yet this narrative that juxtaposed the Chinese American diversity in the San Gabriel Valley to Chinatown as a Cantonese-dominated area did not take into account that there was an intra-ethnic cultural shift in Chinatown. As one community leader who worked in social services since the 1970s explained:

There is a balance that needs to be struck because it's sort of the question about diversity. . . . [Chinatown] is not going back to something that's not diverse. Chinatown has been diverse. It became diverse in the '70s when the first wave of Vietnamese Chinese came from Saigon. . . . And then the Cambodian Chinese, you can see their signs all over, as well. And so, Chinatown is diverse. . . . So, what's the balance and what is the core of Chinatown?

These new Chinese immigrants and refugees were also opening businesses in Chinatown. They established businesses along Broadway, the main commercial street, and the southern area of Chinatown during the time that the San Gabriel Valley was growing as the new suburban Chinatown. Many of these new business owners, who were ethnic Chinese immigrants and refugees from Southeast Asian countries were entrepreneurs and business owners. When walking through Saigon Plaza and Chinatown Plaza on Broadway, shop owners are often speaking in Cantonese Chinese, Teo Chow Chinese, Vietnamese, and Khmer, among the different languages and dialects. By the 1990s, many of the small businesses in Chinatown were owned by ethnic Chinese immigrants from Southeast Asia.[24] These businesses helped to diversify, maintain, and revitalize Chinatown as an ethnic Chinese space for at least two decades.

However, these newer ethnic businesses have also been a point of critique about the economic imbalances of Chinatown as a place of "cheap goods," reinforcing that the concerns about the lack of diversity in Chinatown among business leaders were largely class based. Chinatown business leaders who have supported some of the new upscale retail in the neighborhood have struggled to challenge this perception about Chinatown. These newer businesses, which sell cheap household goods, apparel, and ethnic entertainment have relatively lower prices and appeal to those who tend to be of lower income, which is Chinatown's primary residential demographic, as well as to people who like to "bargain hunt." A few business leaders in Chinatown who owned commercial properties spoke about how Chinatown businesses, and restaurants in particular, were in a "race to the bottom," where they "compete on the basis of price instead of competing on the basis of quality." This rhetoric of quality spoke to how business leaders wanted to appeal to a relatively affluent consumer to sustain Chinatown, especially within the Chinese American community. They viewed the migration of middle-class Chinese Americans to the San Gabriel Valley, both as residents and consumers, as contributing to the economic decline of the neighborhood. However, the narrative also centered this more affluent segment of the ethnic community as integral to sustaining the neighborhood, whether residentially or economically, and minimized the importance of Chinatown's other primary purpose as a home for low-income, working-poor immigrants.

Chinatown is an immigrant neighborhood and has always been one, even prior to being recognized as a Chinatown. Following traditional assimilationist arguments, Chinatown should be a transitional neighborhood for Chinese Americans to help them obtain socioeconomic and residential mobility. This was a common sentiment among community leaders, especially as they discussed Chinatown's relationship to the San Gabriel Valley. However, there were also counterarguments about the immigrant neighborhood identity of Chinatown that instead emphasized how it should serve as a long-term home for working-class immigrant families and seniors who had less opportunities and access to mainstream resources.

Community leaders who worked with and on behalf of residents emphasized how the working-class immigrant community should always be centered in any development plans for Chinatown. Some expressed possibilities that this could happen alongside visions for economic development with business leaders. One young community leader who was involved in the organizing against the co-location of the Castelar Elementary School shared how she supported revitalization efforts, but was cautious about these changes:

> The low-income, particularly, immigrant families, that come here from elsewhere and don't have much, they have very limited resources. I don't know where they're going to go. They can't afford to live here anymore.... How can we find that balance? Of course, we want to see Chinatown revitalized. We do want people to come in.... So how do we strike that balance of preserving our history and honoring it?

Another young community leader who became involved with CHSSC and CACA explained in her understanding of balance, that this includes the goal of "diversifying the economic base," but in doing so the "business-minded folks end up making decisions [that] cater to certain markets." She then mused about what many in Chinatown were wondering, "How do you leverage that in your favor to serve the community?"

Some took a more critical stance of the role of business leaders and their support of new developments. One older community activist explained her position in resisting most, if not all, market-rate housing in Chinatown. She explained how Chinatown's core identity is "a place that welcomes early immigrants" and that the new developments would shift Chinatown away from this identity. She argued passionately about her views on gentrification and the current trend toward market-rate housing in Chinatown as a form of marginalization and imbalance:

> [The current pattern of development] is not fair because it's not as if we don't have enough market-rate housing, from what I could see. And yet they keep saying that there's a shortage of housing. But then there doesn't seem to be any real interest in making sure that everybody is given opportunity to live somewhere that they want to live. It's sort of constant. . . . The problem is [that] not everybody in this world has that much money to pay for housing. And so there should be some balance where people who need affordable housing have those opportunities just as equally as the ones who have money, so that everybody can live together rather than saying, "This is exclusive, like a gated community. This is a gated community for only people who are rich. And then you guys who are poor, you move out of here because you don't fit in. You're too poor for us. And the types of businesses. The type of services. "You demand too many social services, so therefore we don't want to serve [or] provide you with more."

Even those who owned property in Chinatown acknowledged that only a select segment of the community was benefitting from the current changes. One long-term resident who owned their property explained:

> What's going to happen? It's happening in downtown. It's happening in Echo Park. It's very chichi now to move back into the inner city. . . . And of course, Chinatown is going to be the same way. people are going to move back in here who can afford it. And the people who live here are going to get displaced. The property values are going to go up—and hey that's okay. My property value's going up too! But that's not the way it should be. Because who's going to afford to be able to live here?

To these community leaders, Chinatown was one of the remaining neighborhoods where poor and working-class immigrants could afford to live in the city, and this was slowly shifting as Chinatown's development became more aligned with the city and downtown development trends. They were critical of these changes, and the community leaders who supported this trajectory that was making Chinatown increasingly unaffordable. They believed that Chinatown needed to balance these economic pressures by uplifting the needs of working-class immigrants.

Activists who worked in housing issues were also critical of narratives that positioned the San Gabriel Valley as the new center for Chinese Americans. The San Gabriel Valley was also experiencing changes and pressures that limited socioeconomic and residential mobility. Given the population growth of the San Gabriel Valley, multifamily housing construction has increased along with the construction of large-scale mansions, which may make single-family homeownership even rarer in this area.[25] One older community activist expressed her skepticism about the attainability of moving to the San Gabriel Valley, especially as the affordable housing crisis was not just located in the city of Los Angeles. She noted, "people think that they can move to San Gabriel Valley, but then they're finding that it's not cheap over there." Despite the image of the San Gabriel Valley as a place where Chinese Americans could settle once they achieved upward mobility, the area was still subject to the region's housing pressures, making it increasingly unaffordable, even among those who are not considered working class or low income. Thus, this American Dream of homeownership continues to be unattainable for many, whether in Chinatown or the San Gabriel Valley.

While many see how the relationship and competition with the San Gabriel Valley has arguably weakened Chinatown's purpose as a hub for the ethnic community, progressive activists continuously emphasized that poor and working-class Chinese and Asian Americans still lived and worked in Chinatown, even if they were a numerical minority within the ethnic community across the region. They argued that housing, economic development, and social services thus needed to be geared toward those who remained in Chinatown rather than serving those who lived outside the neighborhood. One CCED member who grew up in San Gabriel Valley questioned the narratives that Chinatown no longer mattered for the Chinese American community:

> And then at a certain point, [the] theory, or the assumptions are people are just skipping over Chinatown. They are just moving into these ethnoburbs [in the San Gabriel Valley] as port of entry.... That narrative has kind of neglected the importance of Chinatown. people are like, "There's no value to Chinatown anymore." [But] I don't think so.

These perceptions about upwardly mobile Chinese Americans leaving or skipping over Chinatown for the San Gabriel Valley obscured the continued importance of Chinatown for working-class Asian immigrants. For example, Chinatown was one of the few remaining places that provided resources for older Chinese immigrants who were of Cantonese background. Sharing her observations from decades of professional and volunteer work in China-town, one older community activist pointed out that "there's a lot of people that still speak Toisan, and I don't think that they could go to some of those agencies [in the San Gabriel Valley] where the people are mainly Mandarin speakers." While there were criticisms that Chinatown did not reflect the cultural diversity within the Chinese American community, these counter-arguments illustrate that the strong Cantonese Chinese cultural identity, and in particular, the regional Toisan identity of Chinatown was still needed for the community. Chinatown continued to be home for services and ame-nities for specific segments of the Chinese American community that the San Gabriel Valley did not necessarily provide.

Furthermore, the decentering of Chinatown as an important site for the ethnic community obscured the forced displacement that many tenant or-ganizers and community leaders in social services witnessed through their work. Individuals associated with CCED, SEACA, and CSC shared numer-ous stories about residents who faced rent increases and were served eviction notices.[26] Additionally, the affordable housing covenants of the CRA devel-opments were also starting to expire in 2018. Progressive activists who were critical of the CRA designation and subsequently never engaged with the CRA or CCAC thus questioned the positive impact of the CRA in creat-ing stability for the neighborhood. They were supportive of the affordable housing construction, but critical of how it lacked a long-term mechanism or solution to preserve the existing affordable housing and ensure the devel-opment of future affordable housing. After the dissolution of the CRA in 2011, the city did not have an inclusionary mechanism for affordable hous-ing beyond optional density bonuses for developers. This policy gap led to grassroots activism in two CRA-supported developments, Cathay Manor and Hillside Villa. CCED worked with tenants in both developments to address housing quality and affordability issues. Most notably, the tenants of Hillside Villa organized with CCED members to pressure the city to use eminent domain as a mechanism to preserve it as an affordable hous-ing complex. This strategy was a complete reversal of how cities have used eminent domain to forcibly displace communities in urban renewal projects.

The reframing of eminent domain as a potential protective tool for communities among contemporary housing activists is indicative of the impact of neoliberal housing policies since the 1980s that supported private actors in the ownership and management of affordable housing developments. Regardless of the policy tools or solutions, the housing activism to preserve the current affordable housing developments was a means to try to maintain a balance amid the increased proposals for market-rate apartments and downtown pressures facing Chinatown.

·   ·   ·

As the term *gentrification* has become ubiquitous in describing urban change, it also has become inconsistent in its meaning in everyday usage. The ambivalence in defining and discussing gentrification among community leaders in Chinatown reflects the murkiness of how gentrification is defined in the public and policymaking, as well as among scholars.[27] With the inevitability of change, Chinatown community leaders were trying to discern what was good or bad for the neighborhood rather than preventing change altogether. They also were doing so without always directly using the word *gentrification*. Because gentrification has been publicly perceived as communities being anti-change, it would appear to be a strategic choice of community leaders to not always embrace this term. Instead, they adopted a rhetoric about balance and diversity to discuss the changes in the neighborhood.

But these narratives were still not apolitical. The use of the terms *balance* and *diversity* were still a means to justify their beliefs and understandings of the neighborhood and Chinese American community. Business leaders, in particular, invoked this term to encourage development that brought more affluent residents and consumers to the neighborhood and to justify a move to follow broader downtown trends. They argued that this helped with the economic revitalization of Chinatown. They also were trying to diversify the neighborhood so that it was no longer a predominantly low-income, working-poor community, a defining characteristic of the neighborhood that was supported through the affordable housing development from the CRA designation. Further adding complexity to these arguments was how Chinese Americans could contribute to neighborhood diversity. While there was recognition of the cultural diversity within the Chinese American community in Chinatown, ultimately, the focus was more on promoting diversity among Chinese American residents and consumers based on socioeconomic status and class, which Chinatown lacked due to competition from the San Gabriel Valley. However, the counternarratives to these business leaders also stressed balance and diversity by arguing that without any regulations or community control, following downtown trends and emphasizing the importance of relatively affluent Chinese Americans would lead to an imbalance and displacement of working-poor immigrants. This framing of balance and diversity thus was more protective of the current community to resist external forces that would contribute to displacement.

The rhetoric of diversity and balance revealed how community leaders were responding to contemporary urban revitalization trends that encouraged diversity and what that meant in the context of Chinatown, a historically low-income immigrant community. As Chinatown continues to be recognized as an important neighborhood for both the Chinese American community and the city, it will be part of ongoing policy conversations that try to promote socioeconomic equity and multiculturalism across the city, both of which are defining aspects of urban diversity. Given the competing ways that policymakers and urban planners—and even communities—may approach diversity, their rhetoric and practices can superficially celebrate an image of diversity that does not recognize the history and legacies of racial and class exclusion that have also historically defined urban spaces like Chinatown. They may not directly address ongoing systemic inequities, reinforcing liberal colorblind approaches to diversity and multiculturalism. Thus, achieving diversity is not simply about the outcome of achieving a numerical "balance" of people, housing, or businesses; it is also about the political process to ensure racial and economic equity in the neighborhood and beyond.

FIVE

Sustaining an Ethnic Culture of Place

Chinatown is much more than a district of great bones; it is a cultural treasure—both as a home of many Chinese Americans and as a unique cultural experience intriguing to people of all backgrounds. It hosts many historical places and institutions, yet it is also in the process of redefining itself as an attractive location for boutique shopping, avant garde art, and high end [sic] hotels. The district's public spaces are the platform where this new identity can be negotiated.

—Excerpt from the "Making Chinatown a World Class Cultural Capital" report for the Community Redevelopment Agency, 2010

THE NEIGHBORHOOD CULTURE of Los Angeles Chinatown is intrinsically linked to a Chinese American community identity. Chinatown is known for its unique architecture that recalls traditional Chinese culture, whether real or imaginary. Events such as the Miss Chinatown Pageant, Golden Dragon Parade for Chinese New Year, and the Autumn Moon Festival have become annual traditions in Chinatown for both the community and tourists. Immigrant small businesses also contribute to neighborhood culture as sites for cultural tourism and resources for the community. However, Chinatown's neighborhood culture is also dynamic and changing, representing the histories of different communities' in- and out-migration in the neighborhood. The layers of history and culture are visible throughout Chinatown today, as each building can represent different eras of immigration history in the neighborhood and city. These physical spaces, along with the activities that occur in them, represent the needs and tastes of different generations of immigrants, and particularly the generations of Chinese Americans in Los Angeles for almost a century. They also help to define Chinatown as a unique space and "cultural treasure" amid the urban landscape.

Cultural development, preservation, and heritage are thus critical to how community leaders address gentrification in Chinatown. This chapter examines how community leaders engaged in these strategies to try to sustain Chinatown as a unique ethnic space amid displacement pressures that are contributing to both cultural erasure and socioeconomic disparities. As Chinatown lacked a formal policy mechanism for preservation, community leaders were reconstructing and regulating the built environment, businesses, and neighborhood activities to maintain Chinatown as an important space that would continue to represent a Chinese American community identity. The perceived loss of a Chinese American cultural presence underlaid the concerns about gentrification and the death of the neighborhood as Chinatown increasingly becomes "less Chinese." Thus, these cultural activities and strategies were critical to sustaining the neighborhood as a Chinatown. They contributed to an assertion of a collective ethnic community identity and heritage that helped to anchor Chinatown as both a physical neighborhood and a cultural community.

Yet, as Sharon Zukin argues about the symbolic economy of cities, the production of neighborhood culture also invokes specific representations to influence the consumption of space.[1] Cities have increasingly employed strategies that seek to maintain the cultural heritage and authenticity of neighborhoods as a part of their economic development strategies.[2] These cultural strategies may be intentionally produced and managed to influence economic investment that appeals to outsiders rather than to empower and build capacity for the current community to sustain their neighborhoods.[3] Economic development and revitalization strategies for urban Chinatowns have been especially linked to the production, and at times commodification, of ethnic culture.[4] In non-White racialized spaces like urban Chinatowns, these strategies also may overemphasize ethnic difference to promote these spaces as distinct destinations that boost both the local and regional economy.[5] They can result in creating a palatable and homogenized image of community culture to promote economic consumption in these spaces, which marginalize working-class residents and workers who might be impacted by the possibilities of cultural and economic displacement that come with these cultural strategies. Thus, expressions of neighborhood culture are not politically neutral; they are racialized and class-based representations that can uplift specific images of the community over others to promote economic development.

The production of neighborhood culture in Chinatown highlights the tenuous relationship that Chinese and Asian Americans can have with the neighborhood. The involvement of Chinese and Asian Americans, and in some cases the global Chinese community, were critical to maintaining the culture of Chinatown, whether they were property owners, business owners, or visitors and consumers in the neighborhood. They were prioritized as important to neighborhood preservation through their economic activity in Chinatown, especially among business leaders. While some actively sought to preserve the heritage of Chinese Americans and the neighborhood, there were questions about "modernizing" and upscaling Chinatown to reflect a contemporary Asian American and global Chinese culture, with some business leaders purposely shifting Chinatown's identity to cater to a relatively affluent, upwardly mobile audience. By emphasizing the economic contributions of Chinese and Asian Americans in sustaining a Chinatown culture, it also reinforced neoliberal governance and consumer citizenship.[6] From this perspective, a sense of belonging in Chinatown is centered on the economic contributions to the production of space rather than through other forms of political engagement that build community and uplift the current working-class residents and small businesses to maintain the neighborhood. Thus, there were limitations to these co-ethnic ties and the situating of Chinese and Asian Americans as the primary producers and consumers of Chinatown, as cultural and economic displacement was still a threat.

THE CHALLENGES OF PRESERVING AND BUILDING HERITAGE SPACES

As one of the oldest neighborhoods in the city, Chinatown's physical infrastructure holds much cultural and historical significance. The buildings in the neighborhood vary in design, from the plazas that established Chinatown in 1938 along Broadway to the industrial brick warehouses and pedestrian-scale retail spaces along Spring and Ord Streets. These different buildings represent the layers of immigration history of Chinatown, with some remaining infrastructure from the European immigrants prior to the establishment of New Chinatown. Thus, it is perhaps not surprising that when it was a CRA project area, they promoted Chinatown as a "cultural capital" for the city.

However, during my fieldwork, there was a lack of historical designations to preserve these buildings, as well as a cultural center to act as an anchor signifying the ethnic heritage and historical significance of the neighborhood. As Suellen Cheng, a community leader who has been involved in different cultural heritage projects for over forty years, noted about the challenges of both securing a designation and establishing a cultural center, "Cultural development is fluid. It all depends on the time, the space, and the people. And so, the time changes, the people change. [The] space is always there, but even the usage of the space depends on the needs of the people, depends on the timing." Heritage leaders thus acknowledged that their work is context-dependent, steered by the trends of the ethnic community along with those who have economic and political power. The lack of these spaces symbolized how Chinatown's cultural development and heritage efforts were largely shaped by the motivations of individual community members and organizations, particularly property owners.

Designations and Ownership in the Neighborhood

Historic and cultural designations can be protective tools for communities to preserve their neighborhoods in the face of rapid development.[7] While designations are oftentimes symbolic, this form of place-based advocacy for Asian Americans and other marginalized groups has been an integral part of the ongoing activism to address racial and social inequities as it asserts both a physical and political visibility of the community.[8] Currently, the Chinatown in Los Angeles lacks a comprehensive planning tool that provides restrictions or guidance on preserving the neighborhood as a whole. The preservation efforts have been piecemeal, with few sites officially preserved in the neighborhood. Instead, preservation has been informal among property owners, especially institutional property owners, who have personal motivations and interests in community heritage.

There were concerted efforts to preserve historically significant structures in Chinatown when it was designated a CRA project area in 1980. One of the first activities of the CRA was to rehabilitate Central and West Plaza with the intent to nominate the plazas for the National Register of Historic Places. However, during my fieldwork, the only historically designated structures were the two entryway gates in Central Plaza; none of the buildings in the two plazas were designated. The closest to a cultural designation that Chinatown has received was the national Preserve America designation in 2009. This was a collaboration with other Asian American community leaders in Little Tokyo, Historic Filipinotown, Koreatown, and Thai Town in Los Angeles and initiated through the CRA. This designation was not a regulatory mechanism that protected historical sites. It was a program that helped to provide resources for cultural tourism. By 2017, the program was inactive, as the funding was precarious due to the presidential administration's budgetary changes to support preservation efforts. As mentioned in chapter 2, cultural heritage leaders who are active in the Chinese Historical Society of Southern California (CHSSC) and Chinese American Museum (CAM) were working with the city on their SurveyLA project to recognize various historical sites in Chinatown.[9] While these sites are now part of an inventory, the next steps to actively preserve them have yet to proceed.

As it has been difficult to secure a historical designation that helps to anchor the neighborhood preservation efforts, community leaders were skeptical that Chinatown will ever have one. Much of this skepticism was due to the power of property owners, especially commercial property owners, which includes the owners of Central and West Plaza, the plazas that established Chinatown. A member of CHSSC explained how Chinatown property owners may not have a collective vision for their properties to evolve into historical sites. He reasoned that they may instead be motivated by what he called "an entrepreneurial spirit" and "not because of any moral obligation to maintain or protect a culture or community." Property owners who were concerned about gentrification and were actively preserving the original character and uses of their buildings also were hesitant about the use of zoning overlays, designations, or specific plans that would limit their ability to develop their properties. Some commercial property owners and business leaders have even argued that from an architectural design standpoint, there was no building worth historical preservation status that should restrict how they should use or develop their properties. Their arguments reflected a traditional perspective of historic preservation in which buildings and sites should be preserved because they have mainstream historical and aesthetic significance, which minimized the symbolic importance of everyday sites that provide a sense of community and belonging for historically marginalized groups.

Institutional property owners have thus become important for preservation efforts. Organizations like CHSSC, the Chinese American Citizens Alliance (CACA), Chinese Consolidated Benevolent Association (CCBA), and the various family and regional mutualist associations own their own properties. Some associations also own other properties scattered throughout Chinatown. In some cases, their property ownership directly helped with historical preservation. CHSSC purchased two of the oldest Victorian houses remaining in the neighborhood built by Alsace immigrant Emerson Fritz in the late 1800s. The CHSSC ownership and use of these spaces is symbolic of the layers of immigration history in Chinatown that make heritage efforts often complex; they are preserving the older European immigrant history by maintaining the buildings in their original form, but also using it toward the promotion of Chinese American history.

While not purposeful historical organizations, CCBA, CACA, and the family and regional associations are also considered cultural anchors because of their history in Chinatown and the Chinese American community. An article from the *New Yorker* profiled the changes in the historic Chinatown in Manhattan and specifically cited the family and regional associations as a major reason why it has been able to resist change and preserve its character.[10] In Los Angeles Chinatown, Community leaders also cited the presence of these older mutualist organizations as critical to the preservation of Chinatown. Representatives from CCBA and the family and regional associations openly expressed concerns that Chinatown is slowly becoming "less Chinese." However, there was no indication of any vision among them to preserve their properties for the broader community beyond maintaining their individual organizations as a space for their members.

Without a designation, many heritage leaders experienced limits in building collective community power to preserve and sustain the cultural identity of Chinatown. The power of preservation disproportionately lay with property owners, many of whom were Chinese Americans but not involved with the Chinatown community beyond their claim as a property owner. Yet, because they are property owners with control over the physical spaces in the neighborhood, they had more political power in cultural efforts than the community leaders actively engaged in these efforts. While ethnic property ownership in Chinatown may maintain Chinatown as a place controlled by Chinese Americans, this does not necessarily prevent the displacement of working-class immigrants. They may serve as symbolic anchors of preservation, but Peter Kwong also specifically critiqued the older New York City Chinatown mutualist organizations as part of the community elite that have a history of neglecting and exploiting working-class Chinatown residents and workers.[11] As these older organizations became symbolic organizations representing an older heritage of Chinese America, their role in preserving that older culture of the neighborhood, and the implications of their efforts on the current community, will become more critical over time.

The Ongoing Fight for a Cultural Center

In contrast to other urban Chinatowns across the United States, Los Angeles Chinatown has yet to establish a cultural center. This is a space that is distinct from both CHSSC and CAM, which are organizations and spaces that primarily promote Chinese American heritage and history. Community leaders envisioned a Chinatown cultural center to be a major site within the current neighborhood boundaries that would have physically asserted an ethnic cultural identity of the neighborhood, while also supporting contemporary arts and community activities. The establishment of a cultural center in Chinatown was a major initiative for over three decades in Chinatown, especially during the CRA designation, and, similar to obtaining a historic designation, was an ongoing conversation during my fieldwork. However, the negotiations of determining the scope of this project reflected the ongoing tension of whether a cultural center was meant to support current residential needs or contribute to economic growth.

A cultural center was one of the major projects proposed for Chinatown when it was a CRA project area. As noted in previous chapters, during this time, cities in the San Gabriel Valley were threatening Chinatown as the primary place to experience Chinese American culture. The cultural center was meant to revitalize cultural tourism in the neighborhood, but it was also promoted as a space that could reclaim Chinatown's value for the Chinese American community across the region. In a fundraising brochure, the Chinese Cultural and Community Center of Greater Los Angeles, the local non-profit organization that was formed to manage the proposed cultural center, explained the purpose of the site:

> The recent expansion of the Asian American population with a common Chinese heritage led to the need for a spiritual home to celebrate common cultural traditions with a shared history grounded in an ancient civilization. Such a resource is also needed for saluting diversity in background and culture. Many persons come directly from China to settle in Southern California; others, more recently, from different countries the world over. Many are descendants of men and women who arrived several generations ago; others migrated from different places within our nation and the Western hemisphere.[12]

Recognizing the layers of history, diaspora, and distinct experiences that now defined Chinese American culture, community leaders positioned the cultural center as a space for the community to engage in cultural productions that would promote a unified, but diverse Chinese American community. The cultural center was a means to assert the ongoing significance of Chinatown as an ethnic space across generations and cultural differences.

Despite this vision of unity, the Chinatown Community Advisory Committee (CCAC), disagreed about the scope of the cultural center. Those representing the residential interests envisioned it as a multipurpose community center, with spaces to support various types of recreational activities for the local community. Another vision was for it to be a cultural and entertainment destination, including spaces for a contemporary art gallery and theater, that would attract those who were already visiting downtown for culture and the arts. Both spoke to the dual identities of Chinatown as a residential and tourist neighborhood. The tensions also speak to how these types of community-based cultural institutions that seek to resist cultural displacement can still be constrained by broader development policies and trends, especially ones that push for cultural tourism.[13] The leaders of this effort attempted to negotiate all the potential uses but ultimately did not have a unified vision for the center. In December 1987, the city council member representing Chinatown at the time, Gloria Molina, wrote an open letter to the community, urging them to "put aside their differences" and unite under "one agenda" and development proposal.[14] The conflict and slow process of developing the cultural center was situated as part of the ongoing conflict among community leaders participating in the CCAC.

While the community conflict was often cited as the reason why the cultural center was not built, the cultural center was also never planned as a freestanding development. It was always tied to various commercial developments in the 1980s and 1990s that never came to fruition. One proposal was a major commercial development designed by David Hyun who was the architect for Little Tokyo's Japanese Village Plaza, a CRA-initiated development that was built in the 1970s. While this development in Chinatown was proposed on a county-owned lot that was utilized as a parking lot and not directly displacing any small businesses, there was still concern from CCAC members that this would set a precedent in prioritizing economic development over housing development. Another commercial development proposed by Lippo Bank promised to house a cultural center, but never came to fruition as the bank faced financial losses and James Riady, the chairman of the Lippo Group, faced a political scandal regarding campaign donations to the Democratic Party. Both these developments were never built, and the spaces are currently surface parking lots. The only physical remnant of the proposed CRA Cultural Center is in Blossom Plaza, the most recent development in Chinatown. As noted in chapter 4, Blossom Plaza has had a long and contested history in the community. It switched developers several times, faced resistance from the CCAC, and was delayed by the 2007–2008 Great Recession. The CRA stepped in to help finance it after the recession, and the cultural center was proposed as a community benefit. However, throughout the years of development, the square footage of the cultural center diminished, and the promise of an indoor space changed to an outdoor performance space. The cultural center is now a small patio area with a tree placed in the middle of the space, reducing its functionality.

With the opening of CAM in 2003, a museum space dedicated to Chinese Americans in Southern California, a cultural center may no longer be relevant for the community. CAM was established by the efforts of some of the community leaders who were active in the cultural center efforts. However, it is also not located in the current Chinatown neighborhood. CAM is in El Pueblo de Los Angeles Historical Monument, where Old Chinatown was located, and it has its own separate political representation.[15] Thus, a cultural institution within the current neighborhood boundaries may still appear to be a need, and several community leaders are still holding on to the vision of a cultural center in Chinatown. Toward the end of my fieldwork, community leaders from CCBA, CHSSC, Chinatown Community for Equitable Development (CCED), and Southeast Asian Community Alliance (SEACA) were initiating conversations to support a mixed-use development that would house a cultural center. The county-owned lot that was planned as the original site has been targeted as a possible location and these representatives have started conversations with Chinatown's county supervisor, Hilda Solis. Through their conversations, they were also finding ways to include affordable housing as a part of the development, the other major historic community need. The goal to bring a cultural center to Chinatown continues. But the salience of this space and its ultimate purpose for Chinatown today remains an open question, especially as the Chinese American community's relationship to Chinatown continues to evolve.

DEFINING THE CHINATOWN AESTHETIC: TENSIONS OF ETHNIC HERITAGE AND GLOBAL MODERNITY

While Chinatown does not have a site that is specifically dedicated as a cultural center for the neighborhood or a historical designation, the architectural design and form have helped to create a sense of place that asserts a culture unique to Los Angeles Chinatown. In immigrant and refugee spaces, architectural design has been critical for establishing and communicating a community identity amid forced migration and displacement.[16] The neighborhood aesthetics have drawn people to Chinatown throughout its history, and thus it is part of the preservation debates on how to maintain Chinatown's cultural identity amid downtown change. However, other than the standard regulations on form and density in the zoning laws, there are no specific guidelines or community plans to guide the architectural aesthetics and design of new buildings for the neighborhood. As community leaders attempted to define the neighborhood aesthetics, they were also navigating issues of cultural authenticity and modernity in Chinatown.

The new developments proposed for Chinatown often did not have what many older community leaders saw as any defining Chinatown characteristics. When asked about these characteristics, they often cited the architectural details of Central Plaza, which included buildings with traditional Chinese rooftop designs, as emblematic of the typical Chinatown design (See Figure 12). Central Plaza helped to establish a sense of belonging and community during the early era of explicit racial exclusion against Chinese Americans. Thus, it served as an important physical anchor and design reference point for the neighborhood.

However, the mixed-use housing and retail developments in Chinatown that have been built since the 2000s, including the Orsini, Jia Apartments, and Blossom Plaza have what many cited as a "modern" aesthetic that is in stark contrast to older buildings (see Figure 13). Those involved with heritage and preservation efforts tended to be most critical of this type of architectural design threatening the cultural character of the neighborhood. They often described these new buildings as massive and imposing, with a property owner across from Blossom Plaza calling it an "eyesore." While there were other mid- and high-rise developments that have already been built by downtown developers, such as the Orsini and Jia Apartments, they were all in the outskirts of Chinatown, along Cesar Chavez Boulevard, the major boundary between Chinatown and the rest of downtown. Some even see the Orsini development as not part of Chinatown and part of the "north downtown boundary." As Munson Kwok, one of the founding members of CHSSC who has been active in historic preservation since the 1970s, observed, those developments were "still palatable because it wasn't in the core location. But now with Blossom Plaza being literally, virtually in the heart of this core Chinatown neighborhood, . . . we can

FIGURE 12. K.G. Louie store and the Hop Sing Tong Association in Central Plaza, 2016. Photo taken by author.

FIGURE 13. Blossom Plaza, a mixed-use, mixed-income development located across from Central Plaza, 2019. Photo taken by author.

see ... major physical changes." The mass and design of these new buildings that were now in the core of Chinatown visually disrupted the current neighborhood character. They have become aesthetic symbols of gentrification and unwanted change in Chinatown.[17]

However, there were some in the community that supported the design of these new buildings. The business leaders who primarily spoke of Chinatown from a speculative perspective and wanted to further develop the neighborhood often argued that Chinatown was not viewed as a modern urban neighborhood which was hurting its economic growth. One young business leader involved with the Business Improvement District (BID) explained how Chinatown needed to modernize their look to be more aligned with both downtown and global Asian aesthetics:

> [In downtown], you have the Broad, you have the Walt Disney Concert Hall, you have MOCA ... and then you come to our side [of Cesar Chavez] and you have nothing that's architecturally interesting. And I just feel like that's not fair to Chinatown. That all this development kind of stops at this individual boundary because of the way that everything was zoned. And going back to if you actually go back to China or Taiwan or Hong Kong, I mean those cities in Asia are marvelous. ... Shouldn't we be the best of the Chinese culture and heritage and not the dumps?

Other business leaders have expressed similar sentiments of wanting Chinatown to have similar aesthetics to modern China to assert a more authentic cultural identity. Another young business leader, who was also involved with the BID, also countered the criticisms of the designs of the newer developments by critiquing how the older developments were inauthentic and meant to appeal to tourists:

> If you want to say more Chinese, what do you mean by that? ... Go to Beijing, go to Shanghai, go to Hong Kong. All their buildings look like downtown L.A. You know, they're more modern. They don't have the same Chinese pagoda architecture. That's only in movies. [chuckles] And if you want to preserve that, we have Central Plaza for that!

Their comparisons to economically powerful cities in China highlighted the precarious position of Chinatown in attracting global Chinese investment. Many urban Chinatowns have now become transnational spaces that facilitate the flow of global capital, especially from China.[18] In the 1970s, Asian capital flight led to land speculation, but business leader Wilbur Woo also felt that it led to a "false market" in Los Angeles Chinatown.[19] Since then, the overseas Chinese investment has been primarily located in the San Gabriel Valley and downtown. Chinese investors have been developing high-rise skyscrapers in downtown and contributing to what the press have called a "building boom."[20] The questioning of ethnic authenticity in the older built environment from business leaders hinted at their uncertainty and frustrations as to whether Chinatown could be a modern neighborhood and a part of the economic power of the global Chinese community.

Yet some maintained that the architecture of Chinatown's older buildings was not just a part of maintaining the local history but helped maintain a traditional Chinese identity that was slowly disappearing globally. This sentiment tended to be supported by business leaders who inherited businesses and properties but were not professionally involved in real estate development, nor did they express any speculative plans for their properties or the neighborhood in general. One second generation business and property owner in Chinatown remarked that the architecture is what continues to bring people to all urban Chinatowns:

> I think Chinatown is losing its uniqueness. . . . The only component that we wish that [these new mixed-use developments] would include is a Chinese roofline. . . . Because that is one of the few things that this Chinatown and other Chinatowns throughout the US actually have. I mean people say, "When you look at Shanghai and Beijing—now look at Hong Kong—you don't see any of this!" . . . If you take that component away, there is no more Chinese architecture left. . . . The apartments on Cesar Chavez and Broadway, Blossom [Plaza], you can have all the glass you want, all the modern stuff, just put a little of Chinese wrinkle on top. . . . And I think that's when all the Chinatowns, this Chinatown, San Francisco Chinatown, will lose their uniqueness. Then they will just blend into everything else.

Given the rapid pace of development in China, he saw Chinatown as a space of a global Chinese heritage through its architecture, which was a unique asset. While some business leaders framed the modern architecture of new developments as indicative of economic progress in Chinatown to attract new investment, others saw these designs as a homogenization of the neighborhood and loss of history that would ultimately hurt Chinatown's economy. To them, the local economy was dependent on cultural tourism that is based on Chinatown as a reflection of the historical traditions of China.

There were also variations among newer property owners about maintaining the design and architecture of Chinatown. The developers and property owners whose buildings had this modern aesthetic were purposeful in distinguishing their spaces from the older Chinatown buildings. In some cases, this was seen as disrespectful to the community. The Orsini, a mixed-use retail and market-rate apartment development that opened in the early 2000s, was a contested site, and many in the community have negative recollections of the developer and property owner, Geoffrey Palmer. During the initial stages of development, representatives for Palmer visited the CCAC board meetings. Community representatives and the public consistently critiqued its design as incongruous with Chinatown, along with Palmer having very little transparency with the community about the progress of the development. Past CCAC representatives spoke of how he disregarded almost all community requests, including minor requests, such as adding Chinese design elements to the pedestrian bridges that connected the different buildings. This was in addition to the general criticism about the symbolism of the bridge. While it arguably is to ensure pedestrians' safety along Cesar Chavez Boulevard, it is only accessible to the Orsini residents, which encouraged a further disconnect with those living in the Orsini with the larger residential community. The Orsini continues to command a striking and jarring presence along Cesar Chavez Boulevard, which is part of a major street that connects west and east Los Angeles. Its presence does signal that one may be entering a new neighborhood, but arguably not Chinatown, despite it being the first building one sees after seeing the official Chinatown neighborhood sign when traveling eastward along the boulevard.

While not considered as disconnected from the community as the Orsini, the Blossom Plaza design was also a deliberate move away from old Chinatown to an urban Chinese aesthetic. The architect, Johnson-Fain, is a prominent US-based architectural firm that has designed buildings in China. The firm partner shared that they did not want the Orientalist architecture historically used in Chinatowns and, instead, drew inspiration from their own buildings in China. He explained that they wanted the building to be more "contemporary" and were not creating a "Disneyland for young adults" in the downtown area.[21] Those outside of the Chinese American community were also problematizing the Orientalist aesthetics historically associated with urban Chinatowns. They distinguished their designs not simply as more modern, but also more authentic to a contemporary global Chinese identity. Property owners and developers were thus working with architects who were designing buildings that were aligned with their personal preferences and assumptions about Chinese and Chinese American cultural identities. Yet, it is questionable how much community input goes into these designs as the lack of local voices also raises important questions about who determines these spaces as authentic or inauthentic.

There were differences between the new corporate property owners and individual property owners moving to Chinatown in their efforts to maintain the aesthetics of Chinatown. The property owners who owned smaller properties in the neighborhood were making changes, but they also spoke about the need to preserve the architectural heritage and uniqueness of the neighborhood. One relatively newer Chinese American property owner shared that when he bought property in Central Plaza, he intended to preserve the building to maintain the cultural integrity and character of Chinatown. He often referred to himself as a "custodian" more than a property owner. In addition to preserving the original design of the building, he spoke of his "community service," as he was selective about what businesses would be housed in his property. He shared that the business does not generate profit and instead was chosen because it was "the right fit" that continued the Chinese American retail culture of the neighborhood. Despite his intentions, he also grappled with what he saw as Chinatown being stagnant and said that he could envision Chinatown as similar to the Arts District because it had a growing presence of creatives, but that some elements of a Chinatown culture and aesthetic had to be maintained so that it would remain a distinct neighborhood.

This sentiment to preserve the older architectural aesthetics also extended to some of the non-Chinese American property owners. Alexis Readinger was one of the newer property owners in West Plaza who also became active in the BID. She jokingly identified as "that White girl" in the community and had no prior attachments to Chinatown before moving to the neighborhood. She shared that she was drawn to the architectural character and design of the building as a live-work space. Readinger expressed a protective attitude toward the neighborhood, and remarked, "How do you preserve a lot of aspects in the neighborhood? 'Cause it won't be as charming if it flips too much." Munson Kwok, who critiqued the corporate property owners for creating massive, imposing buildings, also noted this trend in which Chinatown's aesthetics may be appealing to newer stakeholders who do not identify as Chinese American. He noted that "the people who are falling in love with [this low-density neighborhood character] . . . maybe increasingly, they aren't all Chinese." Despite perspectives about non-Chinese Americans and other perceived "outsiders" wanting to change the neighborhood, these newer individual property owners did recognize the assets of Chinatown that made it a unique place in the city, especially within downtown. These individuals, labeled as *gentrifiers*, express a desire for authenticity in the neighborhoods they move into, and they can become preservationists who proactively maintain the older cultural characteristics of these spaces.[22] Readinger, as well as a few other newer property owners, have been credited by community leaders as making concerted efforts in preserving the older building character, while also renovating them to both modernize and meet current building standards, which past property owners did not necessarily do. They were now tenuously part of the efforts to preserve the character of the neighborhood.

The post-1965 Chinese immigrants and refugees from Southeast Asia also developed major cultural monuments in Chinatown that both maintained and disrupted the traditional Chinatown aesthetic, while also establishing a sense of belonging for themselves. One of the most notable changes in Chinatown was the establishment of major temples, whereas before the major religious institutions were Christian churches, including the First Chinese Baptist Church and the Chinese United Methodist Church.[23] The Thien Hau Temple (see Figure 14), was a Taoist temple established in the 1980s by the Cà Mau Association of America, a mutualist association that represents immigrants and refugees who have ties to the Cà Mau region of Vietnam. The temple is a major cultural monument in Chinatown and has the traditional architecture of Asian temples, which was one of the historical influences for the Chinatown aesthetic. In contrast to the older Chinatown aesthetics, which incorporated Chinese elements to European-influenced American architecture, this temple, as well as the Guanggong temple established by the Teo-Chew Association, does not blend these cultures to assert a presence. Their visibility in the neighborhood indicated an important turn in Chinatown's contemporary history. The cultural practices in these temples were not new in the Chinese American community; there were shrines and altars in mutualist associations and people's homes. However, the notable physical presence of temples reflected the embrace of multiculturalism in the post-1965 context, which allowed for these institutions to have a distinct and major public presence in the neighborhood that did not necessarily have to conform to an assimilated aesthetic. The Thien Hau Temple is now considered a major neighborhood attraction and hosts a Lunar New Year's Eve event that has become heavily publicized and draws large crowds to the neighborhood during this time.

FIGURE 14. Thien Hau Temple, June 2023. Photo taken by the author.

Other monuments from this contemporary wave of immigration have a more modern-looking design, contributing to the debates about asserting an authentic Chinese identity in Chinatown. The Teo-Chew Association was the major financier for the Chinatown Gateway, a major neighborhood landmark built in 2003 with the backing of the CRA. Other donors included the Southern California Fukienese Association, CCBA, and the Chinese Chamber of Commerce, but the Teo-Chew Association provided most of the funding and leadership. The establishment of these gateways in Los Angeles and other cities were important placemaking markers that identify the space as Chinatown, distinct from the rest of the downtown neighborhood. These gateways were also often a reference to the traditional gateways that serve as entrances to villages in China. However, many of these gateways are relatively recent constructions built in the post-1965 era almost a century after Chinatowns were built as a part of contemporary cultural tourism and placemaking efforts.[24] They were aligned with the tradition of self-orientalism and cultural tourism in Chinatown, distinguishing the neighborhood as an exotic but palatable place of difference in the city to attract visitors and tourists.[25] They have also been built with the support from

FIGURE 15. Los Angeles Chinatown Gateway on Cesar Chavez Boulevard, which is the southern entrance to Chinatown, 2023. Photo taken by author.

cities in China, indicating expectations that Chinatown should have a role in strengthening transnational links between the United States and China. Yet, the Los Angeles Chinatown Gateway, which was designed by a Chinese American of Chaozhou heritage, is a modern, minimalist design (see Figure 15). Some in the community have criticized the aesthetic, including some Teo-Chew Association leaders, who thought that it should have recalled more of the traditional Chinese designs, similar to other urban Chinatowns. Thus, even when the aesthetics and design originate from Chinese and Chinese Americans, the community still must grapple with whether Chinatown should express a "traditional" Chinese aesthetic that speaks to the heritage of Chinatown or have a modern design to evolve Chinatown along contemporary global trends.

LEGACY BUSINESSES AS SITES OF HERITAGE

As historic designations and a cultural center in Chinatown never materialized throughout the decades, other spaces emerged as informal sites of heritage. In particular, ethnic businesses have become important cultural anchors in the neighborhood. Chinatown has experienced waves of changes, but with the exception of a few chain stores, it has also remained a neighborhood of small businesses, specifically one that is home to generations of ethnic and immigrant-owned businesses. These businesses have the potential to be cultural assets for Chinatown, not necessarily because they are competitive in the current economy or because of any specific political intent to maintain an ethnic culture. They were and continue to be everyday sites where people across generations develop sentimental attachments and a sense of belonging in Chinatown that can resist gentrification.[26] As Natalia Molina argues, because ethnic businesses are one of many sites of everyday culture in the neighborhood, the loss of these businesses contributes to a cultural loss in the community.[27]

Community leaders and the media have labeled these sites as "legacy businesses," a term that indicates that they have been in Chinatown for several decades and have held significance for residents and visitors across generations. The older generation of legacy businesses were part of the New Chinatown development. This includes K.G. Louie, a souvenir gift store in Central Plaza, and Phoenix Bakery, which was originally in Central Plaza but moved to a location around the corner from the plaza. Both of these shops are the oldest Chinese American family-owned businesses in the city. They continue to be operated by the second and third generation of family members, but unlike their parents, operating the business is not their primary job or profession. Ron Louie, who was born and raised in Chinatown and shares the current ownership of K.G. Louie with his siblings, was an architect. Even though he moved to Pasadena, he explained that he never "left Chinatown" in that he and his siblings still manage the store. In contrast, Phoenix Bakery, which continued to be managed by the Chan family, has been able to expand their business and employ individuals outside of their family to operate the business. Ken Chan, the youngest son of original owner and prominent Chinatown business leader Fung Chow Chan, explained that like the Louie family, many in his generation became professionals and only a few family members remain fully committed to the business as their primary job.

Despite experiencing social and residential mobility, both Ken Chan and Ron Louie expressed hesitation in closing their establishments. Their generation's ongoing presence and management of their shops demonstrated that these small businesses have become sites of heritage, both personally and for the community. They shared that the businesses symbolized their parents' hard work that allowed for their generation to have a better life. Chan explained that "if we ever closed . . . then all the hard work that my parents, my uncle did was basically gone for nothing. . . . So, we think it's still a thriving business; it just needs to be tweaked here and there a little bit more." While Louie did not rely on their store as his family's primary source of income, he explained a similar motivation among his siblings to keep the store:

> We all thank my mom and dad. If it wasn't for them, none of us would be [successful]. I'm an architect. My brother's a teacher. Another one is an engineer. If it wasn't for our parents, we wouldn't have had any of this stuff. And so that's why we're keeping the store there. It is to just keep the tradition. Because none of us really live on the store or business. It's just doing it to keep the family name going and tradition.

Louie and Chan's experiences were not unique. Among those who were a part of this generation of small business families, they spoke about working in the shops as a part of their daily routine and family obligations. But they were not necessarily trained to be future entrepreneurs and shop owners. As first-generation, family-owned immigrant businesses, these spaces were primarily to help ensure that the next generation would have better life opportunities, which did not necessarily mean that they would inherit the business. Yet sentimental attachment and family legacies still mattered for the next generation, regardless of upward mobility, and was why these older establishments continued to be in Chinatown.

These legacy businesses also hold sentimental value for generations of customers, some of whom do not identify as Chinese Americans. Ken Chan explained that while Phoenix Bakery may not appeal to recent Chinese immigrants, it has a loyal customer base that consists of people who frequently visited Chinatown in the past:

> Our customer base is basically more of the Americanized ABCs [American Born Chinese], more *lo-fan* Caucasian, more Hispanic. . . . But we still have people coming in from way up from Inland Empire, from all the way down from Orange County. I mean they still drive that distance. . . . The grandkids coming in and say, My grandparents say, "It has to be a Phoenix cake." They don't want a Costco cake. I'm driving fifteen miles one way, and my grandparents insist I get it.

These legacy businesses remained important destinations for the older generation of Chinese Americans and tourists. They were a part of family traditions and appealed to a sense of familiarity and nostalgia that was now being passed down to a younger generation.

While these legacy businesses have become sites of cultural heritage that were helping to sustain Chinatown, the lack of entrepreneurship within the next generation led to criticisms from other business leaders about how they may be stalling the local economy. Some business leaders associated with the BID explained that because the later generation family members keep their properties but do not necessarily use them as their primary source of income, they were less motivated to innovate and keep up with the competitive urban economy. In contrast, community activists who work with the residential and business tenants have pointed out the possibilities of the "changing of hands" of older commercial properties. Several community leaders spoke about how the younger generation who will inherit these spaces will most likely have little interest in holding on to them, being too emotionally and physically distant from Chinatown. As these older businesses begin to leave, Chinatown will also lose spaces that have come to hold much sentimental and historical value for the Chinese American community as well as generations of local visitors.

In addition to the older legacy businesses, new ones that were established in the 1970s through the mid-1990s also have become important sites for both newer immigrants and the younger generation in the neighborhood. They represented the arrival of ethnic Chinese immigrants and refugees from Vietnam, Cambodia, and other Southeast Asian countries. They were also different from the older ethnic businesses, especially the ones in Central and West Plazas that were specifically designed to appeal to tourists and assert an assimilated, modern identity of Chinese Americans in the 1930s. While these new immigrant businesses still appealed to tourists, they were primarily community-serving businesses that sold a range of goods at cheap prices, including apparel, homewares, toys, and jewelry. Some of them were also swap meets in which vendors operated in densely packed stalls that were spread across several buildings in Chinatown's commercial core, including Saigon Plaza, Dynasty Center, The Shop, and Chinatown Plaza (Figure 16). When they first opened, these businesses were described as so densely packed that their goods were "piles on tables" that "spill into pedestrian corridors," creating an image of disorganization that some of the older Chinese American business owners critiqued.[28] Some associated with the BID accused these businesses of creating unsafe conditions. Thus, the BID was agnostic, and at times supportive, of the displacement pressures

FIGURE 16. Swap meets in Saigon Plaza, 2018. Photo taken by author.

facing these businesses. This perception of disorder disrupted the image of an orderly, clean community that BIDs often try to convey in their marketing of the neighborhood.[29]

This newer generation of legacy businesses were the most vulnerable ones to forced displacement in Chinatown. The owners of these establishments have cited the demographic changes within the neighborhood, along with the competition from the San Gabriel Valley, as impacting their customer base and operations.[30] A 2017 article in the *Los Angeles Times* highlighted how the loss of these immigrant-owned businesses would not just have an economic impact for the business owners and customers, but a cultural and sentimental impact that would threaten a sense of belonging for both visitors and residents in Chinatown. The article noted how customers, many of whom were of different Asian ethnicities, expressed a sentiment of feeling at "home" when walking through the swap meets:

> Even though there are no Filipino shops [in Saigon Plaza], Lizette Dejesus, 38, of West Covina said the meets make her feel as if she's back in Manila shopping in the open-air Divisoria Market. On a recent weekday, she sipped iced sugarcane juice as she browsed the markets with her children, one of whom was clutching a new toy, a shiny plastic gun Dejesus bought for $17. "It's way cheaper than you can find anywhere else," Dejesus said. "And it kind of reminds you of home."[31]

Similarly, some younger Chinese and Asian Americans who grew up visiting Chinatown in the 1990s onward have significant attachments to these post-1965 immigrant spaces and businesses. They often see them as their "legacy businesses." Sophat Phea, a Chinatown resident who has been involved with SEACA and CCED, spoke about how he grew up shopping in these businesses. Phea mentioned how he never left Chinatown when he was a youth, and these specific spaces in the neighborhood were parts of the "small box" defining his family life in Chinatown. He and his family lived and only shopped in Chinatown. Another young Chinese Vietnamese American whose family settled in the San Gabriel Valley explained that she would only visit that area of Chinatown and did not visit Central and West Plaza until she became more active in the community. She spoke of that area as being unfamiliar. As she and her family walked north along Broadway and arrived at College Street, which is where Central Plaza is located half a block north, her family would not "cross" to the other side. She also shared that these swap meets were the places her family would visit for "bargain shopping." Her mother saw these stores as reminiscent of old Hong Kong and distinct from ones in the San Gabriel Valley. While criticized for their "disorderly" appearance, these swap meets also brought a different type of cultural authenticity and familiarity to Chinatown that reflected the contemporary urban local outdoor markets in Asia.

The feeling of authenticity associated with these swap meets and small businesses contrasted with the authenticity arguments that other business leaders used when advocating for more contemporary building designs that were aligned with a modern, global Chinese identity. These places were for the local community, but they also attracted immigrants and refugees living in other neighborhoods who saw these places as familiar sites. The "disorderly" design and activities were comforting, not disruptive. These new businesses have become spaces for the assertion and maintenance of a Chinese diasporic community identity for many of the post-1965 immigrants and refugees.[32] Though the shops may lack the defining architectural markers of Chinatown seen in Central and West Plazas and the longer local history, they have become important spaces of everyday use and interactions that define the contemporary neighborhood culture.

As these spaces were now sites of everyday culture for those who frequently visit and live in Chinatown, there was increased recognition and activism to center these spaces in both economic development and preservation efforts. As a part of the Angel Walks LA program that promotes historical walking tours, the city installed signs in front of major neighborhood sites. In addition to places like Central Plaza, Phoenix Bakery, and CHSSC, there is a sign in front of the Dynasty Center as it symbolized the post-1965 community and businesses of Chinatown. Recognizing the post-1965 neighborhood history and their importance for the working-class residents of Chinatown, CCED expanded their definition of legacy businesses to include these relatively newer businesses in their advocacy efforts. However, unlike Phoenix Bakery or K.G. Louie, most of these newer business owners and swap meet operators do not own the buildings in which they are housed, and property ownership changes were occurring. Redcar Properties, which was represented on the BID board, was slowly purchasing the properties in that area, including Dynasty Center in 2021. These changes led many to wonder not just if and when the businesses would be displaced, but also how they planned to assemble their different lots for development that might further change the cultural character of Chinatown. It remains uncertain if many of these post-1965 businesses will survive and continue to be legacy businesses and cultural institutions or will instead be a faded memory of a specific generation who lived and visited Chinatown.

SUBCULTURES AND THE CREATIVE
CLASS IN THE PLAZAS

As the cities in the San Gabriel Valley continue to overshadow Chinatown as the major economic and residential centers for the Chinese American community, business leaders have developed new cultural strategies to try to economically sustain Chinatown. The San Gabriel Valley was not only home to newer ethnic businesses, but it also was home to many of the upscale chains from Taiwan, Hong Kong, and China, such as Din Tai Feng,

Haidilao, and various boba tea shops, as well as a popular night market, 626 Night Market, which hosts Asian food vendors. Rather than trying to keep up with the San Gabriel Valley by offering similar ethnic businesses and activities, business leaders have attempted to carve out a distinct identity that instead appealed to a creative class aesthetic, but one that is defined and driven by Asian Americans, whether as business owners or property owners. A term that was introduced by Richard Florida, *the creative class*, refers to artists, students, and others in professional and creative industries who have high levels of education, as well as cultural and social capital, but may not always have relatively high incomes.[33] While an intersection of urban policies and economic restructuring have contributed to the emergence of the creative class as contemporary drivers of urban growth, their presence is often a signal that a neighborhood is gentrifying.[34]

These trends to appeal to a creative class have impacted Chinatown, as there has been a shift in cultural activities and businesses to attract creative entrepreneurs and creative class consumers. These shifts have been supported by the BID and were located in the major commercial plazas in Chinatown within the BID designation, whose owners sit on the BID board, including Central Plaza, West Plaza, Mandarin Plaza, and Far East Plaza. While these new events and businesses may contribute to a rearticulation of a cultural identity and heritage of Chinatown that situates it as a modern ethnic space defined and led by Asian Americans, it also has the potential to contribute to cultural displacement of the working-class heritage that also defined both the ethnic and neighborhood culture.

The Music and Art Gallery Scene in Chinatown

Central and West Plazas are the historical and cultural anchors of Chinatown that serve as ongoing sites of cultural tourism. However, these two plazas have also been sites for counterculture and subculture activities since the 1970s. Most notably, Central Plaza was home to several underground music scenes. In the late 1970s, several Chinatown restaurants in the plaza served as music venues for pioneering West Coast punk bands including the Bags, the Alley Cats, and the Germs.[35] This included Hong Kong Café, owned by Bill Hong, a prominent and respected business leader who once acted as president of the Chinese Chamber of Commerce and supported social services in the neighborhood, as he also offered his restaurant space for senior programs. Madame Wong was another site in the plaza, which was owned by Esther Wong, who became a prominent figure in the punk scene. She was known as a "godmother of punk" but also was derogatorily referred to as a "dragon lady" by musicians and the media because of how she strictly operated her venue. This history continued throughout the 1990s and early 2000s, but with the hip hop music scene. Angelica Lopez Moyes, a Castelar Elementary School parent and representative for the Historic Cultural Neighborhood Council (HCNC), was a waitress at Grand Star in Central Plaza when it hosted an underground hip hop club, Firecracker, and recalled it as an "unintentional revitalization" of Chinatown, as people converged to the area because they were drawn to the music. Thus, while Chinatown was seen as declining and possibly becoming irrelevant to Chinese Americans as the San Gabriel Valley became a new center for the community, these Chinatown business owners were finding new ways to sustain their businesses, which included appealing to an underground culture.

This history of underground and alternative culture in Chinatown—and specifically the older plazas—continued to shape the interest of newcomers to Chinatown, especially those in creative industries. Alexis Readinger, a property owner in West Plaza who owned a hospitality and architectural design firm, spoke of her past and present neighbors, which included Zack De la Rocha, the lead singer of the political rock band Rage Against the Machine, and Mark Mothersbaugh, who is most well-known as a member of the 1980s new wave band Devo. Another musician, Skrillex, who is a DJ popular in the electronic dance music scene, also leased a nearby space that was the site of an abandoned gas station. It was the site of a clothing popup store and would also host night events. This space also neighbored the CHSSC houses, which served as not just a stark contrast of old and new, but also demonstrated how Chinatown continues to be a home for disparate cultures, whether ethnic cultures or countercultures.

This history of Chinatown highlights the complexities of how other subcultures engaged with Chinatown's outsider status as a non-White racialized space that was also defined by working-class culture. Since Chinatown was outside the mainstream, and during this time the city deemed the neighborhood a "slum" to justify redevelopment, it appealed to the punk and underground music culture in its inadvertent alignment with anticorporate and antiestablishment politics. Fiona Ngô argues that Chinatown became a site to negotiate the meanings of punk and alternative culture, including what is authentic versus corporate and manufactured.[36] However, this meaning making among punk and underground musicians was done in a place that was home to a historically marginalized and overlooked community. Their presence in Chinatown arguably helped to support Chinatown in a way that did not forcibly displace businesses or residents, but it also expanded and contributed to a rearticulation of the neighborhood culture, especially for outsiders. As the underground music scene became more visible and commercialized, as evidenced by popular musicians moving into the neighborhood, this cultural production and meaning making potentially threatened the neighborhood's cultural authenticity, which has historically been defined by the residents, workers, and activists in the community.

Chinatown also became a part of the city's art gallery scene in the late 1990s. During this time, art galleries on Chungking Road in West Plaza began to replace the old Chinese trinket stores and vacant storefronts. Community leaders often cite these art galleries as the first wave of contemporary gentrification in Chinatown.[37] They fit the model of many gentrification narratives that identify artists as the first to move into places that have been disinvested and to "revitalize" the neighborhood.[38] Mandarin Plaza, which is across from Central Plaza, is home to some of these art galleries and studios, but their presence was often invisible as many of the studios continued to look like vacant storefronts, appealing to an impoverished aesthetic that signals a sense of neighborhood authenticity.[39] The art galleries were also not consistently open. They opened their spaces and hosted events in the plaza to support the broader art gallery scene, not necessarily to be a part of the neighborhood-based activities and events. Because of this, many in the community saw these artists as being so separate from the community and not having much of an economic or social impact on Chinatown beyond their individual businesses and plazas. However, their isolation from the rest of Chinatown unquestionably contributes to fragmentation within the neighborhood community.

In 2018, two decades after their initial arrival, the art galleries became contested sites again as increasing media attention was given to neighboring Boyle Heights, a Mexican American neighborhood also experiencing gentrification. During this time, community activists, particularly from the group Defend Boyle Heights, held artwashing protests to resist the art galleries in their neighborhood, recognizing that this was a marker of gentrification and raising concerns similar to community members in Chinatown about the art galleries being disconnected from the working-class immigrant community. However, there was also a more direct connection with Chinatown because one of the Boyle Heights art gallery owners, Wendy Yao, also owned Ooga

Booga in Central Plaza, an independent book and music store. Yao eventually left Boyle Heights amid these protests, but her connection to Chinatown, as well as the visibility of these protests in the local media, contributed to the issue reemerging in Chinatown. CCED was at the forefront of critiquing the art galleries and similar businesses that catered to the creative class. In April 2018, several members attended an event at Public School, an independent bookstore housed between the art galleries on Chungking Road. CCED members took the stage and critiqued their presence, explaining how these spaces were contributing to gentrification in Chinatown. While this was aligned with the ongoing anti-gentrification activism of CCED, their turn toward addressing artwashing also highlighted the tenuousness of their organizing in the community. CCED was displaying a strong act of political solidarity with Defend Boyle Heights and other anti-gentrification groups across Los Angeles. It also came at a time almost two decades after the art galleries emerged, with some older members of CCED expressing uncertainty whether this was the best way to address the art galleries given their now long-term presence in the neighborhood. The hesitance raised fundamental questions about how anti-gentrification organizers address the different waves of gentrification coexisting within their neighborhoods.

Chinatown Summer Nights and the Upscaling of Cultural Events

In addition to housing art galleries and other new businesses, the plazas have been the anchoring sites for cultural events. Cultural events have been critical to Chinatown's identity and local economy since the formation of Old Chinatown. The annual lunar new year event, the Golden Dragon Parade, first started in 1899 and continues to be an important event in the neighborhood, drawing both the Chinese American community and tourists to Chinatown.[40] Given the importance of cultural events, the CRA focused on these activities as a part of their economic development strategy for Chinatown. In 2010, with the Project for Public Spaces, they developed a plan for Chinatown that focused on these older plazas as an anchoring point for cultural activities and events that could promote tourism.

As a part of this new plan, the CRA partnered with the BID and owners in Central Plaza to develop Chinatown Summer Nights, which began that same year. The event was a part of the summer nights programming for local national public radio station, KCRW, and included a live band stage, beer gardens, and food trucks, as well as family activities in the early evening

FIGURE 17. Chinatown Summer Nights live band stage and beer garden in Central Plaza, 2015. Photo taken by author.

and a late-night dance stage (see Figure 17). Chinatown Summer Nights was part of a rebranding of the plazas to create a "lively public multi-use destination that brings people back again and again."[41] This strategy recognized these plazas as assets that continue to define Chinatown as a unique space and to draw tourism into the area. During my fieldwork, Chinatown Summer Nights was a popular neighborhood event that appeared to successfully bring people to Chinatown, especially younger people. The BID was especially active in promoting this event in their social media, and the event was symbolic of how their approaches to economic revitalization in the neighborhood often led to promoting gentrification.

Chinatown Summer Nights has brought mixed feelings in the community, highlighting tensions about who precisely benefits from these events. Some of the property owners at Central Plaza have praised the event for bringing in business on weekend evenings; older business owners shared that it reminded them of Chinatown in the 1950s when it had an active nightlife. However, others have criticized these events as only helping certain businesses, some of which were not even from the community. Food trucks were only present for the event and competed with the brick-and-mortar restaurants in Chinatown. As the event is localized to Central and West Plazas and has since expanded to neighboring Bamboo and Mandarin Plazas, other plazas and stores have not necessarily engaged with the event to help their businesses. Notably, the swap meets in Saigon Plaza and Dynasty Center did not extend their hours past 6:00 p.m. to align with the event, which starts at 5:00 p.m. and lasts until midnight. Some associated with the BID argued that it is a personal business decision of shop owners to not engage with these events, citing that, in general, they do not have long-term plans for their businesses to compete with the changes in Chinatown. But given that Chinatown Summer Nights caters to a relatively affluent demographic, these business owners may also feel that they are unable to participate because of the cultural and socioeconomic differences of their typical customers, working-class immigrant families and seniors.

This newer contemporary event also had a ripple effect on other types of cultural programming. Central Plaza is also the hub for the Chinese New Year and Autumn Moon Festival activities, which are the major ethnic festivals in Chinatown. As it has become a popular event, the activities and programming of Chinatown Summer Nights, including the live band stage and beer gardens, are present in the long-standing heritage events. The BID comanages these events and thus is using the same creative class strategies that are used for the nonethnic festival and heritage events to draw a younger audience to Chinatown. The addition of these newer elements to the older festivals raises important questions about the upscaling of these heritage events that may lead to a cultural erasure and displacement of Chinatown. As Brandi Summers argues about gentrification and culture, aesthetics that originated from within a racialized community can become neutralized through gentrification to promote an aesthetically pleasing promotion of diversity, thus making it easier for consumption.[42] These newer changes to the ethnic and heritage events, which were already used toward cultural tourism to attract co-ethnic visitors, was a part of this process to still promote Chinatown as a site of ethnic heritage and diversity, but one that specifically appeals to an upwardly mobile, creative class population.

Appealing to the (Asian American) Foodie Scene

Restaurants have always been a defining part of Chinatown's economic base that have served residents, the ethnic community, and tourists.[43]

Since the 2010s, Chinatown has become a destination for new restaurateurs to open their new businesses. These new restaurants have received media attention and continued the tradition of restaurants as vital to the neighborhood's economic base for tourism. With the growing popularity of these new restaurants, the identity of Chinatown was shifting to cater to a contemporary foodie scene that did not necessarily rely on the traditional Chinese Cantonese restaurants as these restaurants served diverse cuisines. Many were still owned by Asian Americans, but they specifically appealed to the trends and tastes of young, upwardly mobile consumers, which further contributed to an upscaling of Chinatown's amenities and businesses.

While non-Asian American restaurateurs that served non-Asian food established businesses in Chinatown, such as Little Jewel of New Orleans and Howlin' Ray's Nashville Chicken, Asian American restaurateurs also found a home in Chinatown. The first of these new restaurateurs in Chinatown was Roy Choi, a Korean American celebrity chef who opened Chego, a fusion Korean-Mexican restaurant. He was followed by Filipino American Alvin Cailan, head chef of Egg Slut in Grand Market Plaza in Downtown Los Angeles, who opened Ramen Champ, a restaurant dedicated to Japanese soup noodle bowls. Filipino American brothers Chad and Chase Valencia also opened Lasa, a contemporary Filipino American restaurant. Eddie Huang, a Chinese American from Taiwan who is famous for creating the sitcom *Fresh Off the Boat*, opened Baohaus, which served contemporary variations of *baos*, or Chinese bread rolls. All these restaurants are multicultural revisions of traditional Asian food and dishes. They were part of the rebranding of Chinatown's restaurant identity toward a contemporary multiethnic cuisine. Yet these young Asian American entrepreneurs who were part of that rebranding also became the target of gentrification debates in the neighborhood during my fieldwork.

Many of these Asian American restaurateurs have found a home in Far East Plaza, a commercial plaza dedicated to restaurants (see Figure 18). The plaza has a history of bringing in new types of cuisine that were not Cantonese-based, which is the cuisine and culture historically associated with Chinatown. This included Mandarin Deli, which has since moved to Monterey Park in the San Gabriel Valley. These new restaurants that opened in the 2010s were thus arguably part of the Far East Plaza's history of introducing new cuisines to both Chinatown and the city. Instead of reflecting the regional differences in China, these newer restaurants in Far East Plaza also reflected generational differences in cuisine. George Yu, the executive

FIGURE 18. Sign on the side of Far East Plaza advertising new and old businesses, including Wing Hop Fung (closed in 2016) and Chego, the restaurant owned by Roy Choi (closed in 2019), 2018. Photo taken by author.

director of the BID and whose company, Macco investments, owns and manages Far East Plaza, shared that he was selective in choosing these tenants for his plaza. He also encouraged other commercial property owners to provide their spaces to this specific type of young Asian American entrepreneur. Yu explained:

Fifteen years ago, Leonard Chan [Chinese American entrepreneur from Orange County] would not be back here investing in [Apiary Food Hall at Jia Apartments]. Every penny he has in a 10,000-square foot space that's going to employ, I don't know how many people. The Wu Sisters [of Building

Block Design Studio in Mandarin Plaza] are not going to be here. And I'm just specifically thinking of Chinese [Americans]. David [Chang, Korean American restauranteur from New York] is not going to be here. . . . I love seeing the next generation . . . with their friends—of all ethnicities—hanging out in Chinatown. They're not here because of CCBA, CAM, Chinatown Service Center. I can go on and on. They're here because there's some something for them to do and they want to be here. And without that evolution, these Chinese Americans will not be coming back. So, then what?

Yu saw the "return" of young Asian American entrepreneurs and consumers as critical to the revitalization of Chinatown that will maintain it as an important ethnic space and destination. He, and by extension the BID, were centering these Asian Americans in creative class industries as both the producer and consumer of Chinatown. These restaurants were heavily publicized by the BID through their social media, as well as through local media, such as *Downtown News*, *LA Weekly*, and *LA Eater*. They also received mainstream attention, as many of these Asian American restaurateurs are well known within the industry. By opening their restaurants in the neighborhood, Yu and other business leaders saw potential in attracting people to Chinatown who may otherwise not visit and promoting diversity in the neighborhood, a goal that they have for Chinatown, as explained in the previous chapter.

The new restaurants and retail were a sign that Asian Americans were "reinvesting" in Chinatown. Yet, through this reinvestment, they were also modernizing Chinatown into a neighborhood that centered the cultural tastes of a specific segment of young, upwardly mobile Asian Americans. The business changes in Chinatown reflect a broader trend among Asian Americans' consumerism and professionalism within the creative class identity. In Richard Florida's ongoing theorizing about the rise of the creative class, he notes that Asian Americans are heavily represented in the creative class industries.[44] This trend can be seen as a repositioning of Asian Americans as cool trendsetters and "misfits" in creative class industries, including restaurants, who defy model minority stereotypes.[45] These restaurateurs and chefs challenge stereotypes of Asian Americans seeking traditional upper-middle- class professions, such as lawyers and doctors, that are associated with the model minority, by returning to what is normally seen as a type of working-class labor. However, they are noticeably distinct from the immigrant restaurant workers and cooks who have historically defined part of the Chinatown and ethnic economy. They are engaging in work that upscales these industries, which have been critical to defining not just the local economy of Chinatown, but an economy that working-class immigrants and refugees, who at times, experience exploitation, continue to rely on.[46] Additionally, as they are branded as destination restaurants that follow culinary trends and not necessarily everyday, community-serving spaces, these new restaurants are less likely to become spaces that locals frequently visit and engage in everyday cultural production, akin to the legacy businesses in Chinatown. This shift in the restaurant culture in Chinatown thus has the potential to contribute to economic and cultural displacement. The class and labor disparities in the neighborhood are not always addressed by these business changes, which ultimately reinforce the model minority tropes of Chinese and Asian Americans.

The positioning of these new restaurateurs as integral to sustaining the neighborhood has been a precarious endeavor in asserting and developing a shared sense of ethnic community belonging. Many of these Asian American entrepreneurs had limited to no prior familial or sentimental claims to Chinatown. Yet, as Erica Maria Cheung argues, these young Asian American restauranters who have limited ties to Chinatown were emphasizing their racialized identity to invoke discourses of authenticity in their culinary work as a means to claim their right to be in the neighborhood as co-ethnic cultural producers.[47] Furthermore, the BID provided a space for them to assert their claims of belonging in Chinatown. Despite a shared ethnic and panethnic identity and the support from local business leaders, Chinatown's shift away from Cantonese restaurants, a major anchor and reason why the community and tourists visited Chinatown in the past, was an indication for many older community leaders that Chinatown was continuing to lose its distinct ethnic identity.

CCED directly criticized the Asian American restaurateurs' commitment to the neighborhood. In contrast to George Yu's perspective, a younger activist in CCED explained their ambivalence toward these new entrepreneurs:

> I sort of suspend the judgment because, okay, they're Asian American . . . but I think there's something to be said about thinking about the community that's there already. . . . I think the commitment for me is thinking about how to build power for folks who may not understand how things are working.

Further adding to the critiques of their lack of engagement were observations that these entrepreneurs were also inconsistent in how they built community relationships in the different neighborhoods where their businesses were located. When he first opened Chego, Roy Choi shared in the media his respect for Chinatown and wanting to integrate with the legacy businesses in the area.[48] Yet, as another CCED member pointed out, there were notable differences with how Choi engaged with other low-income racialized communities when he started new businesses in the early 2010s. She explained:

> When Roy Choi opened his restaurant in Inglewood [a predominantly Black city], he deliberately tried to emphasize that, "I'm doing it for the community. I want to provide healthier food." . . . But when he opened Chego, he didn't do that for Chinatown. And I kind of feel it's really contradictory to say, "I want to help this community, but then this community I'm in, that I'm not doing anything to really get involved or give back to the community." And to me it's super hypocritical to do that. . . . You don't see him coming to Chinatown and actually meeting with other groups in Chinatown [other than the BID] and saying, "What can I do to help improve things here?"

When newcomers move into Chinatown, a place that represents the history of marginalization among Asian Americans, which is often overlooked and has historically been systematically erased, they may lack an initial understanding and critical engagement with that history and its impact on the current community. This disregard can contribute to how the neighborhood and ethnic culture is being commodified, homogenized, and used toward gentrification. For community activists, this may feel even more hypocritical when Asian Americans lack this engagement in Chinatown. As these Asian American entrepreneurs cannot disentangle themselves from their shared racialized and ethnic identity with the rest of the community, there is an expectation that their actions should serve the community, especially as they are championed by the BID and business leaders as critical to sustaining Chinatown as an Asian American space. By 2020 both Choi and Huang's businesses had left Chinatown, which has fueled the ongoing criticisms that these young Asian American entrepreneurs have a limited understanding and commitment to Chinatown. As of 2022, some of the newer business owners have since formed a collective in response to the criticisms that they have received from CCED to reflect and find possible ways to build better bridges with the community.

COUNTERING THE YOUNG ASIAN AMERICAN GENTRIFIER IMAGE: CULTURAL PRODUCTION AS POLITICAL ENGAGEMENT

Gentrification scholars have observed how newcomers in a community are often in search of an abstract sense of cultural authenticity, which paradoxically leads to the gentrification and cultural loss of the neighborhood.[49] However, these arguments are complicated when considering spaces like Chinatown, which include co-ethnics who are often "returning" to the community, motivated to connect with a personal and community heritage. There were some who primarily see Chinatown as a site for economic opportunity, especially as a relatively cheaper downtown-adjacent neighborhood. For other young Chinese and Asian Americans, this search for authenticity was also more politicized, with a goal to use their artistic and creative skills to build community capacity that addressed social inequities. They were engaging in cultural work that sought to respect the heritage of Chinatown while also recognizing and celebrating how it is a community in constant change.

As Chinatown experienced its first wave of contemporary gentrification in the 1990s with the establishment of the art galleries in West Plaza, there was a group of Asian American artists who were a part of the art gallery scene that actively grappled with gentrification. Steve Wong, a US-born Chinese American artist who was a curator for CAM during the time of the fieldwork, routinely visited Chinatown during his youth and was one of the new property owners in West Plaza during this time. Wong was part of a group of Asian American artists that formed a short-lived group, the Bamboo Collective, in the early 2000s. He explained how they wanted to create a counternarrative to the art gallery scene that was dominated by White artists with economic motivations:

> We tried to start this kind of momentum of not only just White artists and gallerists being in Chinatown but Asian Americans. And so, I really had this vision of creating Chinatown as a place where young people would want to come back, that it would be this cool hip creative place. "Look there's a group of Asian Americans trying to make kind of this cool creative space that's different from the galleries." But then we were [also] aware and conscious of displacement and gentrification.

Bamboo Collective was a way to assert an Asian American presence in the art scene, a scene that was predominantly a White space. But they purposely asserted a politicized presence that was racialized and reflective about their possible role in gentrification.

Through his work with CAM, Wong also developed an exhibit that displayed Chinatown postcards from Castelar students and tourists who wrote on the backside about what Chinatown meant to them. He explained that the exhibit was to show the "symbiotic relationship between the outside and community" in which Chinatown is both a space for both tourists and residents, while trying to question the tourism identity ingrained in Chinatown. He explained that writing on the postcard, rather than keeping them pristine, would "de-commodify a commodity of postcard[s]," contributing to an overall critique about the commodification of Chinatown. Wong deliberately engaged in cultural productions that helped to center community perspectives and experiences, especially the voices of local youth. These types of activities also helped to build their political consciousness about community issues.

Other Chinese Americans were also leveraging the different cultural histories of Chinatown to activate across generations. Martin Wong, who was the founder and editor of *Giant Robot*, an Asian American pop culture magazine, became politically engaged in Chinatown as a parent at Castelar Elementary School, as mentioned in the previous chapter. In addition to being actively involved in resisting the co-location of the school, he and his partner, Wendy Lau, also organized Save Music in Chinatown to help fundraise for the school's music program. These efforts included punk rock concerts held in Grand Star at Central Plaza, honoring the 1970s music history of the neighborhood while also providing benefits to the local community. Wong and Lau incorporated DIY punk culture with Chinatown youth culture, which can be seen in the design of one of the fundraising flyers (see Figure 19). When discussing his contributions to the community as someone with a media and arts background, Wong shared his appreciation for the distinct role Chinatown had in local music history. He enthusiastically spoke of the 1970s punk scene as personally influential to how he approached his civic engagement in Chinatown:

> I'm really familiar with bands [and] underground music culture. Hong Kong Café and Madame Wong's [in Central Plaza] is where a lot of cool bands played in the '70s. Like The Germs, and X, and The Weirdos. So, there's these three different levels of culture in Chinatown. You got the locals, immigrants mostly. And then you have art galleries. And then there's this heritage of cool music. And [my wife and I] have a foot or finger in all three. We can build a bridge.

Wong and Lau have bridged the different cultures of Chinatown through their creative work. Lau's graphic design background also helped in developing visual media to effectively organize and communicate to other parents during their organizing efforts against co-location.

The political engagement of this new generation of Chinese Americans was intentionally intersectional as they acknowledged the layers of

FIGURE 19. Flyer for 2016 Save Music in Chinatown fundraiser concert for Castelar Elementary School. Art by Senon Williams. Flyer courtesy of Martin Wong.

neighborhood culture. They drew on their creative skills to build community capacity that bridged different stakeholders together. Their recognition and engagement with the different subcultures that exist in the neighborhood was in stark contrast to the musicians who bought property in Chinatown and arguably have direct ties to these music scenes but were not as politically engaged with the community and their potential role as gentrifiers.

Other young Chinese and Asian Americans have also deliberately engaged in cultural production as a part of their activism. CCED has held film screenings as a forum for community engagement and created DIY coupon books, zines, maps, and posters as a part of their activism to support working-class residents and small businesses. Sophat Phea, a CCED member, spoke of his interest in design and how he was also able to use those skills toward his organizing as many of the CCED designs were illustrated by him. *WAPOW*, which was started by second-generation Chinese American Wendy Chung, was a short-lived bilingual community magazine that sought to promote civic engagement in the community.[50] Both the CCED materials and *WAPOW* magazine had aesthetics that reflect the tastes of those who are producing the materials—young, college-educated Chinese and Asian Americans. In fact, despite its modern, streamlined aesthetics and bilingual translations, some older community members still critiqued these materials. For example, older generation community leaders shared that *WAPOW* was too difficult to read because the font was too small. These minor—and at times major—critiques show how these methods that use art and media for political engagement can be imperfect and are an ongoing process of learning about the community. However, the deliberate consciousness among these young Chinese and Asian Americans to try to work with the current community separates these acts from other forms of cultural production in the neighborhood, including Chinatown Summer Nights and the new restaurants. They were challenging the citizen consumer expectation of young Chinese and Asian Americans who emphasized economic consumption as a measure of their belonging in Chinatown. Instead, they focused on bridge building through cultural work that serves the community.

. . .

While the concerns about gentrification in Chinatown may center on residential and economic displacement, cultural displacement is also an important concern that underpins the other types of forced displacement in the neighborhood. The unique culture of Chinatown has been an important, defining part of the neighborhood that has attracted co-ethnics and tourists to the area. Both the designs and uses of different spaces contribute to how neighborhood culture is continually redefined and recognized.

However, the neighborhood culture is not simply defined by a shared ethnic culture and heritage. The cultural and socioeconomic diversity that defines the Chinese American community, as well as the history of the physical neighborhood being home to different waves of immigrants and marginalized communities, have contributed to a complex cultural identity of the neighborhood. Community leaders are trying to recognize and represent this neighborhood identity through their work and activism in the neighborhood to assert an authentic culture of place. Some have more power to control neighborhood development than others, particularly those with economic power. This power to control the neighborhood, whether it is through direct activism or ownership of properties, has implications for how culture is produced, consumed, and expressed in Chinatown. The dominant neighborhood culture that is asserted may not always be considered authentic by many community stakeholders and might instead be an aspirational expression of what Chinatown should be among those who have the power to control spaces in the neighborhood.

The tensions of defining neighborhood culture further highlight the contradictions and limitations of relying on Chinese and Asian Americans as the primary producers and consumers of Chinatown. As the neighborhood is a historic Asian American space, it would seem intuitive that Asian Americans continue to be the stewards of the neighborhood. A strong presence of Chinese and Asian American property owners and business owners in Chinatown may indicate that it has remained an Asian American cultural space. However, their presence does not always guarantee that the changes and preservation in the neighborhood are equitable since the neighborhood culture that they create may be within their narrow vision of what Chinatown is and should be. This vision, while formed from within the ethnic community, can still lead to exclusion by fracturing a sense of belonging for some segments of the community in Chinatown, especially working-class families and individuals. Yet cultural work, whether large community-scale events or individual artistic contributions, will always have the possibility to be important political acts that increase the visibility of those who continue to be most marginalized and that can help to address their needs. As subsequent generations become engaged in Chinatown and continue to redefine the neighborhood culture through their presence, whether through their political activism or as business owners, how they act upon this sense of stewardship to honor different histories and to build connections with the local community will become integral in defining what role they have in gentrification.

Conclusion

ENVISIONING POSSIBILITIES
FOR CHINATOWN

It almost requires a dismantling of old types of organizing, old
types of thinking, and implementing new ideas, new directions.
I think people have to start talking about how can we work
together more, talk about the things that unite us rather than
the things that are dividing us. These are highfalutin themes, but
I think they're such basic things that I think it's unavoidable to
progress without them.

—GILBERT HOM, community activist

THE POLITICAL ENGAGEMENT in Chinatown continues to evolve as
community leaders try to find new ways to unite the community amid the
ongoing pressures of gentrification. This includes my own engagement. In
2018, I was a guest editor for *WAPOW* magazine, a community publication
aimed to provide information about neighborhood development to encourage civic engagement in Chinatown. The issue was dedicated to capturing the visions of different stakeholders—some controversial, like the new
business owners—but mainly residents and other long-term stakeholders of
the neighborhood. By capturing these narratives together in one space, the
other contributors and I had hoped to facilitate the conversations about
building a collective vision for the future of Chinatown, a need that was
expressed by many community leaders. Similar to what was discussed in
the preceding chapters, the development of this issue of *WAPOW* reflected
the tensions and challenges in defining not just who should be included
in representing the Chinatown community but, among those, whose voice
should be put at the forefront. Admittedly, the magazine was agnostic in
centering a specific voice; the intent was to dialogue and put disparate
voices on the same page.

As part of the issue launch, I sat on a panel to discuss my involvement with *WAPOW* and received questions that were related to my research, which is more than what could be concisely presented in a magazine. I was not surprised that these questions would be raised. Throughout my fieldwork, I was often asked about my arguments and positions on various issues. For some, it was a way to see what "side" I was on, but also, and probably more importantly, to hold me accountable as an academic researcher in how I represented the community in my work. I shared what I had learned about the history of Chinatown and its leadership throughout time—that while this has been known as a Chinese American space, many of its leaders had arguably weak material ties to the community, especially as residents. A young community organizer who was just starting with the Chinatown Community for Equitable Development (CCED) then posed the question to me, "Do you think any of us, the organizations, should have a say in Chinatown?" The only response I could muster at the time was a sentiment that I began to adopt after it was shared to me by community leaders like Gilbert Hom and many others. "I think that the organizations and its members have to make concerted efforts to do the work in the local community." I said this with the understanding that such an endeavor is always easier said than done.

The organizer's question was one that I had been grappling with throughout my fieldwork, both theoretically and personally, and endures to the present day as I continue to be engaged in the Chinatown community. I am not the only one who contends with this question among those who are actively involved in Chinatown and see the space as a reflection of the complex, intersecting histories and interests that continually (re)define Chinese and Asian America. However, our practices of political engagement and community building in Chinatown did not always translate to spatial justice, regardless of our intentions. We recognize that the community is diverse, and that within this diversity there are some who are more invisible than others. We know that we must grapple with this diversity to tackle the inequities within the community in our visioning for the future of Chinatown. Given these tensions, how do we engage in stewardship of Chinatown that preserves not simply the ethnic heritage of the neighborhood, but also sets up the next generation to no longer be vulnerable to displacement due to racial, social, and economic injustices? How do we continue to fight for Chinatowns that contribute to a just and equitable city?

RESISTING THE NARRATIVES
OF DYING CHINATOWNS:
A HISTORY OF PERSISTENCE AND CHANGE

In both the public and community discourses, Chinatowns are often depicted as dying neighborhoods that are losing significance for Chinese Americans, especially the younger generation. Many of the people that I met through this research often would lament the loss of the Chinatown that they knew and grew up with. They felt that Chinatown was no longer the same as it was in the past and was at the tipping point of truly disappearing. I grappled with this narrative, both as a researcher and personally as someone who has linkages to several Chinatowns in other cities in addition to Los Angeles. All these Chinatowns were also becoming less familiar to me over time. For this reason, early on in my research, I thought that I was capturing the history of Los Angeles Chinatown at a very critical moment—the moment that it was going to be completely lost to the pressures of contemporary gentrification. And it is this sentiment that motivated me throughout my project; to capture a neighborhood that potentially could disappear in my lifetime.

Yet, my experiences in Los Angeles Chinatown have shown that this narrative about Chinatowns and their eventual disappearance, have been present since they formed in the late 1800s. The city and public deemed Old Chinatown an unimportant, blighted space in the early 1900s, which was a part of the racialized othering of Chinese Americans that positioned the community as a barrier to creating the "modern" city of Los Angeles. This framing helped to justify the creation of Union Station at the expense of Old Chinatown. Nonetheless, Chinatown persisted. The community, specifically business leaders, reestablished the neighborhood in 1938. In the 1950s, academics, the media, and policymakers predicted, and arguably even encouraged, Chinatowns to die yet again as Chinese Americans were positioned as model minorities. Because of the striking down of racial segregation, Chinatowns were no longer needed because their residents and businesses could move to the suburbs. Yet Chinatown persisted again because of the flows of new immigrants and refugees and the ongoing involvement of Chinese Americans in Chinatown, whether as consumers, business owners, property owners, or political activists.

In the 1980s, the threats of forced displacement stemmed from both the fears of the Community Redevelopment Agency (CRA) designation and the growth of the San Gabriel Valley. While the CRA provided new affordable housing for the neighborhood that helped to stabilize the residential community, the growth of the San Gabriel Valley continues to contribute to the concerns that Chinatown may hold no real purpose for the Chinese American community, as it is no longer the only hub for community life. By the early 2000s, the Business Improvement District (BID), property ownership changes, and new private investment contributed to an increase in upscale and corporate retail in the neighborhood that further challenged the traditional identity of Chinatown. The spatial dynamics shaping the community's relationship to Chinatown coupled with urban policies that are contributing to gentrification, from the limited affordable housing mechanisms to strategies that promote a cultural upscaling of neighborhoods, are shaping who and what is coming into, as well as leaving, the neighborhood. They are creating an added urgency and anxieties around our current concerns about Chinatowns as dying neighborhoods.

These assumptions about dying Chinatowns are part of the spatialized racial project that reflects the social and political standing of Chinese and Asian Americans and how communities are pushing against, or even at times embracing, their positioning. These narratives continue to situate Chinese and Asian Americans as socioeconomically assimilated model minorities who no longer need or rely on urban Chinatowns. While I did not seek to contribute to arguments about whether Chinese Americans confirm or reject spatial assimilation theories, my experiences in Los Angeles Chinatown show that spatial assimilationist perspectives remain a dominant logic that shape how people, whether Chinese American or not, perceive the changes in the neighborhood and the relationship between Chinese Americans and Chinatown. While this paradigm has been challenged over time, it is still a prevailing way of thinking about race and space, even within the community. The narratives about migration in and out of Chinatown indicated that not everyone agreed that the out-migration patterns were not always forced, which obscured how many interpreted gentrification and whether Asian Americans should be concerned with this issue. The movement of Chinese Americans in and out of Chinatown was not always viewed as a type of forced displacement because of racialized understandings of Chinese American relationship to place, and specifically urban Chinatowns. Concurrently, how scholars and gentrification scholars recognize and measure forced displacement in all communities also continues to be contested. Along with the racialized perceptions of Asian Americans, the uncertainties about identifying forced displacement can lead to misperceptions about neighborhood changes in urban Chinatowns, further contributing to this narrative of neighborhood death.

But Chinatown is not a dying neighborhood. Places such as urban Chinatowns continue to serve as important sites of community bridging and formations as people come together to defend the space. Since the 1960s, the work of Chinatown activists and social service professionals have constantly been challenging the assimilationist perspectives by advocating for those who remain in Chinatown and cannot leave due to economic and cultural barriers. Their counternarrative of Chinatown is one of a living community, but also a working-poor immigrant community whose conditions are a result of broader political and structural forces that shape migration and development. It is home to a community that has been marginalized and overlooked by policymakers, urban planners, and even at times ethnic community leaders, when they are making decisions about the neighborhood. With this reframing of Chinatown, we can begin to see why the neighborhood continues to be important and how it continues to thrive through the people who still live in and care for the neighborhood. These spaces not only are homes for those who are most economically and socially vulnerable within the community, Asian American communities also have sentimental attachments to these places, as they are physical markers of their history which can often be overlooked. When these sites are threatened and erased, the broader ethnic community, not just the local community, will experience a sense of loss, both material and symbolic.

Much of the fieldwork for this book was collected prior to the COVID-19 pandemic, a major event that had devastating consequences for Chinatown. The pandemic had and continues to have an impact on public health, but also had major impacts on the economy, community building, and race relations. These issues shaped the trajectory of urban Chinatowns, which were already grappling with the pressures and actualities of gentrification. Chinatown experienced a further slowing down of the local economy that intersected with increasing anti-Asian sentiment. The pandemic threatened the livelihood of all the small businesses in Chinatown, as well as heightened public safety concerns for many Asian Americans, especially senior citizens living in Chinatown. While some may again see this as accelerating the death of Chinatowns, the mutual aid work that has defined the Chinatown community since its formation was also uplifted by organizations, old and new, during this time. CCED, the Chinese Consolidated Benevolent Association (CCBA), Chinatown Service Center, Chinese American Citizens Alliance (CACA), among other organizations were actively providing social services and support to the Chinatown community. Members of these organizations provided food and resources to the elders living in the neighborhood and promoted Chinatown small businesses, whether through social media or by encouraging members to continue to eat and shop in Chinatown even if they no longer physically convened there for their meetings. The message was that Chinatown continued to be "open for business" and was still very much a living neighborhood. These responses show that there is always an active resistance to the threats that contribute to the death of Chinatown, especially in a time of crisis. The different community stakeholders continue to care for the neighborhood, and their political engagement will find ways to ensure that the neighborhood will be sustained.

This narrative of dying Chinatowns is thus not new. It was present since the establishment of the neighborhood and remained throughout time. Both people from within and outside the community have also been using this narrative to justify specific changes and development practices in the neighborhood. Yet it has also been continuously challenged. Chinatowns are still here, resisting the external pressures to declare Chinatown dead and the sentiments from among Chinese Americans that the neighborhood is losing its purpose for the community. Chinatowns persist, but they also are not the same as they were when they originally formed. Neighborhoods are not static entities. They change due to a confluence of external and internal pressures. Both the precariousness and perseverance of Chinatown as a physical neighborhood and social-cultural community reflect the changing racial positioning of Chinese Americans and the fact that Chinese Americans are both one of the oldest and newest immigrant communities in the United States. Thus, rather than continuing this narrative about the death of Chinatowns, a more important question to ask about the future of Chinatowns is if they are changing in such a way that may challenge our expectations of what we expect a Chinatown ought to be. If it challenges that expectation, then we still must ask if these changes sustain Chinatowns in a way that not only honors our personal attachments and connections to the neighborhood, but also honors and empowers those in the community who have historically been invisible and marginalized.

A NETWORKED COMMUNITY:
THE INTERCONNECTEDNESS OF CHINATOWN

Los Angeles Chinatown is not an isolated community, and arguably was never one. The neighborhood has consistently been a contested site for development that underscores the complexities of connections that people have to Chinatown. Different actors, including the city, private developers, and various members of the Chinese American community have all vied for power to determine the changes in the neighborhood. While a simplistic, romantic view of these struggles would assume that this power should be held within the community, this notion of community is tenuous. Chinatown is not just defined by the neighborhood community, but also the broader Chinese American community in Southern California and, arguably, a global Chinese community. This characteristic of Chinatown as a networked space will continue to shape the ongoing tensions of defining community stakeholdership and who among the stakeholders has the most power to control neighborhood change. It complicates the internal/external and insider/outsider opposition that is common in gentrification conflicts. It raises important questions about who is defining the collective right to the city, or in this case, the right to Chinatown, as it is not necessarily just in the interests of serving current residents but in the interest of the Chinese American community across spaces.

This geographic dispersal of the Chinese American community has had an impact in determining who has the right to control changes in Chinatown. Chinese Americans are important placemakers of Chinatown, but their relationship to this space is arguably guided by symbolic attachments more than material attachments, especially in the Los Angeles context. In historic Black neighborhoods that formed due to legacies of segregation, the Black middle-class are also recognized as active placemakers. But scholars have noted that they may still move to these neighborhood amid ongoing racial exclusion regardless of their upward mobility.[1] While Chinese and Asian Americans still experience everyday and systemic racism, albeit differently than other racialized groups, they are not necessarily moving "back" to Chinatown in response to this exclusion. In the Los Angeles context, multiethnic suburbs, or ethnoburbs, in the San Gabriel Valley have become new economic, residential, and political centers for Chinese Americans.[2] In fact, Chinese and Asian Americans are notably engaging in planning and development politics in these suburban areas that have both re-shaped the physical landscape to assert the multiethnic demographics and, at times, preserved more Anglo designs and culture to assert their belonging and assimilation.[3] Despite this growing influence, Chinese Americans were still in-volved in Chinatown and their impact is still felt in the neighborhood. Given that this is no longer the only space that Chinese Americans have a presence in, what does it mean that they also continue to make claims in Chinatown? Why does Chinatown matter for them given the growth of these spaces?

The political engagement of Chinese and Asian Americans in Chinatown continues to be important for both the politicization of Asian Americans as well as for ensuring representation to those within the community that con-tinue to lack a political voice. Working-class immigrant communities often rely on community leaders to be political advocates and allies who act as me-diators with mainstream political institutions. Language, time, education, and other various socioeconomic and cultural factors act as major barriers to full political participation for Asian American immigrant communities.[4] The geopolitical experiences that shaped trust in government among immi-grants and refugees also further act as barriers. Because of these commu-nity dynamics, local organizations and their members are critical in ensuring that this specific voice of the community is heard. In ethnic communities, these representatives are often later generation co-ethnics who have gained political, cultural, and social capital to navigate mainstream institutions. As representatives, and not always direct stakeholders, they have a collective re-sponsibility for the broader community. They are constantly challenged to ensure that their work reflects community interests and not personal inter-ests or abstract understandings of community that lack a grounding in their lived experiences and realities. Developing and nurturing spaces where lo-cals can be in leadership positions remains critical for these organizations to have that legitimacy in the community. Through these spaces, different com-munity stakeholders can continue to build working relationships, maintain connections, share resources, and work in solidarity together.

Yet the relationships that define the community networks of Los Angeles Chinatown are also characterized by power differentials based on socioeco-nomics, gender, generation, regional identities, and immigration histories. These relationships cannot be overlooked. Class divisions in the Chinese American community are especially salient in understanding the possibili-ties and limits of community power, and this was expressed in the conflict between residential and business interests in Chinatown. Similar to other

Chinatown studies, business interests in Los Angeles Chinatown continue to have the most political power.[5] Their power is held specifically among major property owners in the commercial area, which is distinct from the immigrant small business owners who do not always own their properties. Business leaders and property owners continue to be prominent in organizational leadership and have power in shaping the economic, housing, and cultural development of the neighborhood. The BID represents that interest group and was considered one of the most, if not the most, powerful voices in the community during my fieldwork. It has served as a platform to strengthen the voice of business interests in Chinatown, particularly the voices of specific commercial property owners. Because they are often guided by economic interest, many in the community see the BID's actions as contributing to a physical and cultural erasure of the neighborhood despite it being an entity led from within the community.

The debates about the ongoing engagement of Chinese Americans in Chinatown also illuminate the tension over property ownership in shaping the community's relationship to space and ultimately the trajectory of Chinatown. Property owners not only hold economic and political power, they also have become de facto preservationists. Several of the community organizations in Chinatown, including the mutualist associations, CCBA, CACA, and Chinese Historical Society of Southern California (CHSSC), are not just community representatives, but also acting as preservationists for Chinatown because they own their properties. The presence of these ethnic organizations helps to maintain Chinatown as a "Chinatown." A few older business leaders, especially the later generation who are managing legacy businesses that helped to establish New Chinatown in 1938, have sentimental attachments to Chinatown and understand that their businesses have come to be a defining part of the history and culture of the neighborhood. However, this attitude is not common nor expected among many of the individual business and property owners, especially newer stakeholders. Thus, there is a generational and ideological divide among business leaders as to whether they seek to act as cultural preservationists in addition to promoting economic development in Chinatown, a dynamic that appears to be common in other non-White, immigrant spaces.[6]

As Chinese Americans across generation and immigration cohorts continue to be commercial, institutional, and residential property owners in Chinatown, they will play a powerful role in shaping Chinatown. They may begin to view it as a space of economic investment where they can generate profits, which disregards the fact that it is also a space of heritage and community. With this mindset, they may try to maximize, or even speculate, rent values that reflect neighboring downtown values. Other Chinese Americans who inherit property in Chinatown may simply not want to be property owners because they have limited connections to the neighborhood. The growing detachment and disengagement with subsequent generations places the current tenants in Chinatown at risk of displacement. Both the older and new generation of property owners who inherit properties are thus critical actors who can shape the trajectory of gentrification, whether intentionally or not. It remains a question whether they are making decisions that reflect a collective community interest, and if not, how community leaders, especially heritage leaders, can motivate them to be guided by a collective responsibility to the community, especially if they do not live or work there.

While Chinatown will always be associated with the Chinese American community, it is not only those who identify as Chinese American who will stake claims and be politically engaged in the neighborhood. Urban neighborhoods are sites for the possibilities of cross-racial alliances and coalitions, and Los Angeles Chinatown is one such site for these possibilities. Los Angeles Chinatown has always had a Latine residential presence throughout its history. Today, Chinatown is a majority Asian American community, but close to a quarter of the population identifies as Latine, particularly of Mexican origin. The multiracial demographics of Chinatown reflect the Mexican history of California that predates statehood. Los Angeles, in particular, is recognized as a "Latino city," as Latines make up almost half the total population.[7] The Latine population is not only large, but their political voice in the city and county continues to grow, whether through electoral politics or grassroots organizing. Yet there was a limited Latine political voice or representation in Chinatown, despite other Latine communities, such as neighboring Boyle Heights, becoming politically engaged in similar issues of gentrification. This further complicates the gap in political representation among residents in Chinatown. The leadership in Chinatown, composed of nonresidents, is primarily Chinese American. Their political power therefore raises questions about how they are stewards for the current and future Chinatown community, regardless of racial or ethnic background.

Immigrant and ethnic communities in both urban and suburban ethnic spaces are engaging in cross-racial alliances based on labor and class solidarities to assert political power and representation.[8] Similar issues are facing other Asian ethnic enclaves in Los Angeles, such as Koreatown, where Korean American activists are advocating for Latine laborers and challenging the Korean American economic elite.[9] With the most recent advocacy of CCED in assisting with tenant organizing, we are seeing some of that cross-racial coalition building becoming more visible in Chinatown. Given the Los Angeles context, it should not be surprising to see a more place-based political engagement in Chinatown that extends beyond racial lines to be representative of the neighborhood's residential demographics.

Given both the internal community dynamics, as well as cross-racial dynamics, gentrification in Chinatown cannot be addressed in isolation. As we continue to search for ways to prevent forced displacement that occurs via gentrification, understanding Chinatown's relationship to other neighborhoods and communities will become increasingly important. Some changes in Chinatown will begin to forcibly displace the current residents and possibly force them to move to other areas that may be facing similar displacement pressures. Furthermore, if the Chinatown community leadership can find ways to regulate and restrict specific types of development within the neighborhood, the displacement pressures from the city and downtown could simply shift to neighboring areas, such as Lincoln Heights and Boyle Heights. The external pressures call into question the broader collective responsibility that Chinatown has for other communities in the downtown area that are experiencing the same downtown displacement pressures. It also necessitates an understanding of Chinatown that emphasizes its interconnectedness. This understanding forces us to understand the intersections of ethnic identity, racialization, and class differences in shaping place-based activism in Chinatown that not only have a direct impact on the physical neighborhood but can have ripple effects to other communities.

NOT JUST A COMMUNITY OF THE PAST:
AN INTERSECTIONAL APPROACH
TO SUSTAINING CHINATOWNS

Given the different communities that have shaped Chinatown to what it is today, the arguments about preservation in Los Angeles Chinatown are layered and multifaceted. The dynamics in Chinatown are aligned with assumptions about development conflicts that highlight class differentials within a racialized community in shaping neighborhood change.[10] These dynamics also uplift the salience of immigration trends and regional migration patterns in shaping the politics of preservation and development. Chinatown is recognized as an important historical neighborhood that represents not just Chinese American history but also the different immigration histories that have come to be a defining part of the city. This social and cultural value of the neighborhood further contributes to why Chinatown continues to be an important but contested space for development.

For many Chinese Americans, older urban Chinatowns, like Los Angeles Chinatown, represent an older history of the community; when early Chinese Americans were subject to explicit legal racial exclusion through federal and local policies, which ultimately contributed to the formation of Chinatowns. These neighborhoods are a symbol of the history of systemic racism and community resilience in the face of social and economic exclusion, a history that is not always included in mainstream accounts of US history. Hence, community leaders often present Chinatown as an ethnic space rooted in this early Chinese American history. This cultural identity continues to be present in the neighborhood, from the traditional Cantonese restaurants to the old political power structure of the CCBA, CACA, and the mutualist associations. Consequently, this culture and history also becomes the center of preservation and heritage efforts in Chinatown.

Post-1965 immigration diversified this Cantonese neighborhood identity, raising important questions about ethnic culture and preservation in Chinatown today. Chinese immigrants and refugees who were from other regions in China, especially the Chaozhou and Fujian regions, settled in Chinatown as both residents and business owners. They brought a different experience of Chinese migration to the United States, as many still identified as ethnic Chinese but also had roots outside of the People's Republic of China, including Taiwan, Hong Kong, Vietnam, Cambodia, Laos, and other Southeast Asian countries. They established a physical presence that many would argue are defining characteristics of the neighborhood today, from major monuments, such as the temples and the Chinatown Gateway to the everyday places, such as the swap meets in Saigon Plaza. The diversity within the post-1965 Chinese American community led to the formation of different organizations, informed the conflict in spaces of political representation, and shaped the variations in framing the neighborhood identity and changes. They were not always recognized or a part of the mainstream or older community power structure, but they created new organizational spaces of belonging that have since grown to be important community organizations.

Furthermore, young Chinese Americans whose families immigrated from Southeast Asian countries, as well as Hong Kong and Taiwan, beginning in the 1970s are also now coming of age and becoming civically engaged in Chinatowns. Their identities are directly shaped by the Chinese diaspora more than the "traditional" immigrant identity. These Chinese Americans were developing similar claims and attachments to Chinatown as Chinese and Asian American activists in the 1960s and 1970s, with many situating their perspectives within progressive politics of race and labor. However, as they have a different migration history and experience, they also bring a critical diasporic, transnational perspective to community and place that expands upon the older immigrant experience of Chinese America that traditionally defines the history of Chinatowns. This will have implications for not just the political engagement that happens within Chinatown, but how the neighborhood continues to be viewed as an ethnic space, including whose histories will be recognized in ongoing preservation efforts.

Preservation efforts in Chinatown are not simply about the heritage efforts that seek to capture the complexities of Chinese American immigration history. They also include the ongoing housing advocacy for low-income residents, especially as the affordable housing covenants for the CRA developments in Chinatown begin to expire. Affordable housing preservation goes hand in hand with cultural preservation, as these places are homes to the low-income, working-class immigrant residents who define the everyday culture of Chinatown and make it a unique neighborhood. Toward the end of the fieldwork for this book, tenant organizing emerged in Cathay Manor and Hillside Villa, which were the first CRA housing developments. The tenant organizing, which was supported by members of CCED, made visible how the CRA designation was a short-term solution in addressing housing affordability, further critiquing how state interventions are not providing enough mechanisms to sustain livable, affordable housing. The improper management of these developments, poor housing quality, and the lack of a policy tool to extend the covenants of these developments were now put in the spotlight in both the community and local media. As the covenants for affordable housing developments built in the 1980s through the 2010s begin to expire and different tenant-led groups continue to build momentum across Chinatown, there is also the possibility of building a stronger collective voice for housing preservation that represents the broader neighborhood beyond individual developments.

The diversity that defines the Chinese American community across socioeconomic status, generation, and immigration cohort, necessitates an expansive understanding of how preservation is defined in Chinatown. This diversity has often led to the perception of Chinatown as a conflicted community. Elected officials and media often called upon Chinatown community leaders to act as a "unified voice," with some in the community also echoing this sentiment. Through my fieldwork, I saw that most community leaders were demonstrating that they were trying to be unified, but also were not sidestepping the diversity of the community. Instead, they were openly trying to work within diversity, which led to internal conflicts that were publicly profiled. As several community leaders stated, they understood that healthy conflict was necessary to get to a consensus, and Chinatown leaders appeared to be moving toward that path. The emergence of the Chinatown Sustainability Dialogue Group (CSDG) as the newest, broad-based grassroots formation showed that community leaders were trying to work at the intersection of different preservation interests, specifically traditional ethnic heritage efforts and residential interests. The term *sustainability* was a deliberate choice for many of the people who initiated this group, especially among the older generation, who have seen the ebbs and flows of organizing in Chinatown. They recognize that change is inevitable, but also that there should be a collective voice to steer those changes. This collective voice should aim to preserve the history and legacies of past communities in Chinatown while also centering the current socioeconomic inequalities that are exacerbated by gentrification. This expansive approach to preservation recognizes the broader historical importance of Chinatown without leaving the working-class immigrant residents behind in these conversations.

COLLECTIVE POWER AND RIGHTS
FOR THE FUTURE OF CHINATOWN

Communities, policymakers, and urban planners continue to contend with the forced displacement that can occur with gentrification. But they are also simultaneously trying to create interventions to improve the social and physical conditions of neighborhoods that are responsive to the community. With this tension, there is a question as to whether "development without displacement" is possible. Can we change neighborhoods that provide needed resources and new amenities without threatening the livelihood of the current community? Anti-displacement frameworks are possible, but the implementation of these frameworks necessitates a deep understanding of the community needs and preferences. As the preceding chapters emphasize, the inclusion of community voices and their political participation are important for carving out pathways toward equitable development. However, the dynamics in Los Angeles Chinatown also show that this work is not always easy and is oftentimes fraught.

Since the 1970s, the trend toward public-private partnerships and citizen participation have reshaped the decision-making and service provision practices in urban and neighborhood governance to be inclusive of local communities. Yet, even if the intents of these spaces are to provide community representation and dialogue, in practice this does not always come to fruition and instead can reproduce power imbalances. In Los Angeles Chinatown, ensuring that low-income, limited English proficient residents are included and uplifted in political decision-making processes continues to be a challenge. The formalization of community engagement and public participation in local government decision-making processes tried to address this gap, but it also further complicated the political leadership in Chinatown.

Initially, through their involvement in the Chinatown Community Advisory Committee (CCAC), community leaders representing residential interests were the strongest voices. This was a space that formed through the CRA designation, which challenges assumptions that these voices are usually weak in the decision-making process and that the CRA was a tool for economic development and business interests. While this may be interpreted as a form of empowerment in Chinatown, it also appeared to empower a select few in the community. The process of participating in these redevelopment conflicts contributed to a questioning of community belonging and relationships. Challenging people's sense of belonging and claims to Chinatown was part of the political power struggle to delegitimize specific voices from political decision-making, and this was exacerbated in these formal spaces of citizen participation. Contrary to expectations of citizen participation, the conflict and fragmentation that emerged from the struggle for political power paradoxically contributed to disempowerment, disengagement, and at times, distrust from others in the community.

The BID has also become a powerful voice of the community in their efforts to revitalize the neighborhood. Despite the public-private structure of the BID, they position themselves more as a private actor, and specifically as a legitimate community group. However, it is a community group that represents not only commercial property owners but new downtown interests as well. Many in Chinatown, as well as those outside of the community, view the BID as the community's pro-development voice in that it directly benefits property owners and contributes to the ethnic growth machine politics in Chinatown that support development and infrastructure changes to follow broader downtown trends.[11] The BID, like any other urban policy or community group, can be a space of possibility that can be inclusive of different interests depending on the vision of those in leadership. But for now, in Los Angeles Chinatown, it is reinforcing neoliberal urban governance that prioritizes the economic interests of select commercial property owners and minimizes collective interests that center equity frameworks for economic development.

While it is still important to have these spaces of citizen participation such as the CCAC and neighborhood council systems, as well as other mechanisms for community control that are recognized by the city, grassroots formations and organizing will continue to matter for sustaining Chinatown. These politicized community formations have defined Chinatown since its original formation. CCBA, CACA, and the older mutualist organizations provided governance and a sense of community to early Chinese American immigrants, asserting a political and cultural presence of Chinese Americans during this time of exclusion, and they continue to be important institutions that are seen as the longtime political elites and symbols of that history. Today, organizations like CCED and SEACA continue to represent the segments of the community that remain on the margins of political conversations, challenging both the city, mainstream institutions, and, at times, the old power structure. Chinatown organizations, both old and new, continue to advocate and center specific segments of the community that are overlooked by decision-makers who determine the policies and practices that contribute to neighborhood change. They provide the necessary external pressures on the city and public agencies to ensure that representation is not tokenized, that the decisions the city makes about Chinatown reflect the actualities of the community rather than assumptions and imaginaries.

These formations are also a part of sustaining and preserving Chinatowns. They play an important part as to why these neighborhoods will continue to matter for future generations. The organizations that have been present since the establishment of Old Chinatown and newer organizations like CCED and SEACA continue to be spaces of politicized community building. Urban Chinatowns thus will continue to be defined by the political engagement and grassroots activism of Chinese and Asian Americans to address ongoing racial and economic injustices in the neighborhood.

Grassroots organizations and organizing has also been foundational for developing anti-displacement strategies, such as community development corporations and community land trusts, which have emerged as possible equity-based solutions that ensure community control over change. Los Angeles Chinatown has never officially had either one of these in place. At various points, community leaders and organizations have tried to develop these groups or initiatives within their organizations, but they have been fleeting. During the writing of this book, there were efforts to establish a community land trust, an anti-displacement tool in which a property is owned and managed by a local nonprofit organization on behalf of the community. This coincided with increasing interest from local government, as the Los Angeles County Board of Supervisors passed a motion in 2020 to fund a pilot program to partner with local community land trusts that would provide resources and assess their feasibility. Community land trusts thus may be the next chapter for Chinatowns, especially Los Angeles Chinatown, as they continue to find anti-displacement solutions amid the gentrification pressures.

The interest in establishing a community land trust shows that land ownership continues to be an important way of ensuring community control in Chinatown. Land ownership was and continues to be one method of excluding racialized groups from national and cultural belonging and limiting socioeconomic mobility. Chinese American immigrants were historically excluded from owning properties as "aliens ineligible for citizenship." Shared property ownership of the plazas that established New Chinatown was a mechanism to keep the community together in the face of forced displacement and racial exclusion. These plazas were not simply a space of tourism that catered to outsiders. The development of New Chinatown in 1938 would not have happened if not for the political savvy of both Chinese immigrant and US-born Chinese American business leaders to secure the land where Central Plaza sits today. The property ownership and shares were split across different families, indicating that this was a strategy of collective ownership in New Chinatown. While this was led by the business leaders of the time, this strategy was integral to the community's survival in the face of racial exclusion. Thus, places like Central Plaza may currently be viewed as a site of tourism and heritage, and even inauthentic spaces to some because of its design. But we also can see it as a space that symbolizes a history of resistance, resiliency, and political ingenuity among community leaders who were working within their racialization at the time to respond to forced displacement.

Revisiting and uplifting this history of resistance and collective ownership that established Chinatown will be critical in defining the vision and possibilities of Chinatown's sustainability within our current context of gentrification. The forced displacement that occurs via gentrification is due to poor and working-class communities of color being excluded from the decision-making that shapes their neighborhoods. While some situate the legacy of Chinatown within an evolving Chinese American identity, it is also important to understand that Chinatown formed when Chinese Americans were overtly excluded from mainstream society. The neighborhood continues to be a place for low-income immigrant communities who, although may not always be legally excluded, undoubtedly face barriers to mainstream resources and political participation. Reasserting the history of Chinatown as a space that serves those who are vulnerable to social and political exclusion can help to inform the anti-displacement alternatives for neighborhood development as well as reshape local race relations and political power.

The history of political engagement in Chinatown has shown that Chinese and Asian Americans are not passive actors in our political system, especially in local politics. They have been involved in both the formal and informal politics that determine the urban landscape. The tensions of neighborhood change in Chinatown are also intrinsically linked to the urban politics that seek to address economic and racial exclusion. As our ethnic community politics continue to be grounded in the material conditions and lived experiences in Chinatown, our place-based political engagement has the potential to promote equitable development in Chinatown and the city for the next generation.

———————

Additional Information about the Interviews

The quotes and narratives included in this book are primarily from the fifty-two in-depth, semi-structured interviews with community leaders that I conducted during my fieldwork. These interviews took place from May 2016 to May 2017 and occurred simultaneously with my observations and archival research. The in-depth, semi-structured interviews were with Chinatown stakeholders whom I identified as community leaders, activists, and organizers who had been politically active in neighborhood issues since the 1970s. I distinguished these individuals from other Chinatown community stakeholders based on the following criteria: (1) acted as a formal or informal representative on behalf of an organization or specific interest for the community; (2) served in a leadership role within a community-based organization; and/or (3) engaged in place-based issues related to social services, economic, housing, or cultural development. While I had preset topics for all interviews, I followed the "active interview" approach, which allowed for flexibility in the interview process. Through this process, interviewees guided the flow of the interviews, which allowed for storytelling that highlighted each interviewee's unique experience and knowledge base about Chinatown.[1]

I used purposive and snowball sampling and identified potential interviewees through observations and archives, as well as recommendations from other community leaders. I was able to approach and recruit most interviewees in person during my fieldwork, while for others I was introduced through a community leader whom I had already interviewed. Throughout the analysis and writing of the research, I also revisited and reinterviewed several community leaders to ensure credibility and to address any changes that occurred throughout the years of my fieldwork.

Based on their organizational affiliation and how interviewees spoke about their involvement in Chinatown, I initially classified community leaders into three broad categories that reflected interest groups: residential, business, and culture. Community leaders classified as representing residential interests included those who were involved in groups and activities that focused on improving the conditions for Chinatown residents and workers, including labor, housing, social services, and immigrant rights. Individuals were classified as having business interests if they held economic investments in Chinatown and became involved with business and property owner interest organizations. Lastly, the culture category includes individuals who became engaged through cultural heritage organizations and/or the older organizations in Chinatown, such as the older mutualist associations, that were now perceived as cultural institutions in the community. They contrasted with residential leaders whose political work and activism centered the Chinatown community specifically.

These three categories were chosen to create mutually exclusive categories across interviewees. However, as I spent more time in the community, I found that these categories were not mutually exclusive and that individuals were often involved in multiple organizations and, at times, represented multiple interests. For example, some business leaders also were engaged in heritage work. The intersections of engagement and temporal changes to people's involvement in Chinatown were also incorporated into my analysis and interpretations. Furthermore, while all interviewees identified with at least one organization or institution in Chinatown, only seven interviewees claimed to be current residents of Chinatown and ten to be past residents. This low percentage of resident representation is indicative of the limits of ethnic political power and representation in Chinatown, which is a major tension discussed throughout the book, especially in chapter 3.

Of the fifty-two interviewees, forty-eight identified as Chinese American. Four interviewees were not Chinese Americans but were identified as individuals who have been actively engaged in the community and were viewed by other community leaders as important local figures in Chinatown. A majority of interviewees were also 1.5+ generation (n = 42). I classify 1.5+ generation as individuals who either (1) were born outside the United States but immigrated before attending college or were of college age (roughly eighteen years old) or (2) were born in the United States. In other words, I grouped individuals who spent their childhood or formative years in the United States into one category.

I did not further break down the generational status because of the complex history of Chinese and Asian immigration, where, as explained in chapter 2, government policies restricted Chinese immigration and excluded Chinese Americans from full citizenship. These policies disrupted both physical and cultural belonging in the United States among early Chinese Americans and prevented them from establishing a permanent home even if they had lived and worked in the country for many years of their lives. Due to these flows of in and out migration, as well as the use of paper sons to immigrate to the United States, tracing the family history for Chinese Americans has challenged traditional linear assumptions of generational status often used in immigration studies. Chinese Americans can claim a long history of migration to the United States despite policies that sought to restrict immigration, citizenship, and settlement. This history was articulated by some of my interviewees; when I asked about their generation, some described their family background and immigration history instead of providing a direct answer that easily categorized their status. The different interpretations from interviewees about their background were informative but outside the scope of this research. It also made it difficult to consistently present generational status among community leaders.

Upon the early stages of fieldwork, I also realized that cohort differences in leadership became an important distinction. I thus further divided my interviewees by "engagement cohorts" to capture varying perspectives from older and newer stakeholders. The older engagement cohort (n = 28) included individuals who became more active in Chinatown up until 1990, and the newer engagement cohort (n = 24) included individuals who became active in the community after 1990. I chose the year 1990 after it emerged in the initial stages of data collection and analysis that this decade was a major post-1965 turning point in how community leaders and the media were beginning to frame Chinatown as a neighborhood that was in decline in relation to the growth of the neighboring San Gabriel Valley. This also initiated internal political shifts and new leadership to address these changes in Chinatown, which became formalized after 2000. Throughout the book, I refer to the older engagement cohort as "older leaders" and the newer cohort as either "newer" or "younger leaders."

In addition to the fifty-two community leaders, I also interviewed seven individuals who did not classify as Chinatown community leaders. They included city government staff, former CRA staff, and non-Chinatown community leaders who worked with Chinatown through the CRA and neighborhood council system. These interviewees were recommended by Chinatown community leaders and were important in providing and validating contextual information about these institutions. In addition, two individuals were also classified as city government staff due to their occupation. However, I included them as community leaders rather than outside partners because they were either older community leaders or still directly involved with Chinatown organizations.

Every interviewee was informed of the option to be identified in this study, and almost all consented to be identified. However, as the findings address the various community perceptions of Chinatown and how they relate to ongoing issues of conflict and power, I decided to present some interview quotes as de-identified to protect the privacy of the few individuals who wanted to remain anonymous. I made exceptions when using quotes that were easily identifiable and to highlight personal stories that would help to provide a grounded perspective of the neighborhood's history.

NOTES

INTRODUCTION

1. Throughout the book, I distinguish between Chinese Americans, a specific ethnic community, and Asian Americans, a panethnic community that is inclusive of Chinese Americans. While Chinatowns have been primarily shaped by the history and experiences of Chinese Americans, Chinatowns also serve as important cultural, economic, political, and residential spaces for other individual Asian American communities and collectively for Asian Americans.

2. Acolin and Vitiello 2017; Cheung (in press); Hom 2022; Hom 2023; Huynh 2020; Knapp and Vojnovic 2013; Lin 2008; Pottie-Sherman 2010; Sze 2010; Wilson 2015; Wong 2019.

3. Soja 2009.

4. Lefebvre 1991.

5. David Harvey (2012), Peter Marcuse (2009) and Edward Soja (2014) trace how the right to the city has also become an urban social movement that recenters the needs and voices of working poor in the development of urban spaces. Kafui Attoh (2011) and Margit Mayer (2009) also show how the concept and the messaging of the right to the city is not always clear, and in some cases, has become appropriated and depoliticized.

6. Fainstein 2005; Soja 2009.

7. Harvey 2003; Marcuse 2009.

8. Sheller 2018.

9. Glass 1964.

10. Hackworth and Smith 2001; Slater 2009; Smith 1979.

11. Fainstein 2010; Hyra 2012; Parson 1982; Ross and Leigh 2000; Smith 1979; Soja 1989.

12. Grodrach and Loukaitou-Sideris 2007; Hyra 2012; Lung-Amam 2021; Sullivan and Shaw 2011; Zukin et al. 2009.

13. Freeman 2005; Freeman and Braconi 2004; Vigdor, Massey, and Rivlin 2002.

14. Li 2016; Marcuse 1985.

15. Hyra 2012; Marcuse 1985; Newman and Wyly 2006.

16. Atkinson 2015; Danley and Weaver 2018; Elliott-Cooper, Hubbard, and Lees, 2020; Fullilove 2004; Hom 2022; Molina 2015.

17. Hyra 2015.

18. Marcuse 1997; Schwirian 1983.

19. Massey and Denton 1985.

20. Zhou 1992.

21. Lee 1949; Logan et al. 1996; Massey and Denton 1987.

22. Kwong 1996; Ong 1984.

23. Portes and Jensen 1989; Zhou and Logan 1991.

24. Zhou 1992.

25. Byon 2020; Teranishi, Nguyen, and Alcantar 2015.

26. Harvey 2003; Lefebvre 1991; Logan and Molotch 1997.

27. Smith 1979.

28. Logan and Molotch 1997; Slater 2009; Smith 1979.

29. Hyra 2012.

30. I use the term *Latine* throughout the book as an inclusive panethnic community term to represent individuals of all gender identities who identify as having Latin American heritage. During the time of this book, there were debates about the use of this term and thus I also recognize that *Latine*, as well as other identity terms used in this book, is historically situated to the time my research was conducted and that the conversations within the community about creating an inclusive group identity continue to evolve.

31. Delgado and Swanson 2017.

32. Boyd 2008; Hyra 2008.

33. Aguilar-San Juan 2009; Smith 2006; Li et al. 2006; Oh and Chung 2014; Võ 2004.

34. Light 2002; Lin 2011.

35. Hum 2014; Hyra 2008; Li et al. 2006; Li 2009; Lin 2011; Park and Kim 2008; Sassen 1996.

36. Acolin and Vitello 2017; Knapp and Vojnovic 2013; Lin 1998; Li 2009.

37. Chen 2002; Lai 2004; Zhou 1992.

38. Lai 2004.

39. Park 1950.

40. Kwong 1996.

41. Kwong 1996; Wu 2014.

42. Kwong 1996; Lin 1998; Liu and Geron 2008; Nee and Nee 1986.

43. Kwong 1996; Lin 1998; Nee and Nee 1986; Wilson 2015.

44. Toji and Umemoto 2003.

45. DeFilippis, Fisher, and Shragge 2009; Joseph 2002; M. Shaw 2008; Hom 2023; Huante 2019; Muñiz 2023.

46. Fallon 2021; Huante 2019.

47. Knapp and Vojnovic 2013; Lin 2011.

48. Omi and Winant 2014, 110.

49. Bonilla-Silva 2003; Feagin 2013; Omi and Winant 2014.

50. Lai 2012.

51. Cheng 2013.

52. Liu 2000; Neely and Samura 2011.

53. Fainstein and Fainstein 1989; Huante 2021; Pulido 2000; Saito 2009; Villa and Sanchez 2005.

54. Lipsitz 2011.

55. Gans 1982; Lai 2012; Saito 2009.

56. Harwood 2005; Nguyen, Basolo, and Tiwari 2013; Horton 1995; Saito 1998.

57. Anderson and Sternberg 2013; Huante 2019.

58. Brooks 2009; Kurashige 2008; Lai 2012.

59. Wu 2014.

60. Fujino 2008; Liu and Geron 2008; Maeda 2009; Nee and Nee 1986.

61. Fujino 2008.

62. Ethnography is a qualitative research methodology that seeks to highlight the lived experiences of groups and the meanings behind those experiences toward theory development. Ethnographic research includes in-depth fieldwork and multiple methods of data collection to produce written and visual accounts of the social phenomenon of interest.

63. The boundaries of Chinatown were derived using a variety of methods. I drew from (1) neighborhood observations and noting physical boundaries, (2) archival research on past policy reports on Chinatown to assess the different political boundaries of Chinatown, including the Community Redevelopment Agency (CRA) Project Area, Business Improvement District (BID), and Historic Cultural Neighborhood Council (HCNC), (3) interview responses from a sample of community leaders across interest groups to define the neighborhood boundaries, and (4) analysis of neighboring census tracts to identify which tracts had a residential population that was at least 30 percent Asian American.

64. Fong 1994.

65. When analyzing my data, particularly the interview data, I was also guided by interpretively informed triangulation to further assess the member validity of my data (Roth and Mehta 2002). This process of triangulation considers how the context and background of individuals, including ethnicity, age, generational status, and stakeholder claims, help provide a deeper understanding of the social structure within the community.

66. Smith 1974.

67. Burawoy 1998.

68. Võ 2000; Warren 2001; Zinn 2001.

69. Given my language limitations, I could not fully capture perspectives from various segments of the community who were not comfortable primarily communicating in English. I was able to capture some Cantonese and Mandarin Chinese during my fieldwork, but I could not read materials written in Chinese, nor steadily

converse with members of the community who spoke those dialects. Chinatown is a diverse immigrant community with a variety of languages and dialects that are not just Cantonese or Mandarin Chinese. Thus, regardless, I would have not been able to comprehensively reach all the different segments of the neighborhood given these language differences. This project, however, ultimately focuses on the political culture of Chinatown and its leaders, almost all of whom are bilingual and conversant in English.

70. Forester 1989; Umemoto 2001.

1. THE MAKING AND REMAKING OF CHINATOWN

1. Dear 1996; Dear and Flusty 2002; Fogelson 1993; Kurashige 2010.

2. Ling 2001.

3. I refer to the Guangdong Chinese regional culture and dialect as Cantonese, along with Siyi as Szeyup and Taisan as Toisan (a county in Szeyup), which reflects Cantonese romanization throughout the book. This reflects how these places are referred to within the Chinatown community, especially among Chinatown community leaders. For other Chinese language terms, I use the Pinyin romanization unless specified.

4. Hom 2013; Shah 2001.

5. Avila 2006; Brooks 2009.

6. Brooks 2009; Kurashige 2008; Wachs 2007.

7. Fogelson 1993; Kurashige 2008; Silver 1997.

8. Pulido 2000.

9. Kurashige 2008.

10. Molina 2005.

11. Quintana 2015.

12. Cheng and Kwok 2001.

13. The U.S. Supreme Court case, *United States vs. Wong Kim Ark* (1899), established jus soli, which deemed any individual born in the United States was automatically a citizen. Wong Kim Ark was born in San Francisco to Chinese citizens and initially denied entry back to the United States due to the Chinese Exclusion Act. Because Wong Kim Ark's parents were Chinese citizens, the language in the decision also explicitly mentions parent affiliation to the Chinese government as consideration for his citizenship.

14. Fickle 2010.

15. Quintana 2015.

16. Phil Choy, Lorraine Dong, and Marlon Hom (1994) provide a visual historical analysis of the political cartoons and commercial advertisements that depicted Chinese American immigrants during the era of Chinese Exclusion. The images portrayed Chinese Americans as an economic and moral threat, which contributed to the fear of a "Yellow Peril" in the United States. The images also

include Chinese Americans as eating rats and evolving from pigs to show their racial inferiority.

17. Hom 2013; Shah 2001

18. The number of Chinese Americans who were killed during the Chinese Massacre has changed as more research is being conducted and archives are discovered. Media reports of the massacre at the time officially reported seventeen individuals; however, contemporary research has identified that the number was most likely nineteen, which still may be an underestimate.

19. In *People v. Hall* (1854), the California Supreme Court established that Chinese Americans and Chinese immigrants were legally barred from providing testimony against White citizens.

20. Foglesong 1986.

21. Wachs 2007.

22. Park Official for Plaza Site 1926, A1.

23. Finney 1920, II1.

24. Brooks 2009; Gow 2010; Umbach and Wishnoff 2008.

25. Gow 2010.

26. Open Letter concerning the New Chinatown project. Peter Soohoo Sr. papers, 1883–2007 (bulk 1923–1945), The Huntington Library, San Marino, CA.

27. Gow 2010.

28. Cheng and Kwok 2001, n.p.

29. Home for the Oriental Population Planned 1934, A10.

30. Cohan 1933, n.p.

31. Brooks 2009; C. Cheng 2013; Wu 2014.

32. Chinese Historical Society of Southern California 1984.

33. Lee 1949; Yu 2002.

34. von Hoffman 2012.

35. C. Cheng 2013.

36. Hulse 1959, n.p.

37. Brooks 2009; Massey and Denton 1993; Saito 1998.

38. Kurashige 2008.

39. Fong 1994; W. Cheng 2013.

40. Gans 1982.

41. Parson 1982.

42. Marks 2004.

43. Kurashige 2008; Parson 1982.

44. Estrada 2005; Roth 2004.

45. In the edited volume by Paul Ong, Edna Bonacich, and Lucie Cheng (1994), there are several studies that document how the occupational preferences for Asian immigrants would change according to the decline and growth of the US economy and global competition. This consequently shaped the socioeconomic demographics for Chinese Americans, as well as other Asian American communities.

46. Ma and Cartier 2003.

47. Lee 2022.

48. The demographic data presented in Tables 1 and 2, as well as throughout the book were obtained through tables provided by Social Explorer. Based on the 2010 Census, I chose five census tracts (2071.01, 2071.02, 2071.03, 1977, and 2060.1) that best matched the neighborhood boundaries shown in Map 1. These census tracts were not consistent in the prior decennial Census; however, I attempted to match the overall area each decade by examining past census tract maps.

49. Hirata 1975.

50. The race and ethnicity categories of the US. Census is a political and racial project, as the categories shift and change in response to the political context and advocacy of groups. The Asian American category was not officially recognized until the 1980 Decennial Census. Yen Le Espiritu (1992) and Linda Trinh Võ (2004) both document the advocacy of Asian American groups to include this category and there are ongoing efforts to disaggregate demographic data for Asian Americans. Because of this it is often difficult to assess demographic trends, especially with specific Asian ethnicities, as some groups have not been as consistently captured as others. This led to gaps and limitations in tracking demographic trends and interpreting neighborhood changes in Chinatown. I did not modify the data, as they were used primarily for descriptive and contextual purposes to supplement my qualitative data, but these discrepancies were considered and accounted for in how I presented my analysis.

51. McMillan 1977, B1.

52. McMillan 1984.

53. Liu and Cheng 1994; Lee 2015.

54. McMillan 1977.

55. Ong, Bonacich, and Cheng 1984.

56. The socioeconomic category of "poor" is defined as individuals whose income is 200 percent of the federal poverty level.

57. Hirata 1975.

58. Hernandez 1984.

59. Fong 1994; González 2018.

60. Li 2009.

61. Horton 1995; Saito 1998.

62. Los Angeles Department City of Planning 2000.

63. Los Angeles Department City of Planning 1996.

64. Liu and Geron 2008; Wilson 2015.

65. Sing 1980.

66. J. Revel Sims (2016) analyzed eviction data from the late 1990s as an indicator of forced displacement and found that Chinatown, as well as several other downtown adjacent neighborhoods, was a potential but inconsistent area experiencing forced displacement. Allen J. Scott (2019) also compared gentrification across Los Angeles neighborhoods using income and the presence of white-collar workers as indicators of residential displacement and found that Chinatown was one of

several central and eastern neighborhoods experiencing gentrification from 2000 to 2015. Additionally, Jan Lin (2008) provides a qualitative assessment of how the neighborhood changes are indicators of gentrification, particularly the changes in the business landscape.

67. The Chinatown Metro Station was a part of the Gold Line/L Line and was referred to as the Gold Line by community stakeholders during the time of the fieldwork. In 2023, the Gold/L Line was restructured to become the A Line.

68. Asian Americans Advancing Justice–Los Angeles 2013.

69. Lin 2008.

2. DOING THE WORK IN THE COMMUNITY

1. Chung 2007.

2. Bonus 2000; Chung 2007; Liu and Geron, 2008; Maeda 2009; Toyota 2010; Võ 2004; Wong 2006.

3. Bunyan 2010; Guo and Musso, 2007; Hustedde and Ganowicz 2002; Levine 2016.

4. Breton 1964.

5. These early community organizations in Chinatown and the Chinese American community are often colloquially referred to as family and regional associations. I use the term *mutualist organizations* as a general term for these early organizations, as some were not based purely on a specific shared Chinese ancestry. While not an emic term that is used by the community, this term is also used to describe other racialized communities' organizational formations that historically provided social and financial support in response to systematic exclusion and discrimination. The term also can be associated with anarchist and Marxist politics; however, the use of this term in the book relates specifically to the activities and practices of these groups that represent a mutual, reciprocal sharing of resources, which was not specific to any political ideology.

6. C. Cheng 2013.

7. Many of the major urban Chinatowns in the United States have a CCBA, as well as a CACA chapter which also formed between the late 1800s to early 1900s.

8. Lai 2004; Kwong and Miščević 2005.

9. The spelling of the Teo-Chew and Fukienese associations represents the regional dialect romanization and will be used throughout the book. In Mandarin Chinese, Teo-Chew refers to the Chaoshan region and Fukien refers to Fujian people and region, both in Southern China.

10. Kuah-Pearce and Du-Dehart 2006.

11. McMillan 1984.

12. Torres 1996, n.p.

13. McMillan 1984.

14. I refer to this entity as the BID to reflect how the community referred to them. Community leaders, city staff, and other stakeholders did not often refer to

the LACBC and instead referred to the organization as the BID. Thus, the BID was not seen as an abstract policy tool, but instead was spoken of as a group representing a specific stakeholder interest in the neighborhood.

15. Lin 2019.
16. Lin 2008.
17. Liu and Geron 2008; Maeda 2009.
18. Maeda 2009.
19. Nee and Nee 1986.
20. Kwong 1996; Wu 2014.
21. Throughout the book, I refer to individuals who identify as ethnic Chinese but whose family migrated from Southeast Asian countries, such as Chinese Vietnamese and Chinese Cambodian. This is aligned with common ethnic-national identity labels which tend to place ethnicity first and national origin second.
22. During this time, various community-based Chinese American historical societies and heritage organizations were established across the United States, with some being directly connected to one another. In particular, the establishment of the Chinese Historical Society of Southern California was supported by Paul Louie and Phil Choy, who had just established the Chinese Historical Society of American in San Francisco.
23. Lamont and Molnár 2002.
24. Marcuse 2009.
25. Espiritu 1992; Kwong and Miščević 2005.
26. Walker and McCarthy 2010.
27. Espiritu 1992.
28. Kwong and Miščević 2005.
29. Nicholls 2003; Walker and McCarthy 2010.
30. Kwon 2013.
31. Kwong and Miščević 2005; Nee and Nee 1986.
32. Chung 2007; Gnes 2016.

3. THE LIMITS OF LEGITIMIZING COMMUNITY CONTROL

1. Chinatown is currently part of the Historic Cultural North Neighborhood Council (HCNNC) after the HCNC formally split into two neighborhood councils in 2018. This chapter specifically examines the HCNC in Chinatown that led to the eventual formation of the HCNNC.
2. DeFilippis, Fisher, and Shragge 2009; Joseph 2002.
3. Arnstein 1969; Arroyo, Sandoval, and Bernstein 2023.
4. Cornwall 2004; Fischer 2006.
5. Arnstein 1969; Forester 1999; Quick and Feldman 2011.
6. Source: Chinese Historical Society of Southern California Archives.
7. This quote was taken from a newspaper article written by Bill White entitled "Development Fight Brewing," published on February 22, 1984. which included an

interview with Sharon Lowe. Due to the nature of the archives at the time of the research, the newspaper that this article was published in could not be easily identified or confirmed. Source: Dr. Munson A. Kwok Personal Archives.

8. Excerpt taken from Draft Meeting Minutes for the May 6, 2004, Chinatown Community Advisory Committee Meeting. Source: Dr. Munson A. Kwok Personal Archives.

9. Excerpt taken from Draft Meeting Minutes for the May 6, 2004, Chinatown Community Advisory Committee Meeting. Source: Dr. Munson A. Kwok Personal Archives.

10. Pelisek 2003, n.p.

11. Hom 2023; Hochleutner 2003; Hoyt and Gopal-Agge 2007; Kudla 2022; Morçöl and Wolk 2010; Unger 2016.

12. Zukin 2010.

13. While BID boards are supposed to represent local stakeholders, most state and local laws across North America do not require BIDs to have a governance structure similar to spaces of citizen participation where the board represents different stakeholder groups.

14. Lin 2008; Logan and Molotch 1987.

15. Kwong 1996.

16. Umemoto 2001.

17. Joseph 2002; M. Shaw 2008.

18. Flay 2021.

19. Bautista 2023.

20. Chandler 2020.

21. Selbin et al. 2018.

22. Friedmann 1987.

23. Bunyan 2010.

24. Barnes 2008.

25. Bonus 2000.

26. Bunyan 2010; Dalton 1986; Laskey and Nicholls 2019.

27. Florin and Wandersman 1990.

28. Fullilove 2004.

4. ASPIRATIONS FOR A BALANCED AND DIVERSE COMMUNITY

1. Qadeer 1997; Umemoto and Igarashi 2009.

2. Bridge, Butler, and Lees 2011; Lees 2008.

3. Wilson 1987; Sampson, Morenoff, and Gannon-Rowley 2002.

4. Crump 2002; Lees 2008; Bridge, Butler, and Lees 2011.

5. Brown-Saracino and Rumpf 2011; Freeman 2009.

6. Ahmed 2020.

7. Fainstein 2005.

8. Sarmiento 2021; Summers 2019.

9. Benford and Snow 2000; Martin 2003; Schneider 1997; Small 2005.

10. Hwang 2015; Fraser 2004.

11. Davidson and Lees 2005.

12. Marks 2004; Toji and Umemoto 2003.

13. Marks 2004.

14. The information presented in this chapter, including Tables 3 and 4, were compiled on March 2017 using several sources, including the CRA Implementation Plan 2011–2014, City of Los Angeles Certificates of Occupancy, and the City of Los Angeles Housing and Community Investment Department Redevelopment Affordable Housing Roster from August 2016. The number is inclusive of new construction since 1980 and developments that are noted with received funding from the Community Redevelopment Agency Tax Increment Low and Moderate Housing Funds. It does not include (1) the CRA-funded rehabilitation projects identified in CRA 5-Year Implementation plans and (2) older developments built before 1973 which are also considered affordable as they are protected by the rent stability ordinance (RSO).

15. Hom 2022.

16. In 2019, new city policies were set in place that placed restrictions for community use at all district schools, including Castelar Elementary School, which led to a decline in use of Castelar as a community space.

17. According to the US Census Bureau Decennial Census for 2000 and 2010 and the American Community Survey 2009–2014 5-Year Estimates, the local youth population (under eighteen years of age) decreased approximately 25 percent from 2000 to 2014 and the number of family households had decreased around 9 percent.

18. A "Title I student" refers to a student who comes from a low-income family. Title I is a federal program for K–12 public education that assists schools in providing additional educational support for students who are living at or below the poverty line.

19. Fong 1994.

20. John Horton (1995), Leland Saito (1998), Wendy Cheng (2013), and James Zarsadiaz (2022) discuss the multiracial and multiethnic dynamics and conflicts that have changed the cultural, social, physical, and political landscape of the San Gabriel Valley since the 1980s and the role Asian Americans have had in these changes. Additionally, Asian Americans Advancing Justice–Los Angeles (2018) provides a report that disaggregates data about the Asian American population in the area, showing intra-group diversity and socioeconomic differences.

21. Information was taken from a 1982 Market Analysis Report of Chinatown for the Community Redevelopment Agency of Los Angeles by Kotin, Reagin, and Mouchly, Inc.

22. W. Chung 2013; Horton 1995; Li 2009; Oh and Chung 2014; Saito 1998; Zarsadiaz 2022.

23. Oh and Chung 2014.

24. There is not a precise ethnic and racial breakdown of small business owners in Chinatown that accounts for the diaspora and intracultural differences within the Chinese American community. *Los Angeles Times* reporter Vicki Torres (1996)

indicated that the number of small businesses owned by ethnic Chinese immigrants from Southeast Asian countries was as high as 90 percent by the mid-1990s. A survey conducted by the Chinatown Neighborhood Business Development Center in 2015 indicated that this number was closer to 40 percent and that Chinese Americans, regardless of national origin, owned 90 percent of small businesses, although they did not survey all the businesses in Chinatown for their study.

25. Li 2009.

26. Evictions in Chinatown tend to also be underreported as many of the tenants have limited English skills. CCED and CSC representatives explained how residents did not always fully comprehend these notices, which were often sent in English. In my volunteer work with CCED, I also witnessed how one resident asked a CCED member to help them translate a notice from their landlord, which further confirmed how Chinatown residents may be especially vulnerable for evictions due to language barriers.

27. Brown-Saracino and Rumpf 2011; Freeman 2005; Freeman and Braconi 2004; Vigdor, Massey, and Rivlin 2002; Slater 2009.

5. SUSTAINING AN ETHNIC CULTURE OF PLACE

1. Zukin 1995.

2. Fainstein 2005; Hackworth and Rekers 2005; Lin 2011; Zukin et al. 2009.

3. Grodach and Loukaitou-Sideris 2007.

4. Lin 2008; Pottie-Sherman, 2010; Sze 2010; Umbach and Wishnoff 2008.

5. Aguilar-San Juan 2009; Anderson and Sternberg 2013; Dávila 2004; Knapp and Vojnovic 2013; Lin 2011; Shaw, Bagwell, and Karmowska 2004; Summers 2019.

6. Jubas 2007.

7. Hurley 2010

8. Cheng 2009; Hodder 1999; Lin 2011; Saito 2009; Võ 2004.

9. Technically outside the current neighborhood boundaries, the Chinese American Museum (CAM) is located in the Garnier Building in the El Pueblo de Los Angeles Historical monument, a building that is recognized in the National Register of Historic Places. The Garnier Building is also the only remaining site from Old Chinatown, and CAM's presence in this building has helped to mark that space as a significant historical site for the Chinese American community within El Pueblo, which celebrates the city's multiethnic history.

10. Tabor 2015.

11. Kwong 1996.

12. Source: Dr. Munson A. Kwok Personal Archives.

13. Sze 2010.

14. Source: Dr. Munson A. Kwok Personal Archives.

15. El Pueblo de Los Angeles is a separate department within the City of Los Angeles and has a special commission that oversees that area. In addition, El Pueblo is not part of the same Council District as Chinatown.

16. Aguilar-San Juan 2009.

17. Hom 2022.

18. Acolin and Vitello 2017; Lin 1998.

19. This quote was taken from McMillan (1977) which included an interview with Wilbur Woo.

20. Pierson 2016.

21. Slayton 2016, n.p.

22. Brown-Saracino 2004.

23. While some have argued that ethnic churches have been sites of assimilation, Russell Jeung (2005) also argues that these have and continue to be everyday sites of racial formation for Chinese Americans. These churches were sites to negotiate their identities and political belonging, both in the United States and China, reflecting how they were adopting Western Christian values, but also were racialized outsiders. The built environment of these churches reflects this identity negotiation, as shown with the Methodist Church. Similar to Central Plaza, the Methodist Church has the traditional Chinese rooftop design.

24. The gateways in the major historic urban Chinatowns in the United States were primarily built in the post–World War II era, with many being less than fifty years old at the time of my fieldwork. The San Francisco Chinatown Gate was built in 1970, the Seattle Chinatown Gate was built in 2008, and the Boston Chinatown Gate was built in 1976.

25. Umbach and Wishnoff 2008.

26. Wong 2019.

27. Molina 2015.

28. McMillan 1984; Torres 1996.

29. Dávila 2004; Zukin 2010.

30. Chinatown Neighborhood Business Development Center 2015.

31. Shyong 2017, n.p.

32. Huynh 2020.

33. Florida 2003.

34. Burnett 2014; Grodach and Loukaitou-Sideris 2007; Lin 2019; K. Shaw 2008; Sullivan and Shaw 2011; Zukin, et al 2009.

35. Coleman 2019.

36. Ngô 2012.

37. Lin 2008.

38. Zukin 1995.

39. Burnett 2014.

40. Ethnic festivals in Los Angeles have historically promoted tourism, especially in a way that also capitalized on its proximity to Hollywood and the movie industry. For example, before China City was destroyed, it hosted the Autumn Moon Festival and included celebrity stars and guests as part of the programming. This type of cultural tourism in China City reflected the background of developer, Christine Sterling, who was a socialite connected to the movie industry. Arguably, the Hollywood elements of the local ethnic festivals in China City also further

contributed to the critiques that this specific site, which already included buildings from the movie *Good Earth*, was more of a Hollywood version of Chinatown than a "true" Chinatown.

41. Quotation was taken from an excerpt from the Project for Public Spaces website in March 2018 (https://www.pps.org/article/la-Chinatown-summer-nights), which has been taken down by the agency as of July 2022. This was an agency that specialized in placemaking efforts and was hired as a third-party consultant to assist in the development of Chinatown Summer Nights.

42. Summers 2019.

43. Ong 1984.

44. Florida 2011.

45. Tabares 2021; Lee 2013.

46. Lin 1998.

47. Cheung (in press).

48. Cheung (in press).

49. Brown-Saracino 2004; Zukin 2010.

50. The magazine ran from 2017 to 2019. In 2023, there were discussions to revive the magazine with a youth group in the San Gabriel Valley.

CONCLUSION

1. Anderson and Sternberg 2013; Boyd 2008; Patillo 2007.

2. Li 2009.

3. Horton 1996; Lung-Amam 2017; Saito 1998; W. Cheng 2013; Zarsadiaz 2022.

4. Aoki and Nakanishi 2001; Wong 2006.

5. Kwong 1996.

6. Muñiz 2023.

7. National Association of Latino Elected Officials Education Fund 2021.

8. Hum 2014; Saito 1998.

9. Chung 2007.

10. Boyd 2008; Hyra 2008; Patillo 2007.

11. Lin 2008.

APPENDIX

1. Holstein and Gubrium 1995; Rubin and Rubin 1996.

REFERENCES

Acolin, Arthur, and Domenic Vitiello. 2018. "Who Owns Chinatown: Neighbourhood Preservation and Change in Boston and Philadelphia." *Urban Studies* 55 (8): 1690–710. https://doi.org/10.1177/0042098017699366.

Aguilar-San Juan, Karin. 2009. *Little Saigons: Staying Vietnamese in America.* Minneapolis: University of Minnesota Press.

Ahmed, Sarah. 2020. *On Being Included: Racism and Diversity in Institutional Life.* Durham, NC: Duke University Press.

Anderson, Matthew B., and Carolina Sternberg. 2013. "'Non-white' Gentrification in Chicago's Bronzeville and Pilsen: Racial Economy and the Intraurban Contingency of Urban Redevelopment." *Urban Affairs Review* 49(3): 435–67. https://doi.org/10.1177/1078087412465590.

Aoki, Andrew L., and Don T. Nakanishi. 2001. "Asian Pacific Americans and the New Minority Politics." *PS: Political Science and Politics* 34(3): 605–10. https://www.jstor.org/stable/1353547.

Arnstein, Sherry R. 1969. "A Ladder of Citizen Participation." *Journal of the American Institute of Planners* 35(4): 216–24. https://doi.org/10.1080/01944366908977225

Arroyo, John, C., Gerald F. Sandoval, and Joanna Bernstein. 2023. "Sixty Years of Racial Equity Planning." *Journal of the American Planning Association,* https://doi.org/10.1080/01944363.2022.2132986.

Asian Americans Advancing Justice–Los Angeles. 2013. *A Community of Contrasts: Asian Americans, Native Hawaiians, and Pacific Islanders in Los Angeles County.* Los Angeles: Asian Americans Advancing Justice–Los Angeles. https://advancingjustice-la.org/system/files/CommunityofContrasts_LACounty2013 .pdf.

———. 2018. *A Community of Contrasts: Asian Americans, Native Hawaiians, and Pacific Islanders in the San Gabriel Valley.* Los Angeles: Asian Americans Advancing Justice-Los Angeles. https://advancingjustice-la.org/sites/default/files/A _Community_of_Contrasts_SGV_2018.pdf.

Atkinson, Rowland. 2015. "Losing One's Place: Narratives of Neighborhood Change, Market Injustice and Symbolic Displacement." *Housing, Theory and Society* 32(4): 373–88. https://doi.org/10.1080/14036096.2015.1053980.

Attoh, Kafui. A. 2011. "What Kind of Right Is the Right to the City?" *Progress in Human Geography* 35(5): 669–85. https://doi.org/10.1177/0309132510394706.

Avila, Eric. 2006. *Popular Culture in the Age of White Flight: Fear and Fantasy in Suburban Los Angeles*. Berkeley: University of California Press.

Barnes, Marian. 2008. "Passionate Participation: Emotional Experiences and Expressions in Deliberative Forums." *Critical Social Policy* 28(4): 461–81. https://doi.org/10.1177/0261018308095280.

Bautista, Christian. 2023. "Infamous Chinatown Landlord Gets $97M for Senior Residential complex." *The Real Deal Real Estate News*, July 6. https://therealdeal.com/la/2023/07/06/infamous-Chinatown-landlord-gets-97m-for-senior-resi-complex/.

Benford, Robert D., and David A. Snow. 2000. "Framing Processes and Social Movements: An Overview and Assessment." *Annual Review of Sociology* 26(1): 611–39. https://doi.org/10.1146/annurev.soc.26.1.611.

Bonilla-Silva, Eduardo. 2003. "Racial Attitudes or Racial Ideology? An Alternative Paradigm for Examining Actors' Racial Views." *Journal of Political Ideologies* 8(1): 63–82. https://doi.org/10.1080/13569310306082.

Bonus, Rick. 2000. *Locating Filipino Americans: Ethnicity and the Cultural Politics of Space*. Philadelphia: Temple University Press.

Boyd, Michelle. 2008. "Defensive Development: The Role of Racial Conflict in Gentrification." *Urban Affairs Review* 43(6): 751–76. https://doi.org/10.1177/1078087407313581.

Breton, Raymond. 1964. "Institutional Completeness of Ethnic Communities and the Personal Relations of Immigrants." *American Journal of Sociology* 70(2): 193–205. https://doi.org/10.1086/223793.

Bridge, Gary T., Tim Butler, and Loretta Lees, eds. 2011. *Mixed Communities: Gentrification by Stealth?* Bristol, UK: Policy Press.

Brooks, Charlotte. 2009. *Alien Neighbors, Foreign Friends: Asian Americans, Housing, and the Transformation of Urban California*. Chicago: University of Chicago Press.

Brown-Saracino, Japonica. 2004. "Social Preservationists and the Quest for Authentic Community." *City & Community* 3(2): 135–56. https://doi.org/10.1111/j.1535-6841.2004.00073.x.

Brown-Saracino, Japonica, and Cesraea Rumpf. 2011. "Diverse Imageries of Gentrification: Evidence from Newspaper Coverage in Seven U.S. Cities, 1986–2006." *Journal of Urban Affairs* 33(3): 289–315. https://doi.org/10.1111/j.1467-9906.2011.00552.x.

Bunyan, Paul. 2010. "Broad-Based Organizing in the UK: Reasserting the Centrality of Political Activity in Community Development." *Community Development Journal* 45(1): 111–27. https://doi.org/10.1093/cdj/bsn034.

Burawoy, Michael. 1998. "The Extended Case Method." *Sociological Theory* 16(1): 4–33. https://doi.org/10.1111/0735-2751.00040.

Burnett, Katherine. 2014. "Commodifying Poverty: Gentrification and Consumption in Vancouver's Downtown Eastside." *Urban Geography* 35(2): 157–76. https://doi.org/10.1080/02723638.2013.867669.

Byon, Anna. 2020. *"Everyone Deserves to Be Seen": Recommendations for Improved Federal Data on Asian Americans and Pacific Islanders (AAPI)."* Washington, DC: Institute for Higher Education Policy.

Chandler, Jenna. 2020. "Warrant Issued for Head of Chinatown Business Improvement District." *Curbed Los Angeles*, February 5. https://la.curbed.com/2020/2/5/21125196/Chinatown-george-yu-bid-skid-row.

Chen, Yong. 2002. *Chinese San Francisco, 1850–1943: A Trans-Pacific Community.* Stanford, CA: Stanford University Press.

Cheng, Cindy I-Feng. 2009. "Identities and Places: On Writing the History of Filipinotown, Los Angeles." *Journal of Asian American Studies* 12(1): 1–33. https://doi.org/10.1353/jaas.0.0025.

———. 2013. *Citizens of Asian America: Democracy and Race during the Cold War.* New York: New York University Press.

Cheng, Suellen, and Munson A. Kwok. 2001. "The Golden Years of Los Angeles Chinatown: The Beginning." In *Bridging the Centuries: History of Chinese Americans in Southern California,* edited by Susie Ling, 33–43. Los Angeles: Chinese Historical Society of Southern California.

Cheng, Wendy. 2013. *The Changs Next Door to the Diazes: Remapping Race in Southern California.* Minneapolis: University of Minnesota Press.

Cheung, Erica Maria. In press. "Upscaling Authenticity: Asian American Food Gentrification in Chinatown." In *Eating (More) Asian America,* edited by Martin F. Manalansan, Anita Mannur, and Robert Ji-Song Ku. New York: New York University Press.

Chinatown Neighborhood Business Development Center. 2015. *Los Angeles Chinatown Neighborhood Business Needs Assessment.* Los Angeles: Chinatown Service Center and Asian Pacific Islander Small Business Program.

Chinese Historical Society of Southern California. 1984. *Linking Our Lives: Chinese American Women of Los Angeles.* Los Angeles: Chinese Historical Society of Southern California.

Choy, Phil, Lorraine Dong, and Marlon K. Hom. 1994. *The Coming Man: 19th-Century American Perspectives of the Chinese.* Seattle: University of Washington Press.

Chung, Angie. 2007. *Legacies of Struggle: Conflict & Cooperation in Korean American Politics.* Stanford, CA: Stanford University Press.

Cohan, Charles C. 1933. "New Colorful Oriental Town Projected Here." *Los Angeles Times*, October 22, 19, 21.

Coleman, Madeline Leung. 2019. "How Chinese Food Fueled the Rise of California Punk." *Topic Magazine*, June 25. https://www.topic.com/how-chinese-food-fueled-the-rise-of-california-punk.

Cornwall, Andrea. 2004. "Introduction: New Democratic Spaces? The Politics and Dynamics of Institutionalised Participation." *IDS Bulletin* 35(2): 1–10. https://doi.org/10.1111/j.1759-5436.2004.tb00115.x.

Crump, Jeff. 2002. "Deconcentration by Demolition: Public Housing, Poverty, and Urban Policy." *Environment and Planning D: Society and Space* 20(5): 581–96. https://doi.org/10.1068/d306.

Dalton, Linda C. 1986. "Why the Rational Paradigm Persists: The Resistance of Professional Education and Practice to Alternative Forms of Planning." *Journal of Planning Education and Research* 5(3): 147–53. https://doi.org/10.1177/0739456 x8600500302.

Danley, Stephen, and Rasheda Weaver. 2018. "'They're Not Building It for Us': Displacement Pressure, Unwelcomeness, and Protesting Neighborhood Investment." *Societies* 8(3): 74. https://doi.org/10.3390/soc8030074.

Davidson, Mark, and Loretta Lees. 2005. "New-Build 'Gentrification' and London's Riverside Renaissance. *Environment and Planning A: Economy and Space* 37(7): 1165–90. https://doi.org/10.1068/a3739.

Dávila, Arlene. 2004. *Barrio Dreams: Puerto Ricans, Latinos, and the Neoliberal City.* Berkeley: University of California Press.

Dear, Michael. J. 1996. "In the City, Time Becomes Visible: Intentionality and Urbanism in Los Angeles, 1781–1991." In *The City: Los Angeles and Urban Theory at the end of the Twentieth Century*, edited by Allen J. Scott and Edward W. Soja, 76–105. Berkeley: University of California Press.

Dear, Michael J., and Steven Flusty. 2002. "Los Angeles as Postmodern Urbanism." In *From Chicago to L.A.: Making Sense of Urban Theory*, edited by Michael J. Dear, 61–84. Thousand Oaks, CA: Sage Publications.

Defilippis, James, Robert Fisher, and Eric Shragge. 2009. *Contesting Community: The Limits and Potential of Local Organizing*. New Brunswick, NJ: Rutgers University Press.

Delgado, Emanuel, and Kate Swanson. 2021. "Gentefication in the Barrio: Displacement and Urban Change in Southern California." *Journal of Urban Affairs* 43(7): 925–40. https://doi.org/10.1080/07352166.2019.1680245.

Elliott-Cooper, Adam, Phil Hubbard, and Loretta Lees. 2020. "Moving beyond Marcuse: Gentrification, Displacement and the violence of un-homing." *Progress in Human Geography* 44(3): 492–509. https://doi.org/10.1177/03091325198 30511.

Espiritu, Yen Le. 1992. *Asian American Panethnicity: Bridging Institutions and Identities*. Philadelphia: Temple University Press.

Estrada, Gilbert. 2005. "If You Build It, They Will Move: The Los Angeles Freeway System and the Displacement of Mexican East Los Angeles, 1944–1972." *Southern California Quarterly* 87(3): 287–315. http://www.jstor.com/stable /41172272.

Fainstein, Susan. 2005. "Cities and Diversity: Should We Want It? Can We Plan for It?" *Urban Affairs Review* 41(1): 3–19. https://doi.org/10.1177/1078087405 278968.

———. 2010. "Redevelopment Planning and Distributive Justice in the American Metropolis." *SSRN Electronic Journal*, August. https://dx.doi.org/10.2139/ssrn .1657723.

Fainstein, Susan, and Norman I. Fainstein. 1989. "The Racial Dimension in Urban Political Economy." *Urban Affairs Quarterly* 25(2): 187–99. https://doi.org/10.1177/004208168902500201.

Fallon, Katherine F. 2021. "Reproducing Race in the Gentrifying City: A Critical Analysis of Race in Gentrification Scholarship." *Journal of Race, Ethnicity and the City* 2(1): 1–28. https://doi.org/10.1080/26884674.2020.1847006.

Feagin, Joe R. 2013. *The White Racial Frame: Centuries of Racial Framing and Counter-Framing.* London: Routledge.

Fickle, Tara. 2010. "A History of Los Angeles City Market:1930–1950." *Gum Saan Journal* 32(1): 24–38.

Finney, Guy W. 1920. "Wanted: New Chinatown Site." *Los Angeles Times*, February 22, 1920.

Fischer, Frank. 2006. "Participatory Governance as Deliberative Empowerment." *American Review of Public Administration* 36(1): 19–40. https://doi.org/10.1177/0275074005282582.

Flay, Sophie. 2021. "City Attorney Files 16 Criminal Charges against Chinatown Building Owner." *ABC7 Eyewitness News*, October 29. https://abc7.com/Chinatown-seniors-elderly-cathay-manor/11179300/.

Florida, Richard. 2003. "Cities and the Creative Class." *City & Community* 2(1): 3–19. https://doi.org/10.1111/1540-6040.00034.

Florin, Paul, and Abraham Wandersman. 1990. "An Introduction to Citizen Participation, Voluntary Organizations, and Community Development: Insights for Empowerment through Research." *American Journal of Community Psychology* 18(1): 41–54. https://doi.org/10.1007/bf00922688.

Fogelson, Robert M. 1993. *The Fragmented Metropolis: Los Angeles, 1850–1930.* Berkeley: University of California Press.

Foglesong, Richard E. 1986. *Planning the Capitalist City: The Colonial Era to the 1920s.* Princeton, NJ: Princeton University Press.

Fong, Timothy. 1994. *The First Suburban Chinatown: The Remaking of Monterey Park, California.* Philadelphia: Temple University Press.

Forester, John. 1989. *Planning in the Face of Power.* Berkeley: University of California Press.

———. 1999. *The Deliberative Practitioner: Encouraging Participatory Planning Processes.* Cambridge, MA: MIT Press.

Fraser, James C. 2004. "Beyond Gentrification: Mobilizing Communities and Claiming Space." *Urban Geography* 25(5): 437–57. https://doi.org/10.2747/0272-3638.25.5.437.

Freeman, Lance. 2005. "Displacement or Succession? Residential Mobility in Gentrifying Neighborhoods." *Urban Affairs Review* 40(4): 463–91. https://doi.org/10.1177/1078087404273341.

———. 2009. *There Goes the 'Hood.* Philadelphia: Temple University Press.

Freeman, Lance, and Frank Braconi. 2004. "Gentrification and Displacement: New York City in the 1990s." *Journal of the American Planning Association* 70(1): 39–52. https://doi.org/10.1080/01944360408976337.

Friedmann, John. 1987. *Planning in the Public Domain: From Knowledge to Action.* Princeton, NJ: Princeton University Press.

Fujino, Diane C. 2008. "Race, Place, Space, and Political Development: Japanese-American Radicalism in the 'Pre-Movement' 1960s." *Social Justice* 35(2): 57–79. https://www.jstor.org/stable/29768488.

Fullilove, Mindy T. 2004. *Root Shock: How Tearing Up City Neighborhoods Hurts America, and What We Can Do about It.* Baltimore: One World.

Gans, Herbert J. 1982. *The Urban Villagers.* New York: Simon and Schuster.

Glass, Ruth. 1964. *London: Aspects of Change.* London: MacGibbon & Kee.

Gnes, Davide. 2016. "Organisational Legitimacy beyond Ethnicity? Shifting Organisational Logics in the Struggle for Immigrant Rights in Los Angeles." *Journal of Ethnic and Migration Studies* 42(9): 1420–38. https://doi.org/10.1080/1369183x.2016.1145045.

González, Jerry. 2018. *In Search of the Mexican Beverly Hills: Latino Suburbanization in Postwar Los Angeles.* New Brunswick, NJ: Rutgers University Press.

Gow, William. 2010. "Building a Chinese Village in Los Angeles: Christine Sterling and the Residents of China City, 1938–1948." *Gum Saan Journal* 32(1): 39–53.

Grodach, Carl, and Anastasia Loukaitou-Sideris. 2007. "Cultural Development Strategies and Urban Revitalization." *International Journal of Cultural Policy* 13(4): 349–70. https://doi.org/10.1080/10286630701683235.

Guo, Chao, and Juliet A. Musso. 2007. "Representation in Nonprofit and Voluntary Organizations: A Conceptual Framework." *Nonprofit and Voluntary Sector Quarterly* 36(2): 308–26. https://doi.org/10.1177/0899764006289764.

Hackworth, Jason, and Josephine Rekers. 2005. "Ethnic Packaging and Gentrification: The Case of Four Neighborhoods in Toronto." *Urban Affairs Review,* 41(2): 211–36. https://doi.org/10.1177/1078087405280859.

Hackworth, Jason, and Neil Smith. 2001. "The Changing State of Gentrification." *Journal of Economic and Human Geography* 92(4): 464–77. https://doi.org/10.1111/1467-9663.00172.

Harvey, David. 2003. "The Right to the City." *International Journal of Urban and Regional Research* 27(4): 939–41. https://doi.org/10.1111/j.0309-1317.2003.00492.x.

———. 2012. *Rebel Cities: From the Right to the City to the Urban Revolution.* London: Verso.

Harwood, Stacy A. 2005. "Struggling to Embrace Difference in Land-Use Decision Making in Multicultural Communities." *Planning Practice and Research* 20(4): 355–71. https://doi.org/10.1080/02697450600766746.

Hernandez, Marita. 1984. Lincoln Heights: Once Again, the Old Neighborhood Sees Change. *Los Angeles Times,* December 3, 4, 6.

Hirata, Lucy C. 1975. "Toward a Political Economy of Chinese America: A Study of Property Ownership in Los Angeles Chinatown." *Amerasia Journal* 3(1): 76–95. https://doi.org/10.17953/amer.3.1.31q4500018823j65.

Hochleutner, Brian R. 2003. "BIDs Fare Well: The Democratic Accountability of Business Improvement Districts." *NYU Law Review* 78(1): 374–404.

https://www.nyulawreview.org/issues/volume-78-number-1/bids-fare-well-the
-democratic-accountability-of-business-improvement-districts.

Hodder, Robert. 1999. "Redefining a Southern City's Heritage: Historic Preservation Planning, Public Art, and Race in Richmond, Virginia." *Journal of Urban Affairs* 21(4): 437–53. https://doi.org/10.1111/0735-2166.00030.

Holstein, James A., and Jaber F. Gubrium. 1995. *The Active Interview*. Thousand Oaks, CA: Sage Publications.

Hom, Laureen D. 2013. "The Chinese Hospital of San Francisco: How the Early San Francisco Chinese Mobilized to Build the Chinatown Community." In *Handbook of Asian American Health*, edited by Grace J. Yoo and Mai Nhung Le, 353–62. New York: Springer Publishing Co.

———. 2022. "Symbols of Gentrification? Narrating Displacement in Los Angeles Chinatown." *Urban Affairs Review* 58(1):196–228. https://doi.org/10.1177/1078087420954917.

———. 2023. "Revitalizing Chinatown for a New Generation: The Community Politics of the Business Improvement District." *Journal of Urban Affairs*. https://doi.org/10.1080/07352166.2023.2192939.

Horton, John. 1995. *The Politics of Diversity: Immigration, Resistance, and Change in Monterey Park, California*. Philadelphia: Temple University Press.

Hoyt, Lorlene, and Devika Gopal-Agge. 2007. "The Business Improvement District Model: A Balanced Review of Contemporary Debates." *Geography Compass* 1(4): 946–58. https://doi.org/10.1111/j.1749-8198.2007.00041.x.

Huante, Alfredo. 2019. "A Lighter Shade of Brown? Racial Formation and Gentrification in Los Angeles." *Social Problems* 68(1): 63–79. https://doi.org/10.1093/socpro/spz047.

———. 2021. "Planning the Barrio: Racial Order and Restructuring in Neoliberal Los Angeles." *Urban Affairs Review* 58(4): 996–1027. https://doi.org/10.1177/10780874211021332.

Hulse, Jerry. 1959. "Chinatown Changing as Suburbs Call Residents." *Los Angeles Times*, October 26, 2, 22.

Hum, Tarry. 2014. *Making a Global Immigrant Neighborhood: Brooklyn's Sunset Park*. Philadelphia: Temple University Press.

Hurley, Andrew. 2010. *Beyond Preservation: Using Public History to Revitalize Inner Cities*. Philadelphia: Temple University Press.

Hustedde, Ronald J., and Jacek Ganowicz. 2002. "The Basics: What's Essential about Theory for Community Development Practice?" *Community Development* 33(1): 1–19. https://doi.org/10.1080/15575330209490139.

Huynh, Frances. 2020. "From Chinese Donuts to Leek Cakes: Navigating Los Angeles Chinatown's Golden Waters." In *American Chinese Restaurants: Society, Culture, and Consumption*, edited by Jenny Banh and Haiming Liu, 26–43. New York: Routledge.

Hwang, Jackelyn. 2015. "The Social Construction of a Gentrifying Neighborhood: Reifying and Redefining Identity and Boundaries in Inequality." *Urban Affairs Review* 52(1): 1–31. https://doi.org/10.1177/1078087415570643.

Hyra, Derek S. 2008. *The New Urban Renewal: The Economic Transformation of Harlem and Bronzeville*. Chicago: University of Chicago Press.

———. 2012. "Conceptualizing the New Urban Renewal: Comparing the Past to the Present." *Urban Affairs Review* 48(4): 498–527. https://doi.org/10.1177/1078087411434905.

———. 2015. "The Back-to-the-City Movement: Neighbourhood Redevelopment and Processes of Political and Cultural Displacement." *Urban Studies* 52(10): 1753–73. https://doi.org/10.1177/0042098014539403.

Jeung, Russell. 2005. *Faithful Generations: Race and New Asian American Churches*. New Brunswick, NJ: Rutgers University Press.

Joseph, Miranda. 2002. *Against the Romance of Community*. Minneapolis: University of Minnesota Press.

Jubas, Kaela. 2007. "Conceptual Con/fusion in Democratic Societies: Understandings and Limitations of Consumer-Citizenship." *Journal of Consumer Culture* 7(2): 231–54. https://doi.org/10.1177/1469540507077683.

Knapp, Anthony, and Igor Vojnovic. 2013. "Rethinking the Growth Machine: How to Erase a Chinatown from the Urban Core." *Urban Geography* 34(1): 53–85. https://doi.org/10.1080/02723638.2013.778634.

Kotin, Regan, and Mouchly, Inc. 1982. *Market Analysis of the Chinatown Redevelopment Project*. Los Angeles, CA: Kotin, Regan & Mouchly, Inc.

Kuah-Pearce, Khun Eng, and Evelyn Du-Dehart, eds. 2006. *Voluntary Organizations in the Chinese Diaspora*. Hong Kong: Hong Kong University Press.

Kudla, Daniel. 2022. "Fifty Years of Business Improvement Districts: A Reappraisal of the Dominant Perspectives and Debates." *Urban Studies* 59(14): 2837–56. https://doi.org/10.1177/00420980211066420.

Kurashige, Scott. 2008. *The Shifting Grounds of Race: Black and Japanese Americans in the Making of Multiethnic Los Angeles*. Princeton, NJ: Princeton University Press.

———. 2010. "Between "White Spot" and "World City": Racial Integration and the Roots of Multiculturalism." In *A Companion to Los Angeles*, edited by William Deverell and Greg Hise, 56–71. Oxford: Blackwell Publishers.

Kwon, Sooh Ah. 2013. "The Politics and Institutionalization of Panethnic Identity." *Journal of Asian American Studies* 16(2): 137–57. https://doi.org/10.1353/jaas.2013.0016.

Kwong, Peter. 1996. *The New Chinatown*. New York: Hill and Wang.

Kwong, Peter, and Dusanka Miščević. 2005. *Chinese America: The Untold Story of America's Oldest New Community*. New York: New Press.

Lai, Clement. 2012. "The Racial Triangulation of Space: The Case of Urban Renewal in San Francisco's Fillmore District." *Annals of the Association of American Geographers* 102(1): 151–70. https://doi.org/10.1080/00045608.2011.583572.

Lai, Him Mark. 2004. *Becoming Chinese American: A History of Communities and Institutions*. Walnut Creek, CA: Alta Mira Press.

Lamont, Michèle, and Virág Molnár. 2002. "The Study of Boundaries in the Social Sciences." *Annual Review of Sociology* 28: 167–95. https://doi.org/10.1146/annurev.soc.28.110601.141107.

Laskey, Allison B., and Walter Nicholls. 2019. "Jumping off the Ladder: Participation and Insurgency in Detroit's Urban Planning." *Journal of the American Planning Association* 85(3): 348–62. https://doi.org/10.1080/01944363.2019 .1618729.

Lee, Erika. 2015. *The Making of Asian America: A History.* New York: Simon & Schuster.

Lee, Rose Hum. 1949. "The Decline of Chinatowns in the United States." *American Journal of Sociology* 54(5): 422–32. https://doi.org/10.1086/220396.

Lee, Shelley Sang-Hee. 2022. *Koreatown, Los Angeles: Immigration, Race, and the "American Dream."* Stanford, CA: Stanford University Press.

Lee, Youyoung. 2013. "In America, a New Creative Class." *HuffPost*, October 27. https://www.huffpost.com/entry/in-america-a-new-asian-creative-class_b _3822813.

Lees, Loretta. 2008. "Gentrification and Social Mixing: Towards an Inclusive Urban Renaissance?" *Urban Studies* 45(12): 2449–70. https://doi.org/10.1177 /0042098008097099.

Lefebvre, Henri. 1991. *The Production of Space.* Translated by Donald Nicholson-Smith. Oxford: Blackwell Publishing.

Levine, Jeremy R. 2016. "The Privatization of Political Representation: Community-Based Organizations as Nonelected Neighborhood Representatives." *American Sociological Review* 81(6): 1251–75. https://doi.org/10.1177/0003122416670655.

Li, Bethany Y. 2016. "Now Is the Time! Challenging Resegregation and Displacement in the Age of Hypergentrification." *Fordham Law Review* 85(3): 1189–242. https://ir.lawnet.fordham.edu/flr/vol85/iss3/11.

Li, Wei. 2009. *Ethnoburb: The New Ethnic Community in Urban America.* Honolulu: University of Hawaii Press.

Li, Wei, Gary Dymski, Maria W. L. Chee, Hyeon-Hyo Ahn, Carolyn Aldana, and Yu Zhou. 2006. "How Ethnic Banks Matter: Banking and Community/Economic Development in Los Angeles." In *Landscapes of the Ethnic Economy,* edited by David H. Kaplan and Wei Li, 113–33. Lanham, MD: Rowman & Littlefield.

Light, Ivan. 2002. "Immigrant Place Entrepreneurs in Los Angeles, 1970–99." *International Journal of Urban and Regional Research* 26(2): 215–28. https://doi.org /10.1111/1468-2427.00376.

Lin, Jan. 1998. *Reconstructing Chinatown: Ethnic Enclave, Global Change.* Minneapolis: University of Minnesota Press.

———. 2008. "Los Angeles Chinatown: Tourism, Gentrification, and the Rise of an Ethnic Growth Machine." *Amerasia Journal* 34(3): 110–26. https://doi.org/10 .17953/amer.34.3.v545v63lpj1535p7.

———. 2011. *The Power of Urban Ethnic Places: Cultural Heritage and Community Life.* New York: Routledge.

———. 2019. *Taking Back the Boulevard: Art, Activism, and Gentrification in Los Angeles.* New York: New York University Press.

Ling, Susie. 2001. "Our Legacy: History of Chinese Americans in Southern California." In *Bridging the Centuries: History of Chinese Americans in Southern*

California, edited by Susie Ling, 12–29. Los Angeles: Chinese Historical Society of Southern California.

Liu, John M and Lucie Cheng. 1994. "Pacific Rim Development and the Duality of Post-1965 Asian Immigration to the United States." In *The New Asian Immigration in Los Angeles and Global Restructuring,* edited by Paul Ong, Edna Bonacich, and Lucie Cheng, 74–99. Philadelphia: Temple University Press.

Liu, Laura Y. 2000. "The Place of Immigration in Studies of Geography and Race." *Social and Cultural Geography* 1(2): 169–82. https://doi.org/10.1080/146493600 20010185.

Liu, Michael, and Kim Geron. 2008. "Changing Neighborhood: Ethnic Enclaves and the Struggle for Social Justice." *Social Justice* 35(2): 18–35. http://www.jstor .org/stable/29768486.

Logan, John R., Richard D. Alba, Tom McNulty, and Brian Fisher. 1996. "Making a Place in the Metropolis: Locational Attainment in Cities and Suburbs. *Demography* 33(4): 443–53. https://doi.org/10.2307/2061779.

Logan, John R., and Harvey L. Molotch. 1987. *Urban Fortunes: The Political Economy of Place.* Berkeley: University of California Press.

Los Angeles Department City of Planning. 1996. *Los Angeles General Plan Framework Element.* https://planning.lacity.org/plans-policies/framework-element.

———. 2000. *Central City North Community Plan Update.* https://planning .lacity.org/odocument/e06434a6-341a-48ed-97dc-8f6a85780951/Central_City _North_Community_Plan.pdf.

Los Angeles Times. 1926. "Park Official for Plaza Site." April 22, A1.

Los Angeles Times . 1934. "Home for the Oriental Population Planned." September 21, A10.

Lung-Amam, Willow. 2017. *Trespassers? Asian Americans and the Battle for Suburbia.* Oakland: University of California Press.

———. 2021. *Businesses Are Victims of Gentrification, Too.* Washington, DC: Brookings Institute. https://policycommons.net/artifacts/4142868/businesses-are -victims-of-gentrification-too/4950665.

Ma, Laurence J., and Carolyn Cartier. 2003, eds. *The Chinese Diaspora: Space, Place, Mobility, and Identity.* Lanham, MD: Rowman & Littlefield.

Maeda, Daryl J. 2009. *Chains of Babylon: The Rise of Asian America.* Minneapolis: University of Minnesota Press.

Marcuse, Peter. 1985. "Gentrification, Abandonment, and Displacement: Connections, Causes and Policy Responses in New York City." *Washington University Journal of Urban and Contemporary Law* 28: 195–240. https://openscholarship .wustl.edu/law_urbanlaw/vol28/iss1/4.

———. 1997. "The Enclave, the Citadel, and the Ghetto: What Has Changed in the Post-Fordist U.S. City." *Urban Affairs Review* 33(2): 228–64. https://doi.org/10 .1177/107808749703300206.

———. 2009. "From Critical Urban Theory to the Right to the City." *City* 13(2–3): 185–97. https://doi.org/10.1080/13604810902982177.

Marks, Mara A. 2004. "Shifting Ground: The Rise and Fall of the Los Angeles Community Redevelopment Agency." *Southern California Quarterly* 86(3): 241–90. https://www.jstor.org/stable/41172224.

Martin, Deborah G. 2003. "'Place-Framing' as Place-Making: Constituting a Neighborhood for Organizing and Activism." *Annals of the Association of American Geographers* 93(3): 730–50. https://doi.org/10.1111/1467-8306.9303011.

Massey, Douglas S., and Nancy A. Denton. 1985. "Spatial Assimilation as a Socioeconomic Outcome." *American Sociological Review* 50(1): 94–106. https://doi.org/10.2307/2095343.

———. 1987. "Trends in the Residential Segregation of Blacks, Hispanics, and Asians: 1970–1980." *American Sociological Review* 52(6): 802–25. https://doi.org/10.2307/2095836.

Mayer, Margit. 2009. "The 'Right to the City' in the Context of Shifting Mottos of Urban Social Movements." *City* 13(2–3): 362–74. https://doi.org/10.1080/13604810902982755.

McMillan, Penelope. 1977. "LA's Chinatown Turns from Tourists to the Chinese." *Los Angeles Times*, September 18, B1, B4–5.

———. 1984. "Vietnam Chinese Transform Chinatown." *Los Angeles Times*, December 1, A14–15.

Molina, Natalia. 2005. *Fit to Be Citizens? Public Health and Race in Los Angeles, 1879–1939*. Berkeley: University of California Press.

———. 2015. "The Importance of Place and Place-Makers in the Life of a Los Angeles Community: What Gentrification Erases from Echo Park." *Southern California Quarterly* 97(1): 69–111. https://doi.org/10.1525/scq.2015.97.1.69.

Morçöl, Göktuğ, and James F. Wolk. 2010. "Understanding Business Improvement Districts: A New Governance Framework." *Public Administration Review* 70(6): 906–13. https://doi.org/10.1111/j.1540-6210.2010.02222.x.

Muñiz, Janet. 2023. "Conflict and Co-Specialization on Calle Cuatro: How Placemakers Navigate Ethnic Branding." *Qualitative Sociology*. https://doi.org/10.1007/s11133-023-09545-7.

National Association of Latino Elected Officials Education Fund. 2021. *2020 Census Profiles California*. Los Angeles: NALEO Educational Fund.

Nee, Victory, and Brett de Bary Nee. 1986. *Longtime Californ': A Documentary Study of an American Chinatown*. Stanford, CA: Stanford University Press.

Neely, Brooke, and Michelle Samura. 2011. "Social Geographies of Race: Connecting Race and Space." *Ethnic and Racial Studies* 34(11): 1933–52. https://doi.org/10.1080/01419870.2011.559262.

Newman, Kathe, and Elvin K. Wyly. 2006. "The Right to Stay Put, Revisited: Gentrification and Resistance to Displacement in New York City." *Urban Studies* 43(1): 23–57. https://doi.org/10.1080/00420980500388710.

Ngô, Fiona I.B. 2012. "Punk in the Shadow of War." *Women & Performance: A Journal of Feminist Theory* 22(2): 203–32. https://doi.org/10.1080/0740770x.2012.720826.

Nguyen, Mai T., Victoria Basolo, and Abhishek Tiwari. 2013. "Opposition to Affordable Housing in the USA: Debate Framing and the Responses of Local Actors." *Housing, Theory and Society* 30(2): 107–30. https://doi.org/10.1080/14036096.2012.667833.

Nicholls, Walter J. 2003. "Forging a 'New' Organizational Infrastructure for Los Angeles' Progressive Community." *International Journal of Urban and Regional Research* 27(4): 881–96. https://doi.org/10.1111/j.0309-1317.2003.00489.x.

Oh, Sookhee, and Angie Chung. 2014. "A Study on the Sociospatial Context of Ethnic Politics and Entrepreneurial Growth in Koreatown and Monterey Park." *GeoJournal* 79(1): 59–71. https://doi.org/10.1007/s10708-013-9478-x.

Omi, Michael, and Howard Winant. 2014. *Racial Formation in the United States From the 1960s to the 1990s*, 3rd ed. New York: Routledge.

Ong, Paul. 1984. "Chinatown Unemployment and the Ethnic Labor Market." *Amerasia* 1(11): 35–54. https://doi.org/10.17953/amer.11.1.025430w450287253.

Ong, Paul, Edna Bonacich, and Lucie Cheng, eds. 1994. *The New Asian Immigration in Los Angeles and Global Restructuring*. Philadelphia: Temple University Press.

Park, Kyeyoung, and Jessica Kim. 2008. "The Contested Nexus of Los Angeles Koreatown: Capital Restructuring, Gentrification, and Displacement." *Amerasia Journal* 34(3): 126–50. https://doi.org/10.17953/amer.34.3.d03g386u007n286w.

Park, Robert E. 1950. *Race and Culture*. Chicago: University of Chicago Press.

Parson, Don. 1982. "The Development of Redevelopment: Public Housing and Urban Renewal in Los Angeles." *International Journal of Urban and Regional Research* 6(3): 393–413. https://doi.org/10.1111/j.1468-2427.1982.tb00387.x.

Patillo, Mary. 2007. *Black on the Block: The Politics of Race and Class in the City*. Chicago: University of Chicago Press.

Pelisek, Christine. 2003. "Voting Fights." *LA Weekly*, February 6. http://www.laweekly.com/news/voting-fights-2135925.

Pierson, David. 2016. "They Built Towering Cities in China. Now They're Trying It in Downtown L.A." *Los Angeles Times*, August 16. https://www.latimes.com/business/la-fi-0825-china-dtla-snap-story.html.

Portes, Alejandro, and Leif Jensen. 1989. "The Enclave and the Entrants: Patterns of Ethnic Enterprise in Miami before and after Mariel." *American Sociological Review* 54(6): 929–49. https://doi.org/10.2307/2095716.

Pottie-Sherman, Yolande. 2010. "Vancouver's Chinatown Night Market: Gentrification and the Perception of Chinatown as a Form of Revitalization." *Built Environment* 39(2): 172–89. https://doi.org/10.2148/benv.39.2.172.

Project for Public Spaces, Inc. 2010. *Making Chinatown a World Class Cultural Capital Beginning with Central Plaza, West Plaza and Bamboo Lane*. Prepared for the Community Redevelopment Agency of the City of Los Angeles. New York: Project for Public Spaces, Inc.

Pulido, Laura. 2000. "Rethinking Environmental Racism: White Privilege and Urban Development in Southern California." *Annals of the Association of American Geographers* 90(1): 12–40. http://www.jstor.org/stable/1515377.

Qadeer, Mohammad A. 1997. "Pluralistic Planning for Multicultural Cities: The Canadian Practice." *Journal of the American Planning Association* 63(4): 481–94. https://doi.org/10.1080/01944369708975941.

Quick, Kathryn S., and Martha S. Feldman. 2011. "Distinguishing Participation and Inclusion." *Journal of Planning Education and Research* 31(3): 272–90. https://doi.org/10.1177/0739456x11410979.

Quintana, Isabela S. L. 2015. "Making Do, Making Home: Borders and the Worlds of Chinatown and Sonoratown in Early Twentieth-Century Los Angeles." *Journal of Urban History* 41(1): 47–74. https://doi.org/10.1177/0096144214537200.

Ross, Catherine L., and Nancey G. Leigh. 2000. "Planning, Urban Revitalization, and the Inner City: An Exploration of Structural Racism." *Journal of Planning Literature* 14(3): 367–80. https://doi.org/10.1177/08854120022092719.

Roth, Matthew W. 2004. "Whittier Boulevard, Sixth Street Bridge, and the Origins of Transportation Exploitation in East Los Angeles." *Journal of Urban History* 30(5): 729–48. https://doi.org/10.1177/0096144204265187.

Roth, Wendy D., and Jal D. Mehta. 2002. "The Rashomon Effect: Combining Positivist and Interpretivist Approaches in the Analysis of Contested Events." *Sociological Methods & Research* 31(2): 131–73. https://doi.org/10.1177/0049124102031002002.

Rubin, Herbert J., and Irene S. Rubin. 1995. *Qualitative Interviewing: The Art of Hearing Data*. Thousand Oaks, CA: Sage Publications.

Saito, Leland T. 1998. *Race and Politics: Asian Americans, Latinos, and Whites in a Los Angeles Suburb*. Champaign: University of Illinois Press.

———. 2009. *The Politics of Exclusion: The Failure of Race-Neutral Policies in Urban America*. Stanford, CA: Stanford University Press.

Sampson, Robert J., Jeffrey D. Morenoff, and Thomas Gannon-Rowley. 2002. "Assessing 'Neighborhood Effects': Social Processes and New Directions in Research." *Annual Review of Sociology* 28:443–78. https://www.annualreviews.org/doi/abs/10.1146/annurev.soc.28.110601.141114.

Sarmiento, Carolina. 2022. "Not Diverse Enough? Displacement, Diversity Discourse, and Commercial Gentrification in Santa Ana, California, a Majority-Mexican City." *Urban Studies* 59(9): 1782–99. https://doi.org/10.1177/00420980211020912.

Sassen, Saskia. 1996. "Cities and Communities in the Global Economy: Rethinking Our Concepts." *American Behavioral Scientist* 39(5): 629–39. https://doi.org/10.1177/0002764296039005009.

Schneider, Cathy. 1997. "Framing Puerto Rican Identity: Political Opportunity Structures and Neighborhood Organizing in New York City." *Mobilization: An International Quarterly* 2(2): 227–45. https://doi.org/10.17813/maiq.2.2.p6u4657jh0303087.

Schwirian, Kent P. 1983. "Models of Neighborhood Change." *Annual Review of Sociology* 9: 83–102. https://doi.org/10.1146/annurev.so.09.080183.000503.

Scott, Allen J. 2019. "Residential Adjustment and Gentrification in Los Angeles, 2000–2015: Theoretical Arguments and Empirical Evidence." *Urban Geography* 40(4): 506-28. https://doi.org/10.1080/02723638.2018.1500253.

Selbin, Jeffrey, Stephanie Campos-Bui, Joshua Epstein, Laura Lim, Shelby Nacino, Paula Wilhem, and Hannah Stommel. 2018. *Homeless Exclusion Districts: How California Business Improvement Districts Use Policy Advocacy and Policing Practices to Exclude Homeless people from Public Space*. Berkeley: UC Berkeley Public Law Research Paper. https://doi.org/10.2139/ssrn.3221446.

Shah, Nayan. 2001. *Contagious Divides: Epidemics and Race in San Francisco's Chinatown*. Berkeley: University of California Press.

Shaw, Kate. 2008. "Gentrification: What It Is, Why It Is, and What Can Be Done about It." *Geography Compass* 2(5): 1697–728. https://doi.org/10.1111/j.1749-8198.2008.00156.x.

Shaw, Mae. 2008. "Community Development and the Politics of Community." *Community Development Journal* 43(1): 24–36. https://doi.org/10.1093/cdj/bsl035.

Shaw, Stephen, Susan Bagwell, and Joanna Karmowska. 2004. "Ethnoscapes as Spectacle: Reimaging Multicultural Districts as New Destinations for Leisure and Tourism Consumption." *Urban Studies* 41(10): 1983–2000. https://www.jstor.org/stable/43197020.

Sheller, Mimi. 2018. *Mobility Justice: The Politics of Movement in the Age of Extremes*. London: Verso.

Shyong, Frank. 2017. Chinatown's Swap Meets Once Opened a Door to the American Dream. Now, Their Future Is Uncertain. *Los Angeles Times*, July 10. http://www.latimes.com/local/lanow/la-me-Chinatown-swap-meets-20170710-htmlstory.html.

Silver, Christopher. 1997. "The Racial Origins of Zoning in American Cities." In *Urban Planning and the African-American Community: In the Shadows*, edited by June M. Thomas and Marsha Ritzdorf, 23–42. Thousand Oaks, CA: Sage Publications.

Sims, J. Revel. 2016. "More than Gentrification: Geographies of Capitalist Displacement in Los Angeles 1994–1999." *Urban Geography* 37(1): 26–56. https://doi.org/10.1080/02723638.2015.1046698.

Sing, Bill. 1980. "Chinatown Struggles to Balance Dual Community Roles." *Los Angeles Times*, April 13, F1, F13.

Slater, Tom. 2009. "Missing Marcuse: On Gentrification and Displacement." *City* 1(2–3): 292–311. https://doi.org/10.1080/13604810902982250.

Slayton, Nicholas. 2016. "Finally, Blossom Plaza Blossoms." *Los Angeles Downtown News*, September 15. http://www.ladowntownnews.com/news/finally-blossom-plaza-blossoms/article_5ce009f4-7ada-11e6-9868-abfa8f0ea23a.html.

Small, Mario L. 2005. *Villa Victoria: The Transformation of Social Capital in a Boston Barrio*. Chicago: University of Chicago Press.

Smith, Dorothy E. 1974. "The Social Construction of Documentary Reality." *Sociological Inquiry* 44(4): 257–68. https://doi.org/10.1111/j.1475-682x.1974.tb01159.x.

Smith, Neil. 1979. "Toward a Theory of Gentrification: A Back to the City Movement by Capital, Not people." *Journal of the American Planning Association* 45(4): 538–48. https://doi.org/10.1080/01944367908977002.

Soja, Edward W. 1989. *Postmodern Geographies: The Reassertion of Space in Critical Social Theory*. London: Verso.

———. 2009. "The City and Spatial Justice." *Space and Justice* 1(1): 1–5.

———. 2014. *My Los Angeles: From Urban Restructuring to Regional Urbanization*. Berkeley: University of California Press.

Sullivan, Daniel M., and Samuel C. Shaw. 2011. "Retail Gentrification and Race: The Case of Alberta Street in Portland, Oregon." *Urban Affairs Review* 47(3): 413–32. https://doi.org/10.1177/1078087410393472.

Summers, Brandi T. 2019. *Black in Place: The Spatial Aesthetics of Race in a Post-Chocolate City*. Chapel Hill: University of North Carolina Press.

Sze, Lena. 2010. "Chinatown Then and Neoliberal Now: Gentrification Consciousness and the Ethnic-Specific Museum." *Identities: Global Studies in Culture and Power* 17(5): 510–29. https://doi.org/10.1080/1070289X.2010.526882.

Tabares, Leland. 2021. "Misfit Professionals: Asian American Chefs and Restaurateurs in the Twenty-First Century." *Arizona Quarterly: A Journal of American Literature, Culture, and Theory* 77(2): 103–32. https://doi.org/10.1353/arq.2021.0006.

Tabor, Nick. 2015. "How Has Chinatown Stayed Chinese?" *New Yorker*, September 24. http://nymag.com/daily/intelligencer/2015/09/how-has-Chinatown-stayed-Chinatown.html.

Teranishi, Robert T., Bach Mai Dolly Nguyen, and Cynthia M. Alcantar. 2015. "The Asian American and Pacific Islander Data Disaggregation Movement: The Convergence of Community Activism and Policy Reform." *Asian American Policy Review* 25: 26–36. http://proxy.library.cpp.edu/login?url=https://www.proquest.com/scholarly-journals/asian-american-pacific-islander-data/docview/1786881807/se-2.

Toji, Dean S., and Karen Umemoto. 2003. "The Paradox of Dispersal: Ethnic Continuity and Community Development among Japanese Americans in Little Tokyo." *AAPI Nexus: Asian Americans and Pacific Islanders Policy, Practice and Community* 1(1): 21–45. https://doi.org/10.36650/nexus1.1_21-46_tojietal.

Torres, Vicki. 1996. "The Great Wall of Chinatown; Merchants Who Cater to Other Southeast Asian Immigrants Now Outnumber Older Businesses." *Los Angeles Times*, March 31. http://articles.latimes.com/1996-03-31/news/mn-53310_1_teo-chew.

Toyota, Tritia. 2010. *Envisioning America: New Chinese Americans and the Politics of Belonging*. Stanford, CA: Stanford University Press.

Umbach, Greg, and Dan Wishnoff. 2008. "Strategic Self-Orientalism: Urban Planning Policies and the Shaping of New York City's Chinatown, 1950–2005." *Journal of Planning History* 7(3): 214–38. https://doi.org/10.1177/1538513207313915.

Umemoto, Karen. 2001. "Walking in Another's Shoes: Epistemological Challenges in Participatory Planning." *Journal of Planning Education and Research* 21(1): 17–31. https://doi.org/10.1177/0739456X0102100102.

Umemoto, Karen, and Hiroki Igarashi. 2009. "Deliberative Planning in a Multicultural Milieu." *Journal of Planning Education and Research* 29(1): 39–53. https://doi.org/10.1177/0739456x09338160.

Unger, Abraham. 2016. *Business Improvement Districts in the United States: Private Government and Public Consequences*. Cham, Switzerland: Palgrave Macmillan.

Vigdor, Jacob L., Douglas S. Massey, and Alice M. Rivlin. 2002. "Does Gentrification Harm the Poor? [with comments]." *Brookings-Wharton Papers on Urban Affairs*, 133–82. http://www.jstor.org/stable/25067387.

Villa Raúl H., and George J. Sanchez. 2005. *Los Angeles and the Future of Urban Cultures*. Baltimore: John Hopkins University Press.

Võ, Linda T. 2000. "Performing Ethnography in Asian American Communities: Beyond the Insider-Versus-Outsider Perspective." In *Cultural Compass: Ethnographic Explorations of Asian America*, edited by Martin F. Manalansan, 17–37. Philadelphia: Temple University Press.

———. 2004. *Mobilizing an Asian American Community*. Philadelphia: Temple University Press.

von Hoffman, Alexander. 2000. "A Study in Contradictions: The Origins and Legacy of the Housing Act of 1949." *Housing Policy Debate* 11 (2): 299–26. https://doi.org/10.1080/10511482.2000.9521370.

Wachs, Martin. 2007. "Autos, Transit, and the Sprawl of Los Angeles: The 1920s." *Journal of the American Planning Association* 50(3): 297–310. https://doi.org/10.1080/01944368408976597.

Walker, Edward T., and John D. McCarthy. 2010. "Legitimacy, Strategy, and Resources in the Survival of Community-Based Organizations." *Social Problems* 57(3): 315–40. https://doi.org/10.1525/sp.2010.57.3.315.

Warren, Carol A. B. 2001. Gender and Field Work Relations. In *Contemporary Field Research*, 2nd ed., edited by Robert M. Emerson, 203–23. Prospect Heights, NY: Waveland Press.

Wilson, Kathryn. 2015. *Ethnic Renewal in Philadelphia's Chinatown: Space, Place, and Struggle*. Philadelphia: Temple University Press.

Wilson, William J. 1987. *The Truly Disadvantaged: The Inner City, the Underclass, and Public Policy*. Chicago: University of Chicago Press.

Wong, Diane. 2019. "Shop Talk and Everyday Sites of Resistance to Gentrification in Manhattan's Chinatown." *WSQ: Women's Studies Quarterly* 47(1): 132–48. http://doi.org/10.1353/wsq.2019.0032.

Wong, Janelle. 2006. *Democracy's Promise: Immigrants and American Civic Institutions*. Ann Arbor: University of Michigan Press.

Wu, Ellen. 2014. *The Color of Success: Asian Americans and the Origins of the Model Minority*. Princeton, NJ: Princeton University Press.

Yu, Henry. 2002. *Thinking Orientals: Migration, Contact, and Exoticism in Modern America*. Oxford: Oxford University Press.

Zarsadiaz, James. 2022. *Resisting Change in Suburbia: Asian Immigrants and Frontier Nostalgia in L.A.* Oakland: University of California Press.

Zhou, Min. 1992. *Chinatown: The Socioeconomic Potential of an Urban Enclave*. Philadelphia: Temple University Press.

Zhou, Min, and John Logan. 1991. "In and Out of Chinatown: Residential Mobility and Segregation of New York City's Chinese." *Social Forces* 70(2): 387–407. https://doi.org/10.2307/2580245.

Zinn, Maxine B. 2001. "Insider Field Research in Minority Communities." In *Contemporary Field Research*, 2nd ed., edited by Robert M. Emerson, 159–66. Prospect Heights, NY: Waveland Press.

Zukin, Sharon. 1995. *The Cultures of Cities*. Oxford: Blackwell Publishers.

———. 2010. *Naked City: The Death and Life of Authentic Urban Places*. Oxford: Oxford University Press.

Zukin, Sharon, Valerie Trujillo, Peter Frase, Danielle Jackson, Tim Recuber, and Abraham Walker. 2009. "New Retail Capital and Neighborhood Change: Boutiques and Gentrification in New York City." *City & Community* 8(1): 47–64. https://doi.org/10.1111/j.1540-6040.2009.01269.x.

INDEX

Old Chinatown (*continued*)
displacement of, 30–33; downtown
redevelopment of, 42–44
Omi, Michael, 15
Ooga Booga, 201–2
Organization of Chinese Americans–
Greater Los Angeles, 134
organizations: as Chinatown power structure, 12–14, 67–82; business leaders,
71–75; immigrant cohort differences,
70–71, 73–74, 84; legacy of mutualist
organizations, 68–71; politically progressive activism, 75–82; sustaining political
community, 65–66; symbolic political
power of older organizations, 87–89;
tensions of stakeholdership, 85–101
Orsini Apartments, 4, 59, 147, 184, 188

PAC. *See* Project Area Committee
Page Act of 1875, 28
Palmer, Geoffrey, 4, 59
Park, Robert, 12
People v. Hall, 241n19
People's Republic of China, 38
Phea, Sophat, 99, 197, 212–13
Phoenix Bakery, 194, 198
plazas, Chinatown: appealing creative class,
198–99; art gallery scene, 199–202;
cultural events, 202–4; establishment of
New Chinatown, 35; foodie scene in,
204–9; music scene, 199–202; new
immigrant businesses in, 47, 168, 195–
198, 226; tourism as site of, 3, 123,
198–209
political economy, neighborhood change,
10–11
political engagement, Chinatown: cultural
production as, 209–13; drawing from
lived experience, 76–78; neutrality,
130–32; New Left movement, 75–76;
organizational landscape, 67–84; preservation efforts, 82–84, 178–183; service
gaps, 78–79; tensions of stakeholdership,
85–101. *See also* various entries
Preserve America designation, 178
progressive activists: CCAC engagement,
106–12, 146–147, 229; centering
working-class community, 75–82,

97–101, 145–46, 169–74; expanding
political representation, 91–92; institutionalizing organizations, 92–93; internal conflict, 129–30; older generation,
76–80; participation in New Left
Movement, 75–76; positioned as outsiders, 89–91, 94–95; resisting formalization, 93–94; younger generation, 80–82.
See also various entries
Project Area Committee (PAC), 104, 106;
dissolution of, 108–9
Project for Public Spaces, 202
property owners: critiques of, 95, 179–80,
195; political interests of, 118–25; role in
preservation, 96–97, 178–80, 189–90,
231–32. *See also* Business Improvement
District (BID)
Property ownership, laws, 29–30
Proposition 13, California, 52
public education. *See* Castelar Elementary
School and Charter School Co-Location
Public lynching, 32. *See also* Chinese
Massacre of 1871
Public Records Act, 130
punk rock music, Chinatown. *See* music
scene, Chinatown

Quintana, Isabella Seong Leong, 31
Quo, Beulah, 42
Quon, Soon Don, 72

Racial projects, term, 15; ethnic enclaves as
site for, 15–16; gentrification as, 15
Racialization, term, 15; relationship to
space 15–16
Ramen Champ, 205
Readinger, Alexis, 96
Red Car Properties, 74, 198
Refugee Act of 1980, 45
Refugee Relief Act of 1953, 38
Residence District Ordinance, 29, 31
residential mobility, 40–42
restaurants, Chinatown: Asian American
restaurateurs role, 205–9; downtown
pressures, part of, 154–55; as economic
base, 204; gentrification, San Gabriel
Valley, as competition, 165–67
Reyes, Ed, 110

Founded in 1893,
UNIVERSITY OF CALIFORNIA PRESS
publishes bold, progressive books and journals
on topics in the arts, humanities, social sciences,
and natural sciences—with a focus on social
justice issues—that inspire thought and action
among readers worldwide.

The UC PRESS FOUNDATION
raises funds to uphold the press's vital role
as an independent, nonprofit publisher, and
receives philanthropic support from a wide
range of individuals and institutions—and from
committed readers like you. To learn more, visit
ucpress.edu/supportus.

www.ingramcontent.com/pod-product-compliance
Lightning Source LLC
Chambersburg PA
CBHW020840270326
41928CB00006B/496